YOUTH STUDIES

Youth Studies

Fundamental Issues and Debates

James Côté

First published 2014 by
PALGRAVE MACMILLAN

Palgrave Macmillan in the UK is an imprint of Macmillan Publishers Limited,
registered in England, company number 785998, of Houndmills, Basingstoke,
Hampshire RG21 6XS.

Palgrave Macmillan in the US is a division of St Martin's Press LLC,
175 Fifth Avenue, New York, NY 10010.

Palgrave Macmillan is the global academic imprint of the above companies
and has companies and representatives throughout the world.

Palgrave® and Macmillan® are registered trademarks in the United States,
the United Kingdom, Europe and other countries.

ISBN 978–0–230–36844–6 hardback
ISBN 978–0–230–36845–3 paperback

This book is printed on paper suitable for recycling and made from fully
managed and sustained forest sources. Logging, pulping and manufacturing
processes are expected to conform to the environmental regulations of the
country of origin.

A catalogue record for this book is available from the British Library.

A catalog record for this book is available from the Library of Congress.

Printed in China

For Donna, with love and devotion

Contents

Tables

Introduction

The uses of this book

This book presents the primary issues and debates in youth studies as currently found in the overlapping disciplines of sociology, psychology, and cultural studies, with some considerations from anthropology, criminology, and demography. Youth studies is a rapidly growing field worldwide, representing multiple viewpoints from these disciplines, and as such can present a confusing picture to novices and experts alike. This book has been written with the goal of helping readers get to the heart of the principal issues that characterize this maturing field. It is my hope that by seeing the field in this way, readers will gain a clear picture of the underlying structure of the field as well as how the field can move forward in a more comprehensive manner.

To achieve this goal, what follows is an overview of the long-standing and recent fissures and fractures in the field, rather than summaries of recent research as found in conventional textbooks. This book introduces students to the field, and it is also strong at the intermediate and advanced levels, going to the heart of this field by identifying its underlying *paradigms* and theories, as well as seminal and current debates. If used in introductory-level courses, instructors may want to provide additional and ancillary material, in lectures and/or in supplementary readings, such as those recommended at the end of each chapter (most of which are journal articles that are easily available as PDFs). There are plenty of introductory youth-studies texts now available in many countries that could supplement this book, but what is lacking in the field are more advanced books that are suited for issue-oriented courses. Because of the way it is written, this book can be used in courses that range from introductory-level undergraduate to the graduate level. At the same time, professional youth-studies researchers and academics should find this book helpful in better understanding the key fissures and fractures in their specific specializations, as well as in areas outside of their concentrations.

To set the stage for getting at the heart of the fundamental issues and debates in this field, Chapter 1 identifies the "threshold meta-concepts" (cf. Meyer & Land, 2003) governing social-scientific theory and research, and shows how these apply to youth studies. When these types of concepts are grasped, people can undergo "ah ha experiences," after which an approach in question, and the field as a whole, can make more sense. These insightful experiences should also help people think about social-scientific issues in a less dogmatic manner. To augment these pedagogical experiences, pointers are given in subsequent chapters throughout the book in terms of exercising critical-thinking skills. Critical thinking is defined in Chapter 1, and common biases and errors that can interfere with these skills are identified. It is a major goal of this book to illustrate how critical thinking can be applied in various ways to youth studies and thus to help readers refine their skills in ways that are transferable to other fields. As argued in Chapter 1, true forms of critical thinking tend to be underutilized, even by those with advanced forms of higher education.

Threshold meta-concepts are those ideas that one must fully comprehend in order to "move beyond" the limitations of individual perspectives and disciplines, and their factional disputes. In this way, they are "gateways" or "portals" into new ways of understanding. Grasping these concepts can transform the person's mental operations, such that the world is seen in different ways. Thus, they are more than merely "important" concepts, which just add to a person's terminological repertoire (cf. Meyer & Land, 2003).

Threshold meta-concepts are also different from important disciplinary concepts because they are "irreversible" after they transform the person's outlook in some way; they are unlikely to be forgotten and therefore likely to affect the way things are understood by the person in the future. Additionally, threshold meta-concepts are "integrative" in that they open up understandings regarding how other forms of knowledge are interrelated (Meyer & Land, 2003).

These threshold meta-concepts are presented in bold when they are first introduced. Along with the contextual definition given upon introducing each term, a glossary of these terms is provided at the end of the book. Important disciplinary concepts are italicized when first introduced, and are also included in this glossary. (Non-academic words with more complex meanings that can be looked up in dictionaries are not included in the glossary.) The difference between these two types of concepts is that threshold meta-concepts are trans-disciplinary—they do not require accepting disciplinary **boilerplate assumptions** (e.g., terms such as *intersectionality, false consciousness,* or *second demographic transition* have significance mainly within the disciplines in which they were coined). In contrast, "important concepts" come from specific disciplinary perspectives, and while they can transform thinking within that perspective, they are not necessarily irreversible because they may not influence the reader when she or he studies or adopts a different perspective.

Finally, threshold meta-concepts can introduce people to "troublesome knowledge" that goes against their previous taken-for-granted understandings of the world. People can experience a sense of conflict or ambivalence about potentially new understandings because these new ideas are dissonant with their previous understandings (cf. Meyer & Land, 2003). This is because threshold meta-concepts highlight disciplinary barriers and give insight into interdisciplinary approaches that may have previously been avoided for paradigmatic reasons (see *paradigm* in the glossary). It is a premise of this book that grasping the threshold meta-concepts governing the perspectives involved in youth studies is essential to a comprehensive understanding of the field, even if one prefers one perspective over others, for political, ethical, philosophical, or methodological reasons.

When key threshold meta-concepts are grasped, the various fault lines, or fissures and fractures, among the dominant approaches in this field become clearer, in part because they underscore the competing assumptions underlying these approaches. Some fault lines are on the surface: they are discussed and debated in books and articles published in the field. Others are below the surface, out of most people's awareness, and yet others are something that people tacitly agree not to acknowledge. Accordingly, distinctions are made in this book among assumptions, issues, debates, and controversies in the following ways:

- Assumptions entail positions that are usually not explicitly acknowledged in a field, although sides (or factions) have formed or can be identified around them, as in the case of "nominalism" vs. "realism."
- Issues involve open questions that are explicitly acknowledged in a field, but no sides have organized or can be readily identified, as can be the case with the concepts of "structure" vs. "agency."
- Debates refer to positions with two or more sides, with identifiable opponents. The nature–nurture debate is the most readily recognized example of this, but less visible debates are also discussed, as in the case of the status of science in debates between factions ostensibly associated with "postmodernism" vs. "positivism."
- Controversies are open debates that have reached the public realm. There are few of these in the youth studies field, but the Mead–Freeman controversy in anthropology is the most obvious example.

The conceptual plan

The academic field of youth studies is largely a product of the university infrastructures found in Western, developed countries. Over the twentieth century, these infrastructures nurtured the disciplinary studies of the various natural and social sciences, whose intellectual roots lie in the broader pursuit of the liberal arts and humanities, dating back to Greco-Roman antiquity and whose ideals have been embraced by European universities for the past millennium (e.g., Bloom, 1987). Most certainly, universities in developing and "underdeveloped" countries have supported some forms of youth studies, but the field as an international endeavor has been a concerted undertaking mainly in Europe, the United States, Canada, and Australia, with university researchers communicating primarily through English-language journals and conferences. In addition, there are large pools of researchers and research centers in China and the Russian Federation,[1] as well as smaller pools of researchers within other countries around the world. However, because English is the current lingua franca of academia, the product of research available in English has tended to define the field internationally (Helve & Holm, 2005).

As a result, this book relies mainly on English-language publications produced in developed Western countries. It therefore characterizes the field as it has emerged in English-speaking countries, as well as those countries that use English as their lingua franca in international academic conferences, such as the Nordic nations. It is to be understood, therefore, that unless otherwise indicated, claims made in this book pertain to youth studies in these countries. Certainly, note will be made when research has revealed something about or from other types of societies, but stating this scope condition of this book upfront has the advantage of not having to keep qualifying the type of society in which each specific theory or research finding applies. Regional and cultural variations and manifestations are certainly important, but a listing of these would distract from the primary purpose of this book in identifying fundamental issues and discussing them in a reasonably concise manner. When this book is used in courses, class discussions and assignments can explore regional and cultural variations that shed light on these issues (see Arnett, 2008 and Nilan, 2011 for discussions of the relevance of differences among countries in terms of economic development).

We see in Part I of the book that the emergence of disciplinary studies in Western academia has been both "a blessing and a curse." The "blessing" has involved the infrastructures that have produced these forms of research, but the "curse" refers to the "academic silos" that have emerged out of the divergent specialized assumptions and terminology underlying the disciplines involved. As argued below, these silos now constitute an impediment to the further development of the youth-studies field as a whole (and more generally the social sciences and humanities), especially as a form of liberal enquiry compatible with the origins of Western academia.

Within this historical, cultural, and linguistic context, Part I takes readers directly to the fundamentals of the **youth question** that has emerged from the various disciplinary theories of the twentieth century. By systematically introducing key threshold meta-concepts, Chapter 1 provides a discussion of the different ways in which youth-studies researchers approach their work in this field. These approaches, and crucial differences among them, can be understood at the most basic levels in terms of three threshold meta-concepts: **ontologies** (i.e., what do researchers consider to be real?), **political agendas** (i.e., what is the object of their investigations—radical social change or maintaining/improving the status quo?), and **value priorities** (i.e., how do they see their responsibilities as researchers to the young people they study?). These threshold meta-concepts provide the theoretical tools to think critically about youth-studies issues in ways that address the youth question and help to identify the various paradigms that have been developed to speak to the youth question. In Chapter 2, the theories constituting each paradigm are fleshed out. Chapter 3 examines the various disputes that have arisen over the history of youth studies regarding how to characterize and study the youth period.

Parts II and III illustrate applications of these fundamentals to the social structures and processes that define aspects of the youth period, with each chapter examining some fundamental assumptions underlying the opposing positions concerning how these structures/processes have emerged and are changing in countries that provide illustrative case studies. The general topics and specific issues and debates examined in these chapters were selected because they have produced discernible debates with far-reaching implications that span the history of the field and cut across the various disciplines that have contributed to youth studies. Some of the more recent topics (such as "place and space") are not covered because no critical mass of published literature involving discernible debates has yet emerged. (Descriptions of some of these topics can be found in current introductory textbooks such as Furlong, 2013 and White, Wyn, & Albanese, 2011.)

The four chapters of Part II examine the socio-economic influences that define and structure the youth period, beginning with the expansion of school systems to encompass more years of education to qualify for entry into the labor force (Chapter 4). Even with higher levels of education, recent cohorts of young people have found themselves increasingly marginalized in the workplace (Chapter 5). Competing explanations for these macro developments are examined. At the same time, the structure of the youth period is changing in terms of the micro influences on young people's daily lives: the different approaches parents take in relating to their offspring (Chapter 6) and the various mediated technologies that increasingly influence how leisure time is spent (Chapter 7). Different understandings representing illustrative fissures and fractures in the field are examined in each chapter.

Part III then moves to an examination of the debates that have emerged with respect to how the changing youth period is experienced: first, in terms of how to conceptualize "youth culture" (Chapter 8); second, in terms of disputes about youth identity formation (Chapter 9); third, in terms of how various youth social identities are experienced subjectively and objectively (Chapter 10); and, finally, with a consideration of competing interpretations of the political behaviors of recent cohorts of young people (Chapter 11).

Part IV draws conclusions about how the field of youth studies is maturing and what it can offer if cooperative research efforts are undertaken in addressing the various problems and prospects of the youth period as currently constituted in Western societies.

Finally, this book has been written such that, with the understandings of the field laid out in Chapter 1, and aided with a glossary for quick reference to threshold and disciplinary concepts, the subsequent chapters can be read in various sequences. This is because the chapters are cross-referenced, so if readers go to a later chapter without reading earlier ones, they will be referred back to earlier ones for those areas that build on these other ideas. In particular, readers may be anxious to get to the "meat" of the field as presented in the substantive chapters in Parts II and III, skipping the more theoretical Chapters 2 and 3 if they do not suit their interests. When using this book in higher-educational courses, some instructors of introductory courses may feel that their students do not need to understand the fundamental theories and seminal debates to get the gist of the specific issues discussed in the substantive chapters. This leapfrogging is feasible because throughout the subsequent chapters I refer back to the main theories (Chapter 2) and seminal debates (Chapter 3) when relevant issues come up, so students/readers can expand their understandings of the underlying theories and debates to their liking and at their own pace. That said, in my experience, teaching theory and the fundamentals of field is one of the greatest challenges to instructors because students who are new to a field have the most difficulty with abstractions that are novel to them. In point of fact, this is a problem faced by teachers and students at all levels of education (Willingham, 2009). Still, regardless of the course level, I believe Chapters 2 and 3 are helpful to instructors who want to provide the more intellectual challenges in their courses and are worthwhile to students who want to expand their intellectual horizons.

Part I

Threshold Meta-Concepts and the Contours of Youth Studies

This opening part of the book sets the stage for critically examining the key issues and substantive debates in youth studies, which comprise the chapters of Parts II and III. Chapter 1 tackles the youth question that cuts across the various disciplines of this field. It does so by offering the lens of the threshold meta-concepts that are central to this area and by showing how these types of concepts help us understand the different approaches taken by youth-studies researchers. As we see, these approaches differ in terms of the preferred ontologies, political agendas, and value priorities of various factions of researchers. This chapter also shows how these meta-preferences shape the various youth-studies paradigms. With these philosophical understandings of how the youth question is approached in this field, readers are equipped to critically analyze the merits of the various theories debated and the evidence offered in support of those theories.

Chapter 2 goes on to discuss the theories that have shaped the landscape of youth studies for the past century. This discussion is organized in terms of the meta-concepts that allow us to identify the paradigmatic roots of each theory.

Armed with these fundamental meta-concepts and concrete understandings of the roots of the youth-studies theories, the stage is set for Chapter 3, which examines the seminal debates that have arisen over the history of youth studies regarding how to characterize and study the youth period, and thus provide answers to the youth question.

The Youth Question

1

The **youth question** at its most basic level involves how to understand the material and subjective conditions associated with the "youth period"—that portion of the life course between what is defined as childhood and adulthood in a given society. This question can be difficult to answer, in part because the societal definitions of the youth period vary widely over time and place. As we see in the chapters to follow, the various cultural definitions of "youth" have a relatively recent history in Western countries and are still changing. To further complicate matters, those from different disciplines use various names for this age period; for instance, psychologists prefer terms such as adolescence, and more recently "emerging adulthood" (Arnett, 2000). As a working model in this book, the full age range of the youth period as found in the range of world cultures is recognized as spanning approximately from ages 14 to 30, depending on the society in question. Although the field began a century ago with a focus on those in their teens, with greater proportions of people now experiencing prolonged transitions to full-time work roles and starting families later, increasing attention is being paid to those in their twenties.

One way to grasp the complexity of the youth question is to think in terms of the memory aid "W_5": who, what, where, when, and why. In a given society, *whom* is defined to be in the youth period; *what* forms does the youth period take; *where* do various forms of the youth period emerge; *when* does the youth period begin and end; and *why* does a youth period exist in this society?

Another way to approach this question is identify the key debates over the past century about how to conceptualize the relevance of the youth period. Theoretical formulations have emerged to address the youth question, as have empirical traditions intended to test the validity of those formulations. Four phases in this development can be identified that are associated with the rise of youth-studies theories in response to perceived changes in the nature of the youth period and debates about the relevance of those changes (cf. Mørch, 2005):

- 1900s–1960s: Modern adolescents in turmoil:

  - Adolescent psychology emerges in the United States to explain the rise in recalcitrant teenagers in a "nature vs. nurture" framework (theories of child/adolescent development are proposed); delinquency studies emerge in the United States in response to localized urban crime; anthropologists dispute the claims of psychologists regarding the universality of "adolescent storm and stress."

- 1950s–1970s: Modern youth in rebellion:

  - American functionalists explain the adolescent period as a product of new role expectations in modern societies; political economists see youth protests as the harbinger of the overthrow of capitalism; psychologists propose developmental stages, including identity formation as well as cognitive, ego, and moral development, linking difficulties with stage progression to social maladjustment.

- 1960s–1990s: Youth as active agents:

  - Sociologists in the United Kingdom see working-class-youth recalcitrance as a form of resistance to their class oppression; cultural theorists in the United Kingdom import American delinquency studies, finding "resistance" in consumption and identity displays in subcultural analyses; adolescent psychology continues to grow in the United States and Europe, becoming increasingly divorced from other youth-studies perspectives, while focusing on "nature-by-nurture" interactions of individual differences in varied contexts (as opposed to global, dichotomous nature vs. nurture effects).

- 1980s–present: Prolonged youth as a positive identity:

  - Multiple, eclectic perspectives emerge in various regions to account for the prolongation of youth into the twenties age range; theoretical perspectives become more covert as research becomes topic-driven and label-based (e.g., emerging adulthood, social generations), and more explicitly value-driven, looking for ways to celebrate the youth prolongation as a minority "identity" or a new "developmental stage." Adolescent psychology counteracts its "deficit approach" with a "positive youth development" approach and complex research models of human "plasticity."

With this evolving nature of youth studies in mind, in this chapter, we review the various answers that have been proposed to the youth question in general, and the specific W_5 components, in Western societies, especially as these answers are influenced by the various philosophical assumptions, political agendas, and value priorities held by youth researchers. Key threshold meta-concepts are introduced to facilitate critical thinking about how to evaluate youth-studies theories and research. The chapter concludes with the argument that critical thinking itself can constitute a methodology for studying forms of social reality like those suggested by the youth question.

Various answers to the youth question: The ontological debate

Defining youth: Is it "real"?

A starting point in answering the youth question is to ask what people mean at the most fundamental level when they refer to the period of the life course between childhood and adulthood. The most fundamental starting point in this sort of enquiry is ontological in nature.

Ontology is a threshold meta-concept from metaphysical philosophy, referring to the question of reality—the basic nature of an entity's existence and what form it takes. In ontological terms, entities may be defined to exist along a continuum ranging from the abstract to the concrete. On the one hand, some things are so abstract that they exist in name only, such as ideas like "society" or "social forces." One cannot lay hands on these things; one can only speak about them as intangibles. On the other hand, some things have a more concrete, tangible existence; the book or computer tablet you are reading are examples.

In the social sciences and humanities, debates can be found about the ontological nature of abstract entities, with some scholars arguing that even abstractions about intangibles can have an "objective" existence. For example, Durkheim (1897/1951, 1895/1964a) wrote of social forces as "social facts" independent of human motivations whose impact can be reliably measured, as in the case of suicide rates.

The ontological status of abstract concepts, including "youth," can be difficult to grasp because most people have a tendency to reify abstractions—to consider them to have a concrete existence on the same plane of reality as physical objects. For instance, in spite of the abstract nature of the idea of "society," members of societies take the idea for granted because they live in them on a day-to-day basis. In fact, the apparent reality of so much of what we encounter in our daily lives makes it difficult for us to think of something like "society" as merely a concept. Consequently, even the suggestion that the concept of society might be ontologically contestable can be a form of "troublesome knowledge"; even though it is an abstraction, it certainly seems "real." However, it is actually very difficult to demonstrate the existence of abstract entities by putting them to empirical tests that others can observe.

Similarly, how could someone even suggest that the periods of youth, young adulthood, or especially adolescence, are not "real"? We can "see" adolescents every day, and it can be pretty obvious when someone is a "youth" as opposed to an "adult."

This uncertainty of knowledge is reflected in the historical and cross-cultural variability in how young people are identified by the language of the place and time. Before the modern era in the West, there was not a sharp distinction between being an adult and a non-adult. Under the right circumstances, those in their teens could assume certain adult roles without interference, including certain occupations, marriage, and military duty (e.g., Steinberg, 1990). As a matter of fact, the word "adolescent" came into English usage only in the 1400s, taken from the Latin *adolescere*, meaning "to grow up, mature." Perhaps even more surprising, the word "teenager" was coined less than 100 years ago by American marketers looking for ways to increase the consumption patterns of this age group (Côté & Allahar, 2006). For reasons discussed below, over time, the words "adolescent" and "teenager" have become synonymous terms of disparagement, manipulation, and disempowerment; the concept of "youth" seems to be currently taking the same downward route in terms of social status. Consequently, as these words developed a shared cultural meaning, they became increasingly consequential for the lives of young people.

Even today, some non-Western languages do not have terms to designate adolescence or youth (Brown & Larson, 2002), suggesting that there is nothing intrinsic to human nature about the youth period. Moreover, it appears that the period that came to be called adolescence in the 1400s was not considered a big deal even in Western societies until the early 1900s when an eminent psychologist of the day—G. Stanley Hall—claimed that the period between about ages 13 and 25 years was scientifically significant for human development (Hall, 1904). We return to Hall's work and influence in Chapters 2 and 3.

The point to be taken here is that in one sense youth as an age period appears to be socially constructed—dependent on how it is defined in a particular time and place—but in another sense it appears to have a reality of its own, with serious consequences for the realities experienced by those defined to be part of that age period. Thus, determining the difference between these two ontological positions—youth as a social construction or as a reality of its own—is more than just a philosophical exercise. But, how are both things possible? A closer examination of the threshold meta-concept of ontology clarifies this apparent paradox.

Conventional answers: Nominalism and realism

As a threshold meta-concept, the philosophical idea of ontology further opens "the portal" to the question at hand—the youth question. More generally and historically, the debate whether reality is socially constructed or has its own properties dates back at least to the philosophical disputes of Greek antiquity. An opposition between **nominalism** and **realism**, respectively, has persisted over time in debates over the validity of knowledge, and developed into a primary fissure in the social sciences and humanities. Burrell and Morgan (1979) characterize the modern version of this dispute in the social sciences as follows:

> Social scientists...are faced with a basic ontological question: whether the "reality" to be investigated is external to the individual—imposing itself on individual consciousness from without—or the product of individual consciousness; whether "reality" is of an "objective" nature, or the product of individual cognition; whether "reality" is a given "out there" in the world, or the product of one's mind. (p. 1)

When we bring this ontological dispute to bear upon the youth question, nominalists argue that youth is merely a label we apply to people of a certain age (in certain times and places), whereas realists argue that this age period has a reality of its own, independent of how we think about or define it. The primary questions accordingly involve whether social reality is the product of human consciousness and perception (*nominal*, from the Latin for "name") or has an independent, obdurate existence (*real*, from the Latin for "thing"). Applied to youth studies, these questions ask whether the youth period is merely a name we apply to certain people or has an existence independent of how we label it.

These threshold meta-concepts are laid out in Table 1.1, showing differences in the approaches taken to defining social realities by those in the social sciences and humanities. Although for heuristic purposes they can be seen to exist as opposing positions, in reality there is a continuum connecting them, so they should not be seen as (false) dichotomies. Actually, we could identify extremes for both positions wherein, for example, extreme nominalists insist that everything is socially constructed, and extreme realists insist that everything has a reality independent of human consciousness. As it happens, those taking either of these extreme positions tend to reject the opposing ontology, as in the case of "anti-realist nominalism" and "anti-nominalist realism."

Burrell and Morgan (1979) argue that extreme nominalist positions can present "an entirely individualistic and subjectivist view of reality in which no meaningful discourse is possible" (pp. 239–40), noting that Sartre (1969) warned about "the reef of solipsism" associated with extremely relativistic metaphysical positions. Burrell and Morgan note that although extreme

Table 1.1   Ontological positions concerning the nature of the social world

Nominalism	⟷	Realism
Social realities are products of social constructions		Social realities have an existence independent of human consciousness

nominalism reminds us that "social reality and knowledge of the world are based essentially upon shared meanings" (p. 240), this nominalist assertion became pedestrian in the twentieth century as a fundamental assumption of mainstream perspectives, particularly in symbolic interactionism (Blumer, 1969; Hewitt, 2003). Furthermore, this extreme anti-realist nominalism exhibits a shortsighted tendency to reject offhand both realist ontologies and quantitative methodologies.

At the same time, extreme realist positions can be found that reject the necessity or utility of carefully identifying the underlying assumptions of a theory to guide empirical research. Hempel (1966) discussed this position in reference to the natural sciences, arguing that the major advances in science have been based on a priori theories. Burrell and Morgan identify a similar position with Skinnerian behaviorism in psychology and *abstracted empiricism* in sociology (cf. Mills, 1959). These extreme realist positions tend to be "all method," with empirical research driven by quantitative techniques, often "fishing" for statistical significance rather than using theoretically derived hypotheses. As a mirror image of anti-realist nominalism, anti-nominalist realism exhibits a similarly shortsighted tendency to reject offhandedly nominalist ontologies and qualitative methodologies, as well as the importance of theory construction.

In actuality, when we map out the positions taken by various social scientists, we find more nuanced and complex sets of positions. In particular, it is reasonable to take a nominalist position in studying one type of social reality while taking a realist position in studying another, without necessarily being inconsistent (cf. Burrell & Morgan, 1979). Some forms of social reality are more arguably socially constructed, while other forms of social reality seem to have their own properties that no one "invented."

By way of illustration, social organizations such as fraternities and sororities can be studied to trace actual events where people sat down together and made up—socially constructed—rules (norms) governing their organizations. However, it is also possible to study how these social constructions can produce realities beyond—and well after—these collective constructions happened. To illustrate, the constructed rules are intended to create interpersonal bonds that become transformed into "social capital"—networks of reciprocal obligations—that help fraternity and sororities members in their careers after they graduate. Similarly, but more informally, youth subcultures can emerge among like-minded people who jointly construct norms based on shared subjectivities, but membership in these subcultures can have real consequences in their lives (e.g., lifelong friendship bonds, life-altering habits, distinctive language patterns, and trend-setting personal appearance styles).

In these examples, we can see that nominalism and realism apply to different social phenomena, and their validity is not merely a matter of the "standpoint" of the observer. Unfortunately, some academics can become so wedded to one or the other of these ontological positions that they insist one position is always the correct way to approach the field and the other position is always the incorrect way. These stances are dogmatic and show limited critical thinking, even among otherwise enlightened experts. The intransigence in accepting opposing ontologies is similar to what we can find with Left–Right political beliefs in the adherence to dogmas; as a matter of fact, a strong correlation has been found between scientists' political beliefs and their scientific position in certain academic debates, as we see in the next chapter.

This hostility between ontological positions is so serious that the epistemological divide—a fundamental disagreement about the validity of certain forms of knowledge—between nominalism and realism constitutes a formidable barrier to developing a mature field of youth studies. As we see in the chapters to follow, factions have formed across this divide in which adherents on both sides deny the validity of the research produced by other factions that take different ontological approaches to the youth question.

Bridging the epistemological divide: Pragmatic constructionism

Over time, a number of social scientists and humanists have sought ways to handle the antagonism between these two ontological positions by identifying a middle ground that suits a wide range of phenomena. As noted, the idea of ontology can be seen as more of a continuum than a dichotomy, even though it is often treated dichotomously. To illustrate possible waypoints along this continuum, Table 1.2 lists five distinct ontological positions.

Weigert, Teitge, and Teitge (1986) refer to one such middle-ground position as *pragmatic constructionism*. This position identifies ongoing social interactions between constructions of reality and how these constructed realities "act back" on the individual in terms of tangible physical and material consequences; these consequences then influence subsequent constructions, which then have further consequences, and so on, in ongoing iterations. It is the institutionalization of such socially constructed realities that constitutes the grounds for the emergence of codes of order (folkways, mores, laws, rules, codes, etc.) that appear to be necessary conditions for social organizations and structures. In fact, pragmatic social constructionism is essentially what Berger and Luckmann (1966) proposed in their treatise that formed the basis of contemporary social constructionism, and is what governs W. I. Thomas's

Table 1.2 A range of ontological positions concerning the nature of the social world

Anti-realist nominalism	Nominalism	Pragmatic constructionism	Realism	Anti-nominalist realism
Social reality is a product social constructions		Realities can be socially constructed, but those constructions can take on a reality that acts back on individuals	Social reality has an existence independent of human consciousness	

(Thomas & Thomas, 1929, p. 572) classic statement "If [people] define situations as real, they are real in their consequences."

Weigert et al. (1986) argue that it is important to distinguish pragmatic constructionism from "reductionist constructionism." Reductionist constructionists, as extreme nominalists, insist that all social reality is the product of human cognitive and communicative activity. On certain matters, this extreme position is difficult to justify logically and is often taken as a matter of faith.

But, is it plausible that all manner of reality are of the same origin? For instance, all cultures have norms, so norms are *universal* to human existence; however, the *contents* of these norms varies widely, so are *relative*. If a social constructionist were making the point that cultural norms are not the absolute "Word of God," few social scientists would disagree, but this point does not address the universal occurrence of cultural norms, and hence the human need to construct norms. For the realist, issues that are more interesting include the origins and consequences of this human need to construct norms. This important distinction between relativistic cultural contents and universalistic processes affecting humanity emerges as a key issue in debates about identity (Chapters 9 and 10).

As noted above, an additional problem with this form of reductionism is that social reality would logically be different for everyone, so it would be impossible to develop a consensus about anything (everyone would be aground on Sartre's "reef of solipsism"). To illustrate this hazard, if used as a starting point for launching a political agenda or espousing a value priority for youth research, reductionist constructionism makes it impossible to establish agreed-upon ways to solve social problems such as sexism, racism, and classism because logically these forms of oppression would have to be seen merely as social constructions and not "real" beyond this. Yet, we know that many problems, including sexism, racism, and classism, have real consequences and it is important to understand and document these consequences if we are to eradicate them.

To illustrate pragmatic constructionism using a common problem studied by youth researchers, consider the issue of financial marginalization and *social exclusion*. Even as these problems are plausibly the result of cumulative formal and informal social constructions, these collective constructions can have material consequences that are not directly reducible to how people think about the youth period. Homeless youth and socially excluded youth not only have poor economic prospects, but they also face physical consequences in health and well-being tied to their (temporary) membership in this age group (e.g., Furlong, 2013). Even young people in better economic circumstances feel material consequences. For example, affluent young people in many countries currently struggle to acquire increasingly extended post-secondary educations. As we see in Chapters 4 and 5, they face a highly competitive labor force with high unemployment rates, while carrying a burden of personal debt or coping with co-residing with their parents because they cannot earn enough to afford independent living. We examine these and many other objective or material consequences of the youth period in the topical chapters of Parts II and III.

Youth-studies paradigms: Ontologies and political agendas

In addition to the distinction between nominalism and realism, Burrell and Morgan (1979) identify a distinction based on the underlying political agendas of theorists concerning assumptions of "order" and "conflict." Here there is a key fault line between positions advocating "regulation" of the status quo in societies vs. those advocating "radical change" in the basis of societies. In youth studies, this fissure can be detected in often unspoken disputes between positions that advocate controlling the lives of young people vs. those advocating fundamental changes in the position of young people in societies.

In general sociology, Burrell and Morgan identify the "sociology of regulation" to include functionalism and the various interpretive approaches such as symbolic interactionism. These approaches have in common a concern with "explanations of society in terms which emphasize the underlying unity and cohesion" and they assume a "need for social regulation in human affairs" (1979, p. 17). In contrast, theories emphasizing the "sociology of radical change" include the various forms of Marxism, critical theory, and conflict theory, all of which have in common a focus on explanations of "deep-seated structural conflict, modes of domination and structural contradiction" that are believed to characterize modern societies (*ibid.*). The point of pursuing these theories is to make possible human "emancipation from the structures which limit and stunt . . . potential for [human] development" (*ibid.*).

Added to this type of within-discipline fissure are agenda differences between disciplines, as in assumptions underlying adolescent psychology and criminology vs. the political economy of youth, as we see in the next chapter. In the former cases, the political agendas can be defined as "conservative" (supporting the status quo in societies), while in the latter case they are identified as "critical" (challenging the status quo).

Burrell and Morgan developed a two-by-two typology of sociological paradigms by cross-tabulating these contrasting political agendas with philosophical assumptions similar to nominalism and realism. That typology is very useful in understanding sociological paradigms as far as they had developed in the 1970s, before youth studies became a distinguishable field of study, and before the so-called "postmodern turn" (Best & Kellner, 1997; Seidman, 1994). Accordingly, to bring this meta-theoretical framework up to date and relevant to current, interdisciplinary youth studies, the typology provided in Table 1.3 is offered. This framework provides a way of representing all of the disciplines contributing to contemporary youth studies, and thus the positions on various debates and disputes within this field of study. For the sake of simplicity and clarity, the pragmatic constructionist position is not included in this typology of

Table 1.3 Youth-studies paradigms

Political agenda	Ontological assumptions	
	Nominalism	Realism
Critical: Conflict/change	(Radical) Postmodernism; cultural studies	Political economy; late-modernism
Conservative: Order/regulation	Symbolic interactionism; interpretive and narrative approaches; (conservative) postmodernism	Functionalism and demography; adolescent psychology; anthropology; criminology

paradigms, but it can be located in those approaches that combine nominalism and realism.

Burrell and Morgan offered other terms for each of the four sociological paradigms identified by this technique. However, because youth studies is interdisciplinary and its paradigms are not as well formed as in sociology (cf. Puuronen, 2005), the following names will be used as heuristic short forms: critical nominalism, critical realism, conservative nominalism, and conservative realism.

In the next chapter, each of the perspectives identified within the four paradigms is discussed. To set the stage for this, it is useful to distinguish the critical from the conservative approaches.

The critical approach: Conflict/change

Critical theories in youth studies emphasize the need for radical changes in young people's treatment by, and position in, societies, but each theory has its own formulations regarding the changes thought necessary. A **boilerplate assumption** of critical perspectives is that the status quo in a given society is the result of past conflicts among competing interests. Depending on the perspective, there is the assumption that humans are self-interested and in-group oriented. Even then, their actual behaviors may be the result of alienation and/or conformity to cultural logics of the most powerful societal groups; in consequence, the political agenda is one of radical change, a stance that requires recognizing and challenging dominant interests.

Marxism played a strong role in the early development of both the nominalist and realist critical paradigms. Interestingly, nominalists have emphasized the writings of the "early Marx" while the "later Marx" has been emphasized by realists. According to Burrell and Morgan (1979, pp. 32–5), Marx experienced an "epistemological break" when he took on issues of political economy more directly later in his career. In other words, Marx's early writings had more of a nominalist flavor in explorations of forms of "consciousness" (i.e., subjectivities) while his later writings turned to more realist concerns in terms of structural forms of class conflict (i.e., material conditions).

The conservative/liberal approach: Order/regulation

Conservative theories, in contrast, tend to assume that most societies are basically well functioning in their current forms. A liberal variant of "conservatism" regarding order/regulation can be found in views that only minor reforms are necessary to keep up with "progress." In the case of the circumstances defining the current youth period in Western societies, there is the general assumption that only minor tweaking would be necessary in the form of programs and policies, especially through educational systems. Indeed, a common recommendation for maintaining order and regulation is through educational systems, which are seen to have evolved to take over more socialization functions from other institutions. These institutions include the family, religion, and the workplace.

The boilerplate assumptions of conservative/liberal approaches tend to involve the premise that societies naturally evolve according to a "plan" like the "invisible hand of the market." Early theories even made biological/organic analogies, and versions that are more contemporary claim a sort of determinism dictated by demographic age/gender distributions. The conservative political agendas based on these assumptions therefore involve the inference that the status quo in most societies is in the best interests of the mainstream of the population; according to the liberal variant, any changes to this status quo are best achieved by finding a consensus on the basis of the will of the majority.

Political agendas: Distinguishing the critical from conservative/liberal positions

A critical perspective differs from a conservative perspective in that the former advocates and has recommendations for changes to the status quo. In contrast, in its more liberal manifestations the latter may be critical of the status quo, but does not advocate significant change. Instead, it often portrays some conflict, fragmentation, or inequality as endemic to the human condition rather than as specific to forms of social organization, such as capitalism or late-modernity. The line between these two broad agendas is sometimes difficult to draw because of unarticulated views or posturing associated with forms of "pseudo-radicalism" sometimes found in academia. As we see in the next two chapters, a primary fissure in the critical approach is between older neo-Marxist approaches focusing on material conditions and newer postmodernist approaches focusing on subjectivities.

In fact, many of those in the Marxism-based old Left believe that the conservative-Right poses less of a threat than does postmodernism to the political agenda of addressing economically based inequalities, and establishing a common ground upon which equality can be based. At the height of the culture wars in the mid-1990s, Todd Gitlin, an ex-president of the 1960s New Left organization Students for a Democratic Society, published *The Twilight of Common Dreams: Why America Is Wracked by Culture Wars* (1995). In that book, he expressed his disappointment in the New Left, noting how the insistence on "political correctness" by postmodernists was undermining the efforts of the old Left to find a common ground on which to reduce economic inequalities. This infighting thereby made it possible for the Right to dominate American politics. Linking wider political concerns with the politics of the academy, Gitlin's argument is as follows:

> The Left, which once stood for universal values, has come to be identified with the special needs of distinct "cultures" and select "identities." The Right, long associated with privileged interests, now claims to defend the needs of all. The consequences are clear: since the late 1960s, while the Right has been busy taking the White House, the Left has been marching on the English department.
>
> (from the publisher's blurb)

Regrettably, there is evidence that the distraction of this infighting among Left-liberal academics has greatly diminished progressive agendas in many countries in the face of the neoliberal agendas created by the Right. The agendas that have suffered include those that would have improved conditions for young people, especially in terms of government policies that the more radical old-Left fought for in struggles like the union movement (Côté & Allahar, 2011).

With respect to the thread of critical thinking used throughout this book, most adherents of both critical and conservative perspectives can adopt the same formal critical-thinking mental processes (as discussed in Chapter 1). However, the critical paradigms adopt boilerplate oppositions to an unquestioning adherence to any status quo that is characteristic of conservative theories. Hence, the starting point for critical theories is different from conservative ones, with the former first examining the social/economic/historical/ideological underpinnings of conflicts and inequalities in the status quo. It is important to stress, nevertheless, that this conflict-oriented starting point does not give the critical theorist an advantage in avoiding the biases and faulty perspective-taking that undermine advanced forms of critical thinking as a systematic methodology.

The value-priority stances taken in youth studies

The above discussion of ontological assumptions and political agendas brings us to the question of the different value priorities that youth-studies researchers hold regarding the young people they study, namely, the primary responsibilities researchers feel they have regarding the subjective and material benefits of youth research for the young people under study. This can involve a fiduciary (trust) responsibility as authority figures, a (moral) duty to protect and guide the young, and an (ethical) obligation to help empower them. Consequently, there is a sense of how youth research *ought to be* carried out as well as what the ultimate goal of that research *should* be. Value priorities are the prescriptive elements of research, which are often unstated or assumed on a disciplinary basis, as we see below. As such, they constitute formidable fault lines that prevent the field of youth studies from finding common ground.

From a social-scientific point of view, a primary responsibility is to ensure that research produces the most accurate results in characterizing the youth period, including subjective experiences and material conditions. However, from an activist perspective, the first responsibility is to advocate for young people, a position based on the assumption that (certain) young people under study have been mistreated, unfairly characterized, or oppressed.

These two positions—scientific vs. activist—are often in conflict. Still those who identify more as "scientists" tend to assume a value neutrality in their efforts, while those who identify more as "activists" explicitly embrace certain advocacy values. In both cases, though, there are (often implicit) value-priority assumptions regarding what the researcher *ought to do* in studying young people. In other words, the research enterprise inevitably involves elements of *prescription* underlying any *descriptions* produced, even if the prescriptions are implicit. This is the case because logically, even if "descriptions" are offered as validly representing reality, the mere act of offering descriptions and not prescriptions tacitly endorses the status quo, so is not "value-free."

It should go without saying that all youth researchers believe that their research efforts are ultimately for the benefit of young people, intended to improve their circumstances in some way, either individually or collectively. Building on the understandings of the political agendas from the last section, Table 1.4 identifies and lists the assumptions and beliefs associated with four fundamental value-priority stances that characterize the responsibilities youth-studies researchers feel they have with respect to the promotion of the welfare of young people.

These stances include two social-control viewpoints, as well as two social-change standpoints.

The first social-control position adopts a conservative approach that looks for ways to regulate young people (regulation–control), while the second involves a more liberal position, seeking to facilitate positive forms of youth development and to guide young people toward positive individual and collective outcomes (facilitation–guidance).

The first of the two social-change viewpoints is a more radical position that seeks to emancipate young people by helping them understand their oppression while at the same time addressing the root causes of their collective difficulties through "praxis," putting theory into action (critical emancipation). The second of these change-oriented stances advocates for young people in ways that help them liberate themselves from societal constraints (advocacy–liberation).

With respect to the relationship of these stances to the ontological disputes examined above, the regulation–control position tends to embrace realist

Table 1.4 Value-priority stances taken in youth studies: Assumptions and beliefs

Assumptions	Social change		Social control	
	Advocacy–liberation	Critical emancipation	Facilitation–guidance	Regulation–control
The role of values in research	Value-based inquiries to free people from social constraints and power relations	Praxis-oriented inquires to address inequalities and alienation	Value-specific inquiries aimed at optimizing human development	Value-neutral inquiries into naturally occurring human development
Preferred methods	Qualitative	Mixed methods interpreted with critical analysis	Mixed methods guided by disciplinary theories	Quantitative
Perceived place of youth in society	Youth are misunderstood and negatively stereotyped; because of this societies are oppressive to youth, but they are capable of dealing with it themselves when given the chance	Youth are disadvantaged and exploited in various ways, and politically disenfranchised; these conditions need to be corrected with the help of those with more social legitimacy and power, including academics, professionals, and policy-makers	Youth may not know their own best interests; may behave in self-handicapping ways	Youth are still in process of maturing, so need to be managed in specific contexts; require specific forms of socialization

Perceived needs of young people to be met by researchers/ adults	Youth voice must be heard; understanding their subjectivity is paramount	Youth voice should be taken into account, but their subjectivity may be influenced by false consciousness	Youth require programs and policies run by adults; researchers can provide evidence of the interventions needed	Youth self-control is a desired outcome of education and special programs; researchers can evaluate the need for, and outcome of, programs
The role of young people in research	Youth should be included as co-researchers whenever possible.	Youth can help in framing problems, including how they perceive their place in society	Youth input is important, but only one source of information (e.g., from focus groups)	No need for youth input in framing research when variables have been determined
Perceived authenticity and agency of youth	Youth are agentic, but held back by prejudices	Youth are vulnerable to the same ideological manipulations as adults that create alienation and limit agency	Youth can be helped to realize their agentic potentials by matching them with suitable contexts	Youth willfulness is suspect as beyond their self-control
Perceived capacity of youth for self-regulation	Rebelliousness/ resistance to be admired	Youth are manipulated by other interests, including how they resist control and see themselves (false consciousness)	Youth vary in their abilities to manage their affairs; normal development builds this capacity	Rebelliousness/ resistance to be expected, but are symptoms of immaturity, a quality of youthfulness
Common caricature by critics	Believe that youth can "do no wrong"	Believe that youth are "cultural dupes"	Believe that youth should march lockstep with neoliberalism	Believe that youth can "do no right"

ontologies along with the quantitative research methods associated with the natural sciences. In stark contrast, the advocacy–liberation stance tends to embrace nominalist ontologies along with the qualitative methods associated with the social sciences and humanities. Between these two poles are stances that balance so-called "hard" and "soft" scientific methods and adopt intermediate ontological positions.

In the chapters to follow, the value-priority stances taken by various youth-studies researchers will be identified as we attempt to ferret out what are often unspoken assumptions that can have a determining effect on the methodologies taken, and conclusions drawn, by these researchers. As noted, those taking any one of these stances would defend them by claiming that they are intent on improving the lives of young people: all youth researchers believe that they are "on the side of angels."

Moving beyond preconceptions: Thinking critically about the youth period

It should be clear to readers by now that the youth-studies field is rife with divisions. This is a common situation in many fields. In fact, controversies are endemic to the sciences and humanities. Nevertheless, controversies can help fields to grow and mature if they move toward constructive resolutions. Given the many fissures and fractures identified throughout this chapter, just how are these resolutions to be found?

This problem is particularly important in addressing the youth question, because answers vary widely depending on the preconceptions of individual researchers in terms of their ontological assumptions, value priorities, and political agendas. In short, answering the youth question involves multiple fissures and fractures that make it an inherently political matter, "political" in the sense of the personal motivations and basic beliefs that can get in the way of clearly understanding all of the evidence at hand.

In general, we all like to think that we are clever enough to understand what is going on in the world and that we are able to solve most conceptual problems that come our way. The lay public often takes this "know-it-all" position with respect to the types of things commonly studied by social scientists. After all, everyone lives in a society, so we must all be experts about that society. The same situation applies to youth studies, with both younger and older people often believing that they are experts by merit of their experience of the youth period, either currently in their lives or in the past. And, most certainly, youth researchers would count themselves as experts in what is true about the youth period they study.

Unfortunately, as it turns out, many times we are not as good at thinking clearly about the social phenomena in our lives as we believe—this goes for both laypeople and social scientists—and because we do not want to give up our preconceptions, we all can fall prey to a number of biases, misconceptions, and other cognitive shortcuts in arriving at conclusions. Psychologists have been studying these aspects of human partisanship since their discipline's early days, as have others, including philosophers and logicians. Before moving further into this book, it is very helpful to point out some of the things that should be kept in mind to ensure that our reasoning powers are as sharp as we believe them to be. I recommend that all readers consider the following arguments carefully and repeatedly as they engage in a process of self-examination to become aware of their own preconceptions and reasoning shortcuts that interfere with their critical thinking. In this way, critical thinking can constitute a "methodology."

It is important to begin by making it clear what is meant by the term "thinking critically." This concept does *not* mean merely to criticize or to be against the "establishment," authority, capitalism, or what have you. In terms of logic, critical thinking is deep and complex, rather than knee-jerk. But in terms of taking a stance as an informed observer, it involves assessing the merits of something, both positive and negative. A movie critic, for example, does not write or speak only about what is wrong with a movie, but also what is "right" about it; this form of criticism is about identifying both strong and weak points. As noted above, youth-studies paradigms can be distinguished in terms of a critical-conservative divide, but that use of the term "critical" is different from the present usage as a formal type of thought.

Similarly, someone exercising critical thinking in youth studies, as in any serious area of intellectual inquiry, would examine the merits of various forms of evidence and arguments, and give reasons for these conclusions based on more than emotional reactions, gut feelings, or personal belief systems. Imagine a movie critic trying to be credible in evaluating movies based on emotions (e.g., "I liked/didn't like it because it was scary"), intuitions (e.g., "There was something I didn't like about it, but I can't put my finger on"), or personal beliefs (e.g., "This movie shouldn't be seen because it is pro abortion"). Movie critics who relied on such knee-jerk reactions would not be taken seriously, let alone be of much use to prospective movie-viewers because such reactions tell us more about the movie critic than about the movie.

Yet, such faulty practices can be found in the social-scientific and humanities literature, albeit sometimes disguised in high-sounding prose. It is a major objective of this book to help readers become more exacting in their pronouncements by becoming better critical thinkers. Hopefully, the arguments evaluated in each chapter will help readers in this respect by providing illustrations regarding how to adjudicate competing positions.

Common biases that interfere with critical thinking

Higher forms of learning in general, as well as specific disciplinary methodologies in the social sciences, are ostensibly about overcoming prejudices, bigotries, and the like. A methodology has certain procedures that enable the observer to see the world in clearer ways, including ways to show independent observers how to see something more clearly. These procedures should also establish some authority in what scholars describe and conclude—an authority beyond that of a journalist, say, who makes happenstance observations. After all, why should anyone listen to a person who provides findings based on weak procedures or who makes unconvincing arguments? Well, there are a number of biases that can prevent us from providing authoritative arguments and evidence in the first place, as well as from recognizing when someone else actually does provide a compelling argument based on solid evidence. As noted, these biases are found among laypeople as well as experts.

One bias is particularly problematic. Unfortunately, we are all hampered by a natural tendency that psychologists call "the confirmation bias" (e.g., Nickerson, 1998; Oswald & Grosjean, 2004). This bias describes the tendency for people to accept, with little evidence, arguments that confirm their existing beliefs. In contrast, arguments that dispute people's existing beliefs are more likely to be rejected out of hand or are required to have more "evidence," far more evidence than would be asked of confirmatory arguments.

The pervasiveness of this bias in the social sciences and humanities means that it is far too easy to associate with and support those who share our beliefs, especially those from the same discipline or faction within that discipline. At the same time, it is far too easy to dismiss the methodologies and conclusions of those from other disciplines and factions out of hand, without even reading their published material, or if we do read it, to subject it to impossible standards.

Although there appears to be a natural tendency to seek and see confirmations for our preconceptions, this tendency can be exaggerated on individual—as well as a group—levels. Individually, people differ in how dogmatic they are (Rokeach, 1960). A long line of research in social psychology has found that people differ in how ready and willing they are to objectively assess non-confirmatory information. According to Rokeach, non-dogmatic (open-minded) people "can receive, evaluate, and act on relevant information received from the outside on its own intrinsic merits, unencumbered by irrelevant factors" (1960, p. 58), such as their preconceptions or conformity pressures from peers or people in authority.

Dogmatic people also have a difficult time recognizing the dual character of communication—source and content—because they have difficulties resisting time pressures from implied or real pressures from authority sources (persons or ideologies) to accept only pre-confirmed information. Such people have a difficult time even learning about competing belief systems. However, people who are less dogmatic are able to learn about other belief systems, critically examining them for their merits—weighing their strengths and limitations, and not just going straight to their perceived limitations.

This tendency has a number of manifestations at the group level, ranging from "group think" (excessive confidence in the conclusions of one's colleagues) to a "circling of the wagons" (putting up protective barriers) against perceived threats from other factions. These defensive practices are also more common in factions that take more extreme positions, by merit of the fact that the latitude for accepting other positions is more limited by the extremity of the position being defended (sometimes called "painting one's self into a corner").

The gist of this discussion of biases is that all too often there is a premature closure in thinking about alternative beliefs systems, and this closure preempts critical thinking. This can be found at an individual and group level in the social sciences, and unfortunately it appears that the youth-studies field is no exception, as illustrated in the various chapters of this book.

Paul and Elder (2006; Elder & Paul, 2010) have written extensively on critical thinking, and a small booklet they have written for teaching purposes is a recommended reading at the end of this chapter. They suggest the following way of understanding the basics of critical thinking. One way to prevent premature closure is to be mindful of the differences between our underlying assumptions and inferences. Assumptions include our taken-for-granted beliefs with which we make general, automatic judgments. In contrast, inferences are a step in mental processing of events by association: if one thing is true, then a second thing should also be true. To avoid drawing faulty conclusions, Paul and Elder recommend that we first determine what we inferred (e.g., that someone is a communist) in a specific situation (e.g., where a person is seen reading a book by Karl Marx). Drawing such a conclusion would require the inference that all people who read Marx's books are communists. A moment's reflection on other possible reasons for reading Marx's books (e.g., it is part of a course assignment) would tell us that we have made a faulty inference. A good critical thinker would then examine other reasons for reading the book in question.

To take another example, this time from youth studies, a common inference among some academics is that if a researcher studies the concept of agency in a way that suggests people are sometimes capable of overcoming structural obstacles, that researcher must be Right-wing in some way or perhaps in support of neoliberalism. To the contrary, there are other reasons for studying agency, including finding ways in which the disadvantaged can be helped to improve their life-chances by moving "around" or "through" certain structural obstacles, as in the case of social mobility through educational systems. In point of fact, research shows that students who are engaged in their studies are more likely to succeed in their educational systems than if they are disengaged, and highly motivated and proactive students from disadvantaged backgrounds can attain better educational and occupational outcomes than if they are disengaged and inactive, even if academic engagement is not as crucial for students from more advantaged backgrounds (e.g., Côté, 1997, 2002, 2013b, 2014a; Côté & Allahar, 2011; Côté & Levine, 1997, 2000).

Being mindful of our assumptions and inferences requires that we recognize that each specific judgment we make, or conclusion we draw, can either be based on all of the information and evidence at hand, or on information and evidence limited by our biases, prejudices, or stereotypes. If we rely on the latter, and they are faulty, our conclusions will be faulty. Self-examination on these matters can be difficult, particularly when it comes to our most central or cherished beliefs, but is necessary if we are to engage in critical thinking. The threshold meta-concepts discussed above can help us make these difficult transformations.

The structure of critical thinking

As noted above, the structure of critical thinking has been studied for some time, and the results have yielded some useful information for the task at hand. According to Paul and Elder (2006), the first thing the thinker should do is to determine the type of question being considered. One type of question is straightforward and involves reasoning within a closed system in which there is one correct answer. This is often the case in the STEM disciplines (i.e., science, technology, engineering, and mathematics). The objective of asking the question is to accumulate knowledge.

A second type of question has a purely subjective answer and does not involve a system of logic. There is no correct answer, so there is no way of judging the validity of the reasoning, evidence, or conclusion. For example, there is no correct answer to the question, "Which is better: Thai or Indian food?" Within the social sciences, an equivalent question would be "Which political position is better: Left-wing or Right-wing?" Or, "Who do you like better, author X or author Y?" The outcomes of these questions are indeterminate, being dependent on tastes and personal values. Note, though, that if the question is extended to include which answer is better for a specific purpose, a clearer answer can be developed. To illustrate, if the question involves which author of historical fiction provides a more accurate depiction of the past, it is possible to answer this question on the basis of independent historical evidence.

However, a third type of question calls for sharpened critical thinking skills because it involves answering questions within competing points of view, each of which can have its own systems of logic and standards of evidence. In this case, there is no correct answer, just better or worse answers based on judgments of the weight of the evidence and the persuasiveness of the competing arguments. The object of the question is to form a defensible judgment. These are the types of questions most commonly encountered in the social sciences and humanities, and thus youth studies.

A series of studies has examined the third type of reasoning among American university students and identified three levels of complexity (King & Kitchener, 1994). Students reasoning at the most rudimentary level think that all questions have definite answers, usually from an expert or authority. The opinions of these arbiters are taken as sufficient proof. Students' reasoning at this level tends to parrot their instructors, and students feel uncomfortable when multiple views are presented. Those reasoning at this level are prone to the various errors discussed above with respect to dogmatism and the confirmation bias.

According to these studies of levels of reasoning, only when students develop more complex thinking capacities can they begin to develop the analytic skills necessary to reason on their own, including self-criticism. At this intermediate level, students think of knowledge as relative and contextual. While this is an advance above authority-based opinion, students can get stuck at this stage, believing that there is no way to judge the validity of different forms of knowledge and opinions about them. As a result, they may adopt a form of "dogmatic relativism," retreating to the belief that all opinions are equally valid, regardless of the internal structure of, and evidence for, the arguments underlying them.

At the third level of complexity, students come to see ways of judging the relative merits of complex arguments, in part by acknowledging that such judgments are by necessity tentative, awaiting further evidence. In this way of thinking, the validity of arguments can be judged by examining the persuasiveness of evidence, the rigor with which it was assembled/collected, and the strength of reasoning involved. At this level, the person is willing to consider all forms of evidence (e.g., qualitative or quantitative evidence, judged by the soundness of the methodology). Those reasoning at this level are also willing to accept better-structured arguments as substitutes for their own past positions and judgments (regardless of the ontology of the assumptions, if this is an issue), with the awareness that these new positions are themselves provisional, to be evaluated in the future should they be challenged by further evidence or arguments.

Although early research was optimistic that most (American) undergraduates would reach the third level of reasoning-complexity by the time they graduated, the accumulated research suggests otherwise, with most students developing only moderately complex reasoning abilities. If this research is valid, it would appear that most (American) university graduates do not have very well-developed critical-thinking skills when it comes to questions involving multiple systems of thought (cf. Arum & Roksa, 2011; Côté & Allahar, 2011). Although most students may understand that not all questions have simple answers, they apparently have difficulty reasoning through unstructured problems, preferring dogmatic relativism.

We can see from the above discussion that there are numerous factors working against all of us in terms of our abilities to think clearly and optimally about complex issues. Foremost among these factors are the conformation bias, preconceptions about competing ideas, and cognitive shortcuts that lead us to hastily draw faulty conclusions. Thinking critically is a hard work and requires practice and discipline; merely criticizing something does not mean that we have engaged in anything other than defensively supporting our preconceptions by dismissing the views of others.

Conclusion: Critical thinking as a methodology

Much is made in the social sciences in general, and youth studies in particular, about the contrasting merits of various methodologies, especially quantitative vs. qualitative ones. However, this contrast is often merely the surface manifestation of three other more potent underlying sets of assumptions. One set of assumptions involves ontological beliefs about the fundamental realities of the youth period. A second set comprises the political agenda of the research intended to contribute to social change or reinforce social order. A third involves value-priority stances toward young people and what youth research *ought to* accomplish. These assumptions often implicitly drive research agendas and unify groupings of researchers, creating competing paradigms in youth studies and producing a number of disputes and debates.

In the next chapter, we examine the theoretical perspectives within each of the four paradigms identified in this chapter, equipped with an understanding of the tacit assumptions that often drive the types of research questions asked, and the conclusions drawn, by youth-studies researchers. This understanding provides a methodology for a conceptual meta-analysis of the field of youth studies—a methodology of critical thinking that is illustrated throughout the remainder of this book. A methodology is any system of guidelines for answering questions and solving problems, and does not have to involve numbers or interviews. Therefore, critical thinking constitutes a methodology if it follows a systemic set of steps that allows others to understand how a conclusion is reached and to repeat the process. In these ways, it provides some assurances that conclusions are not simply based on the confirmation bias discussed above.

This method also requires that the youth-studies field be seen as complex and multifaceted with a variety of subject matter. This diversity of topics requires that different theories and methods be used that are most suitable for the particular subject matter under study. The analogy of the jigsaw puzzle is helpful here. The task for youth researchers interested in advancing the field as a whole (and not just their own faction) is to cooperate in identifying how to position the various "pieces" (theories/methods) of the puzzle and to communicate with each other in order to determine how they best fit together. With respect to the paradigms identified in Table 1.3, some pieces will fit into one paradigm "cell" by merit of their subject matter, while other pieces fit into other paradigm "cells." Thus, paradigms are not right or wrong in an absolute sense, but rather are different in terms of the topics defined as important by their proponents. The trick is to determine the right application of each, and this is where healthy debate is called for, as illustrated throughout this book.

The takeaway from identifying the subject matter of paradigms is that different researchers are often studying different manifestations of the youth period and they are doing so because their assumptions have pointed them in different directions. Accordingly, each of the four paradigms potentially has valid concerns, and the advancement of the field lies in recognizing these different concerns, and not with one paradigm dominating the field by overshadowing other paradigms. We pick up on this practice of "meta-theorizing" at the beginning of Chapter 3, where means for evaluating the strengths and weaknesses of theories are discussed.

Recommended readings

Sukarieh, M. & Tannock, S. (2011). The positivity imperative: A critical look at the "new" youth development movement. *Journal of Youth Studies*, 14, 675–91.

    An example of researchers who (implicitly) adopt a value-priority position of critical emancipation arguing against the other value-priority positions, especially facilitation-guidance, but also advocacy-liberation.

Unger, R. Draper, R. & Pendergrass, M. (1986). Personal epistemology and personal experience. *Journal of Social Issues*, 42, 67–79.

    An early exploration into how ontological beliefs can affect the other assumptions held by researchers, suggesting that "root" unarticulated assumptions can determine the positions people take with respect to "postmodernism" and "positivism."

Meyer, J. & Land, R. (2003). Threshold concepts and troublesome knowledge: Linkages to ways of thinking and practicing within the disciplines. University of Edinburgh: ETL Project. www.etl.tla.ed.ac.uk/docs/ETLreports4.pdf

    The theory of the utility of threshold concepts in teaching difficult subject matter is explained.

For thoughtful analyses of the nature of critical thinking, consult the following two sources:

Elder, L. & Paul, R. (2010). *The foundations of analytic thinking*. The Foundation for Critical Thinking. Available from http://www.criticalthinking.org/store/products/analytic-thinking/171

Hare, W. (2001). *Bertrand Russell on critical thinking*. Retrieved from http://www.criticalthinking.org/pages/bertrand-russell-on-critical-thinking/477

Theoretical Approaches to the Youth Question

2

In this chapter, the theoretical approaches that have been taken up in, or touched upon, youth studies are briefly characterized in terms of their fundamental assumptions. The substance of these theories is fleshed out, applied, and critiqued in the topical chapters to follow in Parts II and III.

As we see in this chapter and the one to follow, youth studies is still a disparate field—different approaches and disciplines dominate different areas. This heterogeneity raises the question about whether there is really a distinct field of youth studies with a coherent character or whether there are actually multiple fields with some overlap (e.g., adolescent psychology vs. the sociology of youth). For instance, in the United Kingdom, there is a tendency to associate "youth studies" with sociology (e.g., Cieslik & Pollock, 2002; Furlong, 2013; Jones, 2009), while adolescent psychology is in many ways a separate enterprise, with its own journals, conferences, and professional societies, largely in the United States and continental Europe. In this book, a catholic definition of youth studies is adopted to include all theories and empirical research that deal, either directly or incidentally, with the age group positioned between childhood and adulthood, regardless of the terms they apply to this age period (e.g., adolescence, young adulthood, youth, or more recently emerging adulthood).

This definition of youth studies is adopted based on the assumption that for the field to mature to the point where it can fully characterize the youth period in all of its manifestations, both individual and collective, there is a need for broader integrations of assumptions and methods. All approaches are susceptible to criticisms, but all usually have something to contribute, as I attempt to show in the present chapter. The critiques of these approaches in the chapter to follow should not be taken as dismissals of any one perspective, but rather as frank, constructive attempts to bridge faults and fissures in the field by identifying the strengths and limitations of each theory.

Realist perspectives

Adolescent psychology

Adolescent psychology was among the founding disciplines in youth studies (phase 1), largely through the work of Hall and his storm-and-stress theory (1904). In attempting to explain the ostensible "differentness" among those aged roughly 12–24 from those who are younger and older, Hall proposed that their psychological makeup was distinctive, largely because their mental operations were in continual conflict and turmoil.

Hall justified this claim with a Darwinian "recapitulation thesis," namely, that the individual life course repeats the evolutionary history of the human species; in other words, he postulated that human evolution (*phylogenesis*) influences the genetic makeup of people at different periods in their lives (*ontogenesis*). Using this logic, Hall claimed that *adolescent storm and stress* is universal because there was supposedly an era in human evolutionary history characterized by "barbarism" that is, and will always be, repeated (recapitulated) during the developmental stage schedule of each human. Hall was so convinced about the genetic basis of adolescence, and its turbulence, that he advised adults to isolate adolescents in schools until the turmoil had passed. This dictum influenced the secondary-school movement in ways still felt today.

Rice observed that Hall's "views exerted a marked influence upon the study of adolescence for many years" (1992, p. 71), although these views were contested at that time (e.g., Hollingsworth, 1928; Thorndike, 1904) as well as more recently (e.g., Offer & Offer, 1975; Petersen, 1993). Furthermore, as we see in the next chapter in the discussion of the nature–nurture debate, beginning with research in the 1920s, his views were exposed as being faulty by anthropologists (Mead, 1928) and sociologists (Hollingshead, 1949) on a number of empirical and logical grounds, especially in terms of his genetic claims of cultural universality in adolescent turmoil.

Proefrock (1981) critically examined the early history of adolescent psychology, arguing that it had the effect of shaping the ways in which the public views the "adolescent" and has therefore affected the very nature of adolescence as it is currently structured in Western societies. He argued that, based on views advanced by Hall and others, the psychopathology attributed to adolescence by psychologists came to be used as a legitimation for the juvenile justice system in countries like the United States and the suspension of rights imposed by that system. In fact, the storm-and-stress idea stands as one of the most enduring, and difficult to eradicate, stereotypes the social sciences has produced (cf. Coleman, 1978). Thus, Hall's erroneous idea of inevitable storm and stress remains influential today in some circles, especially among the public and journalists in persistent negative stereotypes about young people.

Lerner and Steinberg (2009) provide a useful three-phase history of adolescent psychology, showing how it has moved from these early assumptions characterizing its first phase during the first half of the twentieth century (see also the framework in the evolution of the broader field of youth studies provided at the beginning of Chapter 1). They argue that in the second and third phases, which began in the 1970s, among other advances, the positive youth development movement emerged, which

> is based on the belief that the potential for plasticity among all youth constitutes a fundamental resource for healthy development; if supportive families, schools, communities, programs, and policies could be created for youth, their potential for plasticity could be actualized as change in positive directions. (p. 10)

Plasticity refers to the potential for development malleability. It is the opposite of *essentialism* (i.e., reductionist biological/genetic views of human development). Moreover, this positive view has been supplanting the earlier emphasis on developmental problems. Increasingly the following view is being accepted, according to Lerner and Steinberg:

> [T]he focus on plasticity, diversity, and individual agency—and the strength of capacity of the adolescent to influence his or her development for better or worse—means that problematic outcomes of adolescent development are now regarded as just one of a large array of outcomes. (p. 10)

In point of fact, a non-partisan assessment of this field suggests that adolescent psychology has contributed much to youth studies, especially in the case of cognitive, moral, and identity development. It has also clarified the difficulties experienced by many young people struggling in Western societies, particularly the United States and Europe, in terms of emotional issues, some of which include depression, suicide, anxiety, and eating disorders, providing useful estimates of the prevalence of these issues in the youth population (thereby correcting Hall's contention that emotional issues are universally experienced). Adolescent psychologists have also studied the diversity of experiences during this period, both culturally in terms of gender, ethnicity, class, sexuality, and so forth (see, e.g., Lerner, Brown, & Kier, 2005) and cross-culturally (see, e.g., Brown & Larson, 2002). Additionally, psychologists are showing positive ways in which young people can and do develop as individuals in their own right and in preparation for their futures (Larson, 2000).

In Chapter 6, we examine how adolescent psychologists have studied parenting styles and how this line of research compares with how sociologists have conceptualized and studied similar parenting styles, showing the contrasts in disciplinary approaches to the same subject matter. In Chapter 9, we examine one of the research traditions popular in adolescent psychology, comparing it with a postmodernist approach that ostensibly shares the same terminology (i.e., the term "identity").

Cultural anthropology

Anthropologists were also among the first to address the youth question in the early twentieth century, principally through Mead's study, published as *Coming of Age in Samoa* (1928), which refuted Hall's foundational work in adolescent psychology. Mead's influence continued in her later studies (e.g., in 1930) of youth in other cultures, a research program that culminated in the influential book *Culture and Commitment: A Study of the Generation Gap* (1970). We review Mead's contribution to the nature–nurture debate in the next chapter.

Although many other anthropological studies have included young people, anthropologists' involvement in addressing the youth question has tended to be incidental. Functionalist sociologists (below) and anthropologists have historically had much in common in terms of their underlying paradigmatic assumptions. However, whereas functionalists are interested in the contents and contexts of socialization over the life course, anthropologists study how these learning processes differ among cultures while still producing well-functioning humans. Cultural anthropologists help us better understand the relationships among socialization practices, cultural patterns, and personality characteristics. They have generally concluded from their cross-cultural research that the more individuals are integrated into their culture, behaviorally and emotionally, the greater the chance of that culture perpetuating itself. In addition, cultures adopt childrearing practices that are consistent with their own institutional and behavioral patterns, even though these childrearing practices can differ widely from those found in other cultures. These practices can range from coddling children to being very harsh to them (e.g., Condon, 1987; Mead, 1970; Schlegel & Barry, 1991).

Anthropologists have also documented cultural variations in the length of time people spend in the age periods of adolescence or youth. Schlegel and Barry (1991) studied records of some older 186 tribal cultures, finding that the period we now call adolescence generally was much briefer and more structured. It also occurred during the mid to late teens, in most cases immediately following puberty (puberty is believed to have occurred several years later in these societies than is the case in the West today because of poorer nutrition). Consequently, by the time they reached their late teens or early twenties, most young people were prepared to assume the roles and responsibilities of adulthood.

Consistent with Mead's work, Benedict (1938) wrote a landmark essay contributing to our knowledge of the cultural variability of adolescence, arguing that most pre-industrial societies provide for a continuous passage from childhood to adulthood. By doing so, cultural continuity is safeguarded, and individual members of the society do not experience serious personal difficulties in making transitions through age statuses. In pre-industrial societies, it is easier for younger members to learn adult work roles in childhood and adolescence, while experiencing the realities of life, including sex and death.

Benedict argued that Western societies, in contrast, are age-graded, largely segregating children, adolescents, and adults from each other. Western societies have introduced three sets of discontinuities into the socialization process, as of the 1930s, according to Benedict. First, children were socialized into non-responsible roles, even though adulthood ostensibly requires a self-regulated responsibility. Second, children were socialized to be submissive, despite the expectation for adults to be dominant. And, third, children were shielded from sexuality, while adulthood required a complex awareness of sexuality.

Benedict's question was just when, where, and how are young people in the West to learn these three essential aspects of adulthood? Benedict did not believe Western societies had good mechanisms for transmitting these things, so they left adolescents largely on their own to learn them. As a result, Western adolescence could be a difficult period of adjustment.

Overall, anthropologists take conservative approaches to youth studies in their concern for social integration and cultural continuity to the extent that their criticisms of the Western status quo is to suggest the need for reforms, not radical change.

Criminology/delinquency

Criminologists have been involved in addressing the youth question primarily in terms of the field of "delinquency studies" dating to the early days (phase 1) of youth studies (France, 2007). Much recent work from this perspective can be located on the conservative, regulation–control side of the value-priority range of positions illustrated in Table 1.4, in its general focus on social control and self-control as a means of producing conformity and reducing crime (e.g., Gottfredson & Hirschi, 1990; Hirschi, 1969). In addition to this realist tradition stemming from functionalism, a more nominalist version stemming from symbolic interactionism (below) can be identified with "labeling theory," an approach popular among sociologists of deviance (e.g., Becker, 1963). Biological and psychological approaches have also been undertaken but because delinquency tends to a group phenomenon, sociology models have prevailed in the study of youth deviance (Tanner, 2010).

According to Tanner (2010), this field began in the early 1900s in Chicago, with studies attempting to explain urban crime rates in terms of differing neighborhood social disorganization. The field then evolved through several stages, first with a functionalist influence by Merton (1938), who argued that delinquency is a result of social strain and *anomie*, and then by Cohen (1955), who saw delinquency as a class-based phenomenon. It was next influenced by symbolic interactionism, with the development of labeling theory (Becker, 1963), which focused on the consequences of delinquency rather than the causes. Eventually, these strands of thought morphed into subculture theories of deviance in the United States and the subculture theories of youth "resistance" in the United Kingdom, the latter of which we examine in Chapter 8.

Most recently, as noted, the field has come to be dominated by control theory in explaining "normal" delinquency.

Because none of the debates discussed in this book involve crime or delinquency, and given space limitations, this perspective will not be discussed further here. However, for sociological reviews of the "crime and delinquency" literature, readers are directed to textbooks such as Tyyskä (2009), Furlong and Cartmel (2007), and White, Wyn, and Albanese (2011). For reviews of psychological versions of "problem behaviors," see textbooks by Arnett (2004) and Lerner, Brown, and Kier (2005). The field of delinquency studies also has its own textbooks because of the popularity of university courses on the topic (e.g., Tanner, 2010; Thompson & Bynum, 2010).

Functionalism and demography

Functionalism was also among the founding disciplines in youth studies, sharing its roots and fundamental assumptions with cultural anthropology. As noted in the previous chapter, functionalism's influence increased in the mid-twentieth century during the second phase of youth studies when there was a concern with the rebelliousness of youth threatening social integration and cultural continuity.

In general, functionalists have viewed adolescence (e.g., Hollingshead, 1949; Parsons, 1961) and, more recently, the prolonged transition to adulthood (e.g., Beaujot & Kerr, 2007) as an inevitable "function" of social and institutional changes associated with industrialization and modernization. Functionalists argue that, like other forms of inevitable social evolution, the human life cycle in Western cultures has become increasingly differentiated, ultimately to accommodate a more complex adulthood associated with changes that increase the institutional complexity of societies (Parsons, 1961). In particular, they argue that the period between childhood and adulthood has increased significantly to allow people to better prepare for the complexities of modern life. Accordingly, they conclude that the young need to remain dependent longer while preparing for adult roles.

Arguments posed by those working on the basis of assumptions from the demographic variant of functionalism have more recently posited that the prolongation of youth into the twenties is part "of the evolution of the human life course" associated with the *second demographic transition* (Beaujot & Kerr, 2007, p. 5). Beaujot and Kerr (2007) describe this demographic theory as follows:

The concept of the second demographic transition has especially been used to interpret the fertility trends of the past 40 years. The first transition, from about 1870 to 1945, brought smaller families, especially because of changes in the economic costs and benefits of children, along with a cultural environment that made it more appropriate to control family size. The second transition since the mid-1960s, has been linked to a continuation of low fertility, a further tendency to delay births, as well as an increased flexibility in marital relationships. (p. 8)

Beaujot and Kerr (2007) cite changing norms allowing for greater choice. These include easier entry into and exit from marital relationships, along with greater acceptability of premarital sex and cohabitation. As we see in Chapter 5, demographers tend to see lower workforce participation among the young to be the result of "choices" made by them to delay entry into the labor force full time. They are now able to do so, the argument goes, because they are not normatively pressured to take up marriage and family roles. Moreover, it is argued that some are taking advantage of a period of semi-autonomy afforded by parental support, especially in extending or renewing intergenerational cohabitation.

The theory of the second demographic transition, modeled in some developed countries, obviously does not apply to "underdeveloped" countries or to many developing countries. Beaujot and Kerr (2007) acknowledge that even in developed countries there are variations introduced by State policies that take over some traditional family roles, as in the Nordic case where young people are afforded more government support for their variation transitions to adulthood.

Finally, a recent demographic approach takes evolutionary assumptions even further, speculating that these delays in the transition to adulthood allow for more intergenerational investments in offspring and therefore constitute an improvement in the species. Kaplan (1997) argues that the prolonged transition to adulthood allows people to "invest" more in themselves before having children, especially if they are supported by their parents, and thus have more to offer their children when they have them later in life.

We examine functionalist influences in youth-studies debates in Chapters 4 and 5 on education and work, respectively, but also see its implicit influence in the chapters on the family (Chapter 6) and media and technology (Chapter 7).

Political economy

The above realist perspectives would fall into the paradigm that Burrell and Morgan identify as functionalism in sociology because of the concern with "providing explanations of the status quo, social order, consensus, social integration, solidarity, need satisfaction, and actuality" (p. 26). Burrell and Morgan identify a number of other sociological perspectives that adopt "radical structuralist" assumptions, of which conflict theory is best known.

Within youth studies, conflict theory has been a rather underrepresented perspective, with the political-economy approach emerging during the second phase of youth studies (1950s–1970s), with declining attention to it thereafter. The clearest and earliest statement of the political-economy-of-youth perspective comes from Rowntree and Rowntree (1968), but this approach seemed to "wither on the vine" after the student revolts of the 1960s subsided. Although not necessarily identifying as political economists, others have proposed later versions, such as some of those in the Birmingham School (see Jones, 2009, for a discussion of this neo-Marxist influence on youth studies in the United Kingdom), Cohen and Ainley (2000), Levitt (1984), Mizen (2002), Tannock (2001), and Côté and Allahar (1996, 2006). The common element of these works is that the youth segment is viewed as politically without a voice and economically exploited.

This approach receives special attention here and later in this book because it appears to constitute a serious omission in the youth-studies field to have ignored the issues raised by this perspective after the spectacular events of the 1960s. As we see, although a number of youth theorists and researchers have raised issues central to this perspective, very few have taken this position beyond boilerplate sociological accounts of social exclusion or social-class inequalities. The watered-down version of this perspective can become functionalist and hence conservative, failing to give an account of the roots of these problems in the self-interested activity of specific groups of people that have to be rectified through radical changes.

If it is true to its origins, though, a political-economy-of-youth perspective focuses on the roots of the problems of social exclusion of disadvantaged youth as well as the growing marginalization of the whole age group, seeing the entire youth segment as a special form of class and calling for radical solutions to this class-containment (Côté, 2014b). Without a focus on the root causes of these problems, the youth-studies field risks being used as an "apology" for neoliberalism (cf. Sukarieh & Tannock, 2011, a recommended reading for Chapter 1).

By the same token, in piecing together a political economy of youth that is relevant currently, it is necessary to rely on scholars from other disciplines, including philosophy (Heath & Potter, 2004), media studies (e.g., Rushkoff, 2001), and investigative journalism (e.g., Frank, 1997a, 1997b; Klein, 2000; Schlosser, 2001). In other words, the field of youth studies has been "scooped" in applying one of its founding perspectives to its own subject matter.

I would argue that it is especially timely in the current aftermath of the "Great Recession" to give the political-economy-of-youth perspective renewed attention. For one, corporations have grown in influence in Western societies to the point where their legitimacy and influence over governments rivals that of the Catholic Church in Medieval Europe (Gore, 2013). This global economic depression is ostensibly one of the most severe crises ever of capitalism, yet many major corporations are making record profits. This paradoxical situation of enormous and growing wealth inequalities can be attributed to several decades of neoliberalism, the most recent version of laissez-faire capitalism. As we see, neoliberalism has had severe consequences for young people around the globe, with youth unemployment rates exceeding 50 per cent in some developed countries (e.g., Greece, Spain, and Italy; International Labour Office, 2012, 2013).

This perspective originated with attempts to account for the youth protests and social movements of the post-World War II period. These accounts focused on the changing material conditions of existence produced by economic and political power (e.g., Levitt, 1984; Marcuse, 1972; Rowntree & Rowntree, 1968), contributing to the second phase of youth studies, "modern youth in rebellion." Young people were argued to constitute special form of "class," disenfranchised economically, politically, and socially. These alienated youth were seen as politically destabilizing and a threat to the economic order, so dominant interests needed to mask their oppression to prevent their mobilization. Their increasing warehousing in schools accomplished this in part, providing indoctrination into the capitalist ethos. A *manufacture of consent* was also identified as orchestrated through other institutions, particularly the mass media (Herman & Chomsky, 1988). The Center for Contemporary Cultural Studies (CCCS) of the so-called Birmingham School picked up on these consent-manufacturing trends with Gramsci's (1971) work on cultural hegemony.

Although many of these oppressive trends can be observed today, the perspective is in need of updating. See Côté (2014b), a recommended reading listed at the end of this chapter, for an update of this position to include the influence of neoliberalism. In addition, Côté and Allahar (1996, 2006) have argued that many of the attempts to manufacture consent among youth have paradoxically "manufactured dissent" among more recent cohorts of young people in a variety of ways. These forms of dissent or resistance range from internalizations adversely affecting their psychological well-being to externalizations associated with the venting of anger and frustration, with many in-between forms of resistance involving passive–aggressive stances to the adult authorities managing the daily lives of young people in schools and community settings.

Contemporary evidence for this perspective can be found in the role of corporations in the manufacture of consent through advertising and marketing, as we see in the youth culture chapter (Chapter 8). As we also see in the chapters on education and work (Chapters 4 and 5), there is evidence that the economic disenfranchisement of youth has deepened at the same time that the very wealthy, and the corporations they own or make stock profits from, have further cemented their own interests. The target of the political-economy critique is the manipulation of the youth segment as consumers and workers. Addressing this exploitation requires radical change, beginning with a challenge to capitalism, especially its unregulated, laissez-faire forms, the most recent of which is neoliberalism.

As argued in the youth culture, education, and work chapters, the political-economy perspective offers an account of why the youth phase has changed, as well as the implications of these changes, thereby filling a gap in the youth-studies literature. In those chapters, the political-economy perspective is posed against theories from the three other paradigms. The focus of this perspective is in the macro analyses of institutions most affected by the political and eco-nomic confluence of self-interested power structures that favor certain groups over others, and in the micro consequences of this power on the material con-ditions of those groups. Beyond this focus, however, this perspective loses its explanatory power.

Thus, in spite of highlighting this perspective in several chapters in this book, it is not offered as a *grand theory* overshadowing all other theories, a panacea for correcting youth woes, or a unifying foundation for an interdis-ciplinary youth studies. As noted in the next chapter, all theories have focal points in terms of their ability to explain certain subject matter. Beyond those focal points their ability to explain other subject matter begins to diminish, and at a certain point theories are unable to convincingly explain anything. Other theories should then be used to try to understand that different subject matter.

Late-modernism

Late-modernism has developed in sociology in parallel with, and as a struc-turalist alternative to, postmodernism (discussed in the next section) during the most recent, fourth phase of youth studies. Giddens (1991) and Beck (1992) laid out the general foundation for this perspective, which has been adapted specifically to youth studies by Furlong and Cartmel (2007). As we see in Chapter 9, late-modernist theories share postmodernism's concern with societal problems associated with institutional fragmentation but stress the importance of personal agency in dealing with problematic societal contexts.

Positions like Giddens's can be understood in the field of youth studies in terms of more radical forms of neo-Durkheimian theory. Adapted to youth studies, this perspective views the transition to adulthood in terms of the normative structures that can guide, and be used as guideposts by, young people during this transition. Normative structures refer to the value-based patterns and standards of behavior that can give people's lives meaning. Since Durkheim's writing a century ago about social anomie (e.g., Durkheim, 1893/1964b), a further "destructuring" of institutions is postulated to have taken place in general in late-modernity, with some institutional reconfigura-tions specifically altering the norms that once guided the young into adult roles. This destructuring has resulted in an increasingly anomic (less normed) society in general, and a decline in the social markers of adulthood in particular, espe-cially for those brought up with secular values. Traditional and non-secular societies preserve these norms more successfully. At the same time, certain reli-gious and ethnic families and enclaves in secular societies can preserve these norms, but sometimes to the objection of the young people who are raised in the host, secular society (i.e., second- and third-generation immigrants).

This anomie is argued to have affected the life courses of many people, who can find themselves (1) with little guidance from their families of origin or an organized religion; (2) compensating for fragmented institutional contexts (e.g., disjunctive education-to-work contexts); (3) coping with decoupled and erratic life-transition options (e.g., creating a family of orientation entirely different from their family of origin); or (4) struggling to meet the requirement to individualize their life plans without a sense of purpose rooted in stable values (Côté, 2000). Faced with these challenges, people in general, but young people in particular, need more of the types of agentic resources identified by Giddens (1991) and others (e.g., Côté, 2013b, 2014a; Evans, 2002; Heinz, 2002).

To understand the late-modernist formulations regarding individualization of the life course, it is important to recognize that they are based on the assumption that individualization involves *freedoms from* normative constraints, especially norms that in the past ascribed narrow social roles or stigmatized certain practices. It is not necessarily assumed that there are more *freedoms to* pursue activities independent of systemic barriers such as social class disadvantage or racial and gender/sexuality discrimination. In addition, some of these older normative barriers are under assault in some countries, as in the case of same-sex marriages being legalized in many political jurisdictions over the past decade, a trend that is slowly spreading to other jurisdictions.

In other words, the requirement to individualize has emerged because of *a lack of structure*. This can create serious challenges for some people, as can persistent social stratification processes along class, race, and gender lines that present *too much unwanted structure* for those placed at a disadvantage. Some specific deficits in structure, or relatively normless or anomic spheres affecting the transition to adulthood, include

- diminished norms and ideologies (e.g., personal values associated with what it means to be male or female [gender], how to establish intimate relationships [marriage], and how to deal with one's sexuality);
- disjunctive links among institutions (e.g., ambiguities and dead ends in the education-to-work transition); and
- destructured social markers (e.g., the meaning of key events, including leaving home, securing employment, and establishing a family during the transition to adulthood).

(Côté, 2000, 2002)

Like the political-economy perspective, the late-modernist view in youth studies focuses on the declining fortunes of the young as a result of the shifting institutional structures of society that have allowed market mechanisms to replace traditional religious and familial modes of social control (Côté, 2000). On the one hand, the late-modernist perspective applied to youth studies is concerned with why societies have been normatively destructured in certain ways, as well as the emotional vulnerabilities introduced by these changes. On the other hand, the political-economy perspective is concerned with the declining earning power of the young, identifying a redistribution of wealth and power toward older members of society in the decline of the material conditions of youth, creating economic vulnerabilities.

In other words, the two perspectives are complementary, with the late-modernist position helping to explain how young people became vulnerable to manipulations by capital. The late-modernist position also provides a more micro corrective to the macro political-economy perspective, by examining how young people themselves have been trying to put meaning back in their lives while capital has targeted their vulnerabilities in the quest for profits. It would be a serious misunderstanding of the late-modernist position to think that it celebrates the anomie of late-modernity and its consequences, particularly compulsory individualization. In fact, late-modernists are critical of this current status quo, often pointing to neoliberalism as a current source of the problem (e.g., France, 2007; Furlong & Cartmel, 2007).

While the political-economy perspective may appear to overemphasize structural determinants in people's lives, the late-modern approach may also seem to overestimate the extent to which people can exercise agency. Still, the perception of biases may be a result of differences in perspective vis-à-vis level of analysis, with the political-economy approach taking a decidedly macro approach that looks at broad patterns, and the late-modern approach taking a more micro one, where individual differences in people's behavior receive more attention. Moreover, the late-modern approach highlights *the lack of structure* in certain areas of people's lives (i.e., the destructuring of cultural norms and practices that would have given their lives more meaning and direction), political economists prefer to emphasize economic structures and other structures of opportunity that affect people's life chances. So, while these two critical-realist approaches may appear on the surface to work at cross-purposes, this is not necessarily the case. Additionally, this comparison highlights differences of emphasis, not omission, between theories. As argued in Chapter 3, individual theories cannot, and should not strive to, explain "everything," but rather to focus on those phenomena best explained by their core assumptions.

We see below how the late-modernist approach is useful in understanding issues associated with the family (Chapter 6), youth culture (Chapter 8), and identity (Chapter 9, focusing on agency, and Chapter 10, focusing on structure).

Macro-nominalist perspectives

Postmodernism and cultural studies

Burrell and Morgan (1979) identified several sociological perspectives that adopt "radical humanist" assumptions corresponding to critical approaches favoring nominalist ontologies. However, their treatise was written before the so-called "postmodern turn" (Best & Kellner, 1997; Seidman, 1994). At the time of Burrell and Morgan's writings, the best-known theory in this paradigm was the "critical theory" of the Frankfurt School, which influenced neo-Marxist commentaries on the changing nature of youth during the "modern youth in rebellion" phase of youth studies (e.g., Marcuse, 1972).

Within the most recent, "prolonged youth as an identity" phase of youth studies, nominalist approaches have become increasingly popular, but their status as critical as opposed to conservative theories is questionable. These approaches have been nurtured by cultural studies, especially in rejoinders in the United Kingdom to the work of the CCCS, which produced studies of British youth culture from 1964 to 2002 (Jones, 2009). (The work of the CCCS is discussed in Chapter 8). The older versions of critical nominalism have generally waned in importance, and now appear to have little influence in youth studies at the same time that the cultural studies approach became more popular and "mainstream."

The postmodernist perspective is a difficult approach to characterize because many of those who appear to adopt a postmodernist position (sometimes called poststructuralist) deny that the term fits them (e.g., Hollinger, 1994), and there appear to be a number of open-ended debates about exactly what it represents (e.g., Smart, 1993). Part of the difficulty in defining a postmodernist youth studies may lay with the multiple origins of perspectives that are deemed "postmodern."

This is in part the case because the notion of postmodernism originated in art and architecture to describe new designs based on a rejection of what "modern" art and architecture supposedly represented (Gergen, 1991). The notion found its way to the social sciences through the humanities, in the philosophical works of French poststructuralists, especially Derrida. This literal translation of the boilerplate assumption of a rejection of "modernism" (more aptly named "anti-modernism") from distant fields to the social sciences is bound to be fraught with problems. And, while postmodernist architecture might have been a reaction against modernism, it did give rise to new forms of architecture. It is unclear whether a new approach has emerged in the social sciences that is not contingent on refutation; that is, can stand on its own without constantly justify itself as a correction to "modernism." Thus, rather than proposing theoretical and empirical advances (cf. Mongardini, 1992), much of the "postmodern turn" has involved attempts to refute grand theories, or "grand narratives" as they are sometimes called (Seidman, 1994).

Two other influences have shaped current postmodernist approaches (Seidman, 2004): (1) critiques of *Enlightenment* rationalities associated with modern science (influenced by the Frankfurt School), and (2) the identity politics that emerged from the so-called culture wars over the universality of prevailing knowledge that gave rise to "Afrocentrism, feminism, lesbian and gay or queer theory" (Seidman, 2004, p. 208). The first of these influences has fueled support for nominalist ontologies in general, and anti-realist nominalist ontologies in more extreme approaches, as we see in Chapters 8, 9, and 10, where youth culture and identities are discussed. The second of these influences has encouraged researchers of all stripes to question the validity of their approaches beyond "normative" samples and populations. Yet, the problem with crediting postmodernism for this influence is that this self-examination began before the so-called culture wars attributed to identity politics (e.g., Wexler, 1983).

In cultural youth studies, there is evidence of confluence of anti-modernist assumptions, nominalist ontologies, and radical political agendas with an insistence on politically charged methodologies predicated on a few boilerplate assumptions. These initiatives have exacerbated the epistemological divide in youth studies. Among other things, this has produced a stridently anti-realist nominalism among many postmodernists, where the notion of "objective reality" is rejected as "unknowable" and methods used to assess that objective reality are dismissed out of hand.

As a result of these oppositional preoccupations, the application of postmodernism to youth studies does *not* seem to offer new theories so much as sets of assumptions that are intended to "disrupt" or "de-center" other perspectives by "interrogating" and/or "deconstructing" them (cf. Brock, Raby, & Thomas, 2012; Raby, 2005; Rattansi & Phoenix, 2005; Wetherell, 2009). In some cases, it is evidently not enough to postulate "de-centered" experiences, but some apparently feel it appropriate to recommend ways to de-center those that may not already be in that state (e.g., Raby, 2012). The "take no prisoners"—even internecine—nature of this approach is likely to draw formidable boundaries that few will cross, leaving hostile factions on either side of the boundaries. But, is it really necessary for academics to wage "war" on each other? Many think not.

As it turns out, a number of postmodernist assumptions about the current state of society are viewed as undue exaggerations by youth researchers. For example, based on a late-modernist perspective in the lead textbook in the youth-studies field, Furlong and Cartmel (2006) state that they "are extremely skeptical of the validity of post-modernist theories and suspicious of a tendency ... to exaggerate change" (p. 2). Arguably, many of the changes claimed by some postmodernists to have recently occurred in "post-modernity" actually date back to the early days of sociology and were a major concern of founders of the discipline, in particular Durkheim.

By and large, the verdict is out whether there are entirely new social theories based on postmodernist assumptions (cf. Seidman, 2004); even more tenuous is an assumption that there is a postmodernist youth studies (e.g., Furlong & Cartmel, 2007). For instance, Furlong (2013) argues, "few youth researchers have fully embraced postmodernism" (p. 44). Still, as we see below, the above influences seem to have produced several boilerplate assumptions in the application of postmodernism to identity studies and youth-cultural studies. In the case of identities, the social and psychological realms are viewed as inevitably relational, unstable, oppositional, multiple, contradictory, and fragmented (Rattansi & Phoenix, 2005). In the instance of youth culture, these realms are said to be fluid, multiple, and temporal (Bennett, 2011). We pick up on the debates introduced by postmodernists in the chapters of youth culture and identity.

Micro-nominalist approaches

Burrell and Morgan (1979) also identify an "interpretative paradigm" as comprising approaches that generally correspond to conservative assumptions regarding social order in conjunction with nominalist ontologies. They define it as

> informed by a concern to understand the world as it is, to understand the fundamental nature of the social world at the level of subjective experience. It seeks explanation within the realm of individual consciousness and subjectivity, within the frame of reference of the participant as opposed to the observer of action. (p. 28)

They go on to identify several philosophical traditions associated with this paradigm in sociology, including phenomenology and hermeneutics. These traditions have influenced youth studies through the work of Bourdieu (e.g., Andres & Wyn, 2010; see Jones, 2009) and Touraine (McDonald, 1999). More generally, though, research based on nominalist assumptions seeking "to understand the world as it is" has not had a strong influence in youth studies as a focused attempt to answer the youth question or in generating debates. Instead, there appear to be a large number of somewhat atheoretical studies in the field that are strongly attached to a nominalist approach to understanding micro-level topics and phenomena of local interest to the researcher in question.

The reasons for this preference for nominalist stances in these studies seem to vary. Some studies appear to be part of the reaction against the bugaboo of grand theories noted above, especially among those influenced by postmodernism (cf. Brock, Raby, & Thomas, 2012, p. 13). Many of these studies claim to adopt the methodology of "grounded theory," whereby no theoretical assumptions are made before embarking on data collection (Glaser & Strauss, 1967). Although this may appear to be an open-minded approach that can lead to new discoveries, is it really possible to be totally free of the paradigmatic assumptions examined in Chapter 1? Yet other studies may be adopting nominalist assumptions out of a rejection of realism and all quantitative methodologies (thereby adopting an anti-realist nominalism).

Because these studies do not explicitly link themselves to paradigmatic traditions, the issues they raise tend to be of single issue and/or not linked to an identifiable debate in any of the topic areas discussed in this book. The most relevant debate might be the one between using qualitative vs. quantitative methods, discussed in the next chapter. Because of this, just two currents in this paradigm will be discussed here, and only a few representative studies will be mentioned for the second current, sampled from the *Journal of Youth Studies*. Each of these studies makes an explicit claim to the superiority of some aspect of this paradigm, without engaging in any broader youth-studies debates beyond the single-issue topic of specific study.

Symbolic interactionism

Symbolic interactionism has interdisciplinary roots dating to the nineteenth century, becoming one of the three "pillars" of sociology. Dating back to the earliest delinquency and subcultural studies in the first phase of youth studies, this perspective has provided the assumptive basis for numerous studies. However, there is no "symbolic interactionism of youth," in the way there is a political economy of youth. Most importantly, symbolic interactionists make few age distinctions in how they see realities to be constructed and negotiated. Age distinctions are made mainly in reference to childhood, during which the self is formed; no life stages after childhood are postulated (e.g., Hewitt, 2003). Other than the delinquency/subculture traditions, some of the more notable symbolic interactionist publications relevant to youth studies include Corsaro and Eder (1995) and Rosenberg (1965), but these are not directly related to debates examined in this book. The influence of symbolic interactionism is generally indirect, shaping the assumptions researchers adopt in their micro-level studies.

Interpretive/narrative approaches

Narrative approaches have seen some successes in the study of identity formation where sensitivity is required to understand the emergent expressions of the various subjective aspects of identity in relation to life-history narratives (e.g., Bazuin-Yoder, 2011; Chandler, 2001; McAdams, 1993). Similarly, recent approaches to identity based on the interpretive tradition have adopted a decidedly conservative variant of the postmodern approach, examining the contexts in which certain societal conditions create a fragmentation of identity and an erosion of the sense of a unified core. Notably, these conditions are celebrated and some postmodernists embrace them (e.g., Gergen, 1991; Rattansi & Phoenix, 2005). In Chapter 9, we examine the postmodern position statement by Rattansi and Phoenix (2005), who "threw down the gauntlet" to those who take realist approaches to identity.

Many of the studies that correspond to these assumptions are self-consciously atheoretical, following a shift that began in the 1970s in many fields from studies grounded in well-developed theoretical traditions to atheoretical, topical studies, or middle-range ones that identify a minimal intellectual heritage. As noted above, these studies often proudly claim to be based on "grounded theory" (Glaser & Strauss, 1967). Although conceptually sound in principle, this is a controversial approach because it is unclear how truly free of assumptions researchers can be when they begin their studies. Such studies may simply be implicitly adopting the paradigmatic assumptions examined in Chapter 1 without acknowledging them, while explicitly eschewing any of the formal theories in a field. Given this distancing from any theoretical heritage, it is difficult to compile findings in order to document whatever knowledge base might be growing.

There has been some theoretical coherence in youth studies around Bourdieu's (1973, 1977; Bourdieu & Passeron, 1977) concepts of "habitus" and "cultural capital" in some work on "subjectivities" (e.g., Andres & Wyn, 2010). Bourdieu's framework seems strongest when it is applied as a form of pragmatic constructionism (as in the benefits of cultural capital to the élites), but it is not always used in this way. As we see in the family chapter, Bourdieu's concept of cultural capital is often used in the youth field (as well as other fields) to apply to any sort of resources passed on by a family or cultural context. For example, some researchers (e.g., Irwin & Elley, 2011) now speak of "middle-class cultural capital," which is far from what Bourdieu had in mind in terms of its role in the cultural reproduction of élites. Chin and Phillips (2004) even claim that children can create their own "cultural capital" as part of their insider knowledge regarding how to negotiate childhood. This is a misuse— indeed, an over-extension—of Bourdieu's work because his concept of cultural capital is more specific to the relative value of *high-status* culture knowledge and tastes as a way of establishing distinctions from lower status cultures. As it stands, the consistency and coherence of youth research based on Bourdieu's strand of research is not clear (cf. Jones, 2009, p. 39). Questions have also been raised concerning how well Bourdieu's model of cultural reproduction works outside of France, with its specific class structure and culture rooted in a feudal tradition (e.g., Davies & Guppy, 2006).

In addition, Bourdieu's concepts allow researchers to speak in generalities, but the concept of habitus is so general that it seems to encompass the conceptual structure of entire theoretical perspectives like symbolic interactionism, which would break down "habitus" into myriad concepts to explain people's dispositions, attitudes, values, definitions of the situation, presentations of self, and so forth. The same objection would be forthcoming from adolescent psychologists, whose parent discipline is based on the intensive study of the wide-ranging "dispositions" that would constitute a person's habitus. With these problems in mind, the concept of habitus is unlikely to ever become part of a unified youth studies, where a common language is shared among youth researchers of different theoretical persuasions. Overall, it is unclear what is achieved by simply equating "subjectivities" to forms of habitus. This is the case because the concept of habitus is so general that it has not been operationalized or put to an empirical test with respect to its validity. Instead, it stands as both an assumption preceding observation and an inference for interpreting observations, a violation of critical thinking.

For a sampling of illustrative studies that take interpretive/narrative approaches, as found in the *Journal of Youth Studies*, see

• Allen (2008), "Young people's 'agency' in sexuality research using visual methods";

- Best (2008), "Teen driving as public drama: statistics, risk, and the social construction of youth as a public problem";
- Sanders and Munford (2008), "Losing self to the future? Young women's strategic responses to adulthood transitions";
- Tutenges and Hulvej Rod (2009), " 'We got incredibly drunk...it was damned fun': drinking stories among Danish youth"; and
- Fjær (2012), "The day after drinking: Interaction during hangovers among young Norwegian adults."

Conclusion: Theories as insightful but limited

The youth-studies field comprises contributions from a variety of disciplines: some of these study young people incidentally as a sub-category in other analyses, but their main body lies elsewhere (e.g., functionalism and anthropology); others that have an exclusive focus on the young became sub-disciplines in their own right (e.g., adolescent psychology). This chapter attempted to provide useful, if brief, accounts of the theories that have contributed to youth studies in some way. The various inter-theory critiques are discussed in the next chapter, organized in terms of the debates that have dominated youth studies since its early days.

In Chapter 1, the various youth-studies approaches were categorized into four paradigms for heuristic purposes (Table 1.3), with full recognition that there can be considerable overlap among the various approaches and that individual researchers can use different approaches for different topics. Consistent with this assumption, in this chapter the approaches were presented without emphasizing their critical and conservative implications. This was done because the line is often not clear between whether an approach is truly radical, advocating significant changes to the status quo, or is merely a liberal variant of an otherwise conservative position that affirms the status quo or calls for minor reforms to it. In the next chapter, we take on this issue more directly in a discussion of the disputes among youth researchers that have a political basis.

In reserving most of the critiques of the theories for the next chapter, my hope is that a major takeaway point for the overall discussion is that many approaches do not have to be seen as competitors, as if someday one approach will "win" and become *the* grand theory of youth studies. To the contrary, the takeaway point is that the youth-studies field needs to be able to treat these various approaches as a carefully assembled collage in order to better understand the full gamut of topics, precisely because the assumptive bases of each approach are better suited to some topics than to others. All theories have their strengths and weaknesses, so a mature field needs to identify and apply the strong components of each theory when appropriate, while admitting to and setting aside the weak components. The imperialistic tendencies of some theorists act directly against this need and, in doing so, hold back the youth field from reaching its potential and becoming widely useful to all possible stakeholders—not just career-minded academics, but young people themselves, parents, community leaders, practitioners, and policy-makers.

As argued further in the next chapter, the influence of humanities orientations like postmodernism has introduced considerable confusion into youth studies, as well as other academic fields. Extreme forms of these orientations reject science as an Enlightenment folly, seeing it as grinding Western civilization into the ground, and the planet with it. But, when we step back to recognize that both the humanities and social sciences—in their mature forms— recognize that "truth" can never be absolutely grasped, but only approximated, then the project of improving those approximations can be a joint one, not an oppositional one. Extreme forms of postmodernism can reject even the utility of critical thinking, dogmatically asserting "universal relativism," which can lock everyone into dogmatic and hostile factions. It is difficult to defend such an extreme position.

Seidman (2004) argues that there are three (overlapping) forms of social theory: scientific, moral/critical, and philosophical (humanities). Scientific approaches aim to produce valid knowledge through reliable methods, moral/critical approaches strive to make the world a better place in which to live, and philosophical approaches aspire to develop timeless understandings of the human condition. Following this logic, the way forward for social theory in general, and youth studies in particular, is for academics to be cognizant of all three forms of theory. Instead of viewing them in opposition, each can be a valuable tool for triangulating on the validity claims, and thus developing ways of thinking about the tensions among them without producing paralyzing epistemological divisions.

Recommended readings

James E. Côté (2014). Toward a new political economy of youth. *Journal of Youth Studies.*

This article describes the political-economy-of-youth perspective, including the characterization of "youth as class" and updates it to account for the current position of the youth in the political economy of Western societies, with a focus on the United States.

Richard Lerner et al. (2011). Individual and contextual bases of thriving in adolescence. *Journal of Adolescence,* 34, 1107–14.

This article lays out the most recent advances in the positive youth development movement originating in adolescent psychology. Note the emphasis on developmental contextualism and human plasticity, and compare this "specimen" with the criticisms of positive youth development by Sukarieh and Tannock (2011), a recommended reading for Chapter 1. Is their criticism that positive youth development serves neoliberalism really fair, or would the goals of developing the agentic strengths of young people apply to all societies?

The following series of three papers provide a revealing and useful glimpse into the types of debates that have been introduced into youth studies by the late-modernist approach. As is the case with many complex formulations, youth researchers are still working out the implications of Beck's (1992, 2002) theory of individualization when it is applied to the youth period.

Dan Woodman (2009). The mysterious case of the pervasive choice biography: Ulrich Beck, structure/agency, and the middling state of theory in the sociology of youth. *Journal of Youth Studies*, 12, 243–56.

Woodman argues that Beck's writings concerning individualization and agency have been largely misunderstood by youth researchers employing his work, with the widespread belief that he emphasized agency over structure in how the life course is now played out.

Steven Roberts (2010). Misrepresenting "choice biographies"?: A reply to Woodman. *Journal of Youth Studies*, 13, 137–49.

Roberts objects to Woodman's position, arguing that youth researchers do have it right that Beck emphasizes agency over structure.

Dan Woodman (2010). Class, individualisation and tracing processes of inequality in a changing world: A reply to Steven Roberts. *Journal of Youth Studies*, 13, 737–46.

Woodman responds that Roberts and other youth researchers are too caught up in seeing structure and agency as polarities to fully grasp the nuances of Beck's position about how structure now affects the choices available to young people as they make their way through the life course.

Seminal Debates in Youth Studies

3

With an understanding of the underlying assumptive structure of the paradigms and theories in the youth studies field derived from Chapters 1 and 2, respectively, the seminal debates in the field of youth studies can be discussed in some depth. We see in the sections to follow in this chapter that the basic assumptions regarding ontological status, political agendas, and value-priority stances can be combined into positions that dogmatically draw oppositions to other positions, leading to protracted disputes that divide the field.

To facilitate the evaluation of arguments involved in these debates, this chapter begins with a discussion of "meta-theory," namely, a way of "theorizing about theories." Insights into the basic structural components of theories help us to think critically about the strengths and limitations of theories in general, and thus what we can expect from them in providing answers to the youth question, including evaluating the debates that have arisen in attempts to address that question.

Meta-Theory: Theorizing about theories

In recent decades, many social scientists and humanists have distanced themselves from what are perceived as *grand theories*; they have instead moved to develop myriad middle-range theories. In characterizing this shift in sociology, Giddens (1984, p. xv) argued that theoretical traditions "gave way and [were] replaced by a baffling variety of competing perspectives." Paradoxically, this theoretical distancing is often done without acknowledging an overarching paradigm into which a middle-range theory fits. Yet, all theories, even middling or "petite," are influenced implicitly or explicitly by many of the same underlying assumptions that gave rise to those older grand theories.

As we saw in the preceding chapter, a number of researchers have tried to answer aspects of the youth question. Although each theorist may be convinced of the "rightness" of his or her ideas, can all answers to the youth question be right? Well, logically, no. From a critical-thinking point of view, theories do not vary so much on the "right–wrong" dimension, as on a continuum of usefulness with respect to specific applications. In this section, we briefly consider some approaches that have been taken in evaluating the merits of theories in terms of their validity and usefulness.

One approach to assessing validity is to adopt a time-tested philosophical method that evaluates theories based on **theories of truth** (e.g., Kirkham, 1992). For instance, empirical evidence gathered through observations is typically sought to demonstrate the merits of a theory. Assessing theories in this way follows the **correspondence theory of truth.** Over time, empirical tests of theories build evidence concerning the extent to which the theory corresponds to empirical realities, and if the evidence shows otherwise, the theory should be modified or abandoned. For example, as we see below, the theory of universal adolescent storm and stress postulated by Hall in the early twentieth century has been abandoned by most social scientists because the empirical evidence has failed to validate its premise of being a universal phenomenon.

But, in order for a theory to become the object of intensive empirical testing, it must first gain acceptance among a sufficient number of overseers within a discipline or in one of the disciplinary perspectives. Theories that become widely shared have more credibility in terms of the **consensus theory of truth,** often because their logic seems sound, a requirement of the **consistency theory of truth.**

According to philosophers of science, over time, theories rise and fall depending on how much empirical support is found for them (correspondence), how widely they are accepted (consensus), and how logically coherent they are (consistency) (e.g., Hempel, 1966). This ideal is more easily achieved in the natural sciences because it is usually easier to provide compelling empirical demonstrations of theoretical predictions. In the social sciences and humanities, and certainly in youth studies, a rigorous evaluation of theories like that found in the natural sciences is hampered by the ontological, political, and value-priority disputes noted above, which tend to create academic silos that impede communication.

Consequently, within insular disciplines and perspectives, a sort of groupthink can lead researchers to believe that their theories are entirely coherent and consistent, and so widely applicable, and that there is sufficient empirical evidence to support them. Nonetheless, in an enthusiasm for their own theories, this overconfidence can lead researchers to treat them as "rubber sheets." That is, they try to stretch their theories to cover many more phenomena or contexts than is justified by the assumptions of the theory. Wertheimer (1972) argued that "rubber sheeting" a theory or concept reduces both its conceptual clarity and scientific utility. A few words about conceptual clarity and scientific utility are thus in order.

Like Wertheimer, in proposing a more precise way to speak about the strengths and limitations of theories, Kelly (1955) argued that all scientific concepts have a focal point, but outside that central point, their ability to explain phenomena diminishes. Kelly referred to the former as the *focus of convenience* of a theory and the latter as the *range of convenience*. The focus of convenience constitutes the "realm of events where ... a theory tends to work best" (p. 11). A theory's range of convenience defines its outer boundaries—"that expanse of the real world over which a given ... theory provides useful coverage" (p. 17). Giving examples from psychology, Kelly cited animal learning as the focus of convenience of stimulus–response theories, perception as the focus of field theories, and neuroses as the focus of psychoanalytic theories. From this point of view, then, theories should not be judged in terms of right–wrong dimension so much as a continuum of usefulness in relation to specific subject matter. This formulation is similar to the idea of scope conditions in the natural sciences (Hempel, 1966).

Just as Wertheimer warned about rubber sheeting, Kelly cautioned that it is common for theories to become "inflated" when theorists have emotional attachments to them; they therefore fail "to recognize that what is reasonably true within a limited range is not necessarily quite so true outside that range" (1955, p. 11). When this happens, predictions can become less precise, and hence lose scientific or logical rigor, becoming "so elastic that a wide variety of conceivable events can be construed as corroborative" (*ibid.*, p. 18).

As we see in Parts II and III, few theories have *not* been rubber sheeted or inflated in some way, principally because theorists tend to put too much faith in their own theories (and particular discipline) and too little in other theories (and other disciplines). This error can be the result of the confirmation bias, which leads each of us to put too much faith in what we have previously taken to be valid or true (see Chapter 1 for further discussion of this bias).

Nature vs. nurture: Etiology

The disagreements about the causes of human behavior are among the oldest disputes in philosophy, dating back to Greek philosophers like Aristotle and Plato (Muuss, 1996). In turn, the nature–nurture debate is one of the oldest disputes in the human sciences dating to the early decades of the twentieth century. Although the field of youth studies was embryonic at the time, this debate constitutes its earliest dispute. At the same time, this dispute helped increase interest in how to characterize the transition to adulthood (Côté, 1994). In fact, the nature–nurture debate is a fundamental youth-studies issue from which many other disputes stem, such as whether adolescence and youth are developmental stages or cultural age-statuses, as we see later in this chapter.

The nature–nurture debate in the modern human sciences has been characterized by considerable acrimony. Because of its wide-ranging political implications, it endures today. In actuality, the political stakes are high if one side were to "win" over the other side in terms of influencing public policy, as follows:

- If the claims of the nature side were accepted as valid, and all behaviors and mental capacities were believed to be genetically based and manifested through human biology, societies would find justifications in not taking responsibility for certain social problems. This would be the case because, by implication, these problems would be due to human genetics and thus inevitable as part of the human condition. For instance, if genes caused people to commit crimes, there would be little a society could do to stop or rehabilitate criminals. Likewise, economic privilege would be justified by the belief that the wealthy are genetically superior and that is how they (or their ancestors) acquired their wealth. Hence, the nature position in this debate implies the preservation of the status quo.

  o It is easy to see why beliefs in the genetic basis of behavior are more popular among the wealthy because they justify the privileges accorded to them (i.e., they tend to believe they are wealthy because of genetic superiority and the poor are without wealth because they are genetically inferior).
  o This position tends to rely on ontological realism, take the value-priority position that people need to be regulated and controlled, and maintains a conservative political agenda concerning social order.

- In contrast, if a pure nurture argument were accepted as true, and humans were believed to be born as genetic "blank slates" to be "written on" by experience, then economic privileges would be the consequence of preexisting social inequalities that favor some people over others. Accordingly, the nurture position does not support the legitimacy of a status quo based on inheritance, but rather suggests that social reforms are necessary to address social and economic inequalities, which are held to be responsible for the various social ills that are believed to be at the root of criminality and other forms of deviance.

  o Given the socio-economic implications of the nurture position, and its implicit challenge to the societal status quo, it is easy to see why this position is less popular among the upper classes and more popular among those without economic privilege, or those who identify with the latter.
  o The nurture argument therefore invites a more radical political agenda and the value-priority positions involving advocating for, and emancipating, all people. However, the belief that people are born as "blank slates" does not automatically involve beliefs about nominalism; indeed, social-environmental influences can still be seen as "real," rather than purely socially constructed, as in the case behavioral conditioning.

Clearly, much is at stake in terms of how people explain the causal foundations of human behavior, which is undoubtedly why nature–nurture issues have continually generated controversy (Shankman, 2009). Among the important issues are the justifications for capitalism vs. socialism, social-class distinctions, sexual orientations, gender roles, and social policies to remedy social problems and economic inequalities. Moreover, this is not simply an "ivory tower" dispute: these positions have dramatically influenced political policies in many countries, such as eugenics practices and immigration laws in Europe and the United States (Broad & Wade, 1982).

An interesting historical footnote to the nature–nurture controversy comes from an old study conducted by Pastore (1949). Pastore found that among 24 prominent scientists who were outspoken in the first part of the twentieth century as either hereditarian (nature advocates) or environmentalist (nurture advocates), 11 of the 12 on each side of the debate were found to be respectively either politically conservative (Right-wing) or liberal (Left-wing). This study was conducted on the basis of public pronouncements by leading scientists of the time like Galton, Davenport, and Pearson. Remarkably, when told of the correlation between their political and scientific views, most of these scientists were unwilling to accept that the findings applied to them personally. Their denial suggests just how deeply engrained personal and political biases can be and how they can prevent us for seeing things—and ourselves—more clearly.

Genetics-based arguments had a significant influence of youth studies in its early days, and continue to do so. As noted above, spearheaded by Hall (1904), proponents of the nature faction argued that adolescence is inevitably a period of storm and stress caused by genetically based hormonal disturbances. In response, anthropologists such as Benedict and Mead argued for the importance of nurture, with Mead reporting her findings from a culture where adolescence was not a turbulent period, thereby falsifying the hypothesis of universal adolescent storm and stress (Mead, 1928).

Mead's task in refuting Hall's extreme claims was relatively straightforward logically. Based on the absoluteness of Hall's (1904) claim that adolescence is a genetically based period in which *everyone inevitably* experiences a prolonged period of emotional turmoil, if one culture could be found where this was not the case (the "negative instance" method), then Hall's theory cannot be correct. Mead tackled this issue of the universality of adolescent storm and stress in a remote culture in the South Pacific. She reported her findings in a book that has been the best-selling book in the history of anthropology, *Coming of Age in Samoa* (1928). In one of the early mixed-method designs, in addition to her ethnography of Samoan culture focusing on the transition to adulthood, Mead compared three groups of females based on interviews in a quasi-experimental design: (1) those who had not yet experienced puberty, (2) those who were experiencing it, and (3) those who were past puberty. She reported that the experience of puberty made no significant difference in the character or emotional stability of these girls.

Mead attributed the lack of emotional turmoil among Samoan adolescents to their culture's consistent and continuous socialization practices. In contrast, she argued, the difficulties affecting American adolescents, the population that Hall had used for his generalizations, were caused by conflicting standards of conduct and morality, and "the belief that every individual should make his or her own choices, coupled with a feeling that choice is an important matter." In contrast, she asserted that in 1920s Samoa: "The gap between parents and children is narrow and painless, showing few of the unfortunate aspects usually present in a period of transition . . . essentially the children are still growing up in a homogeneous community with a uniform set of ideals and aspirations" (1928, p. 273). This evidence of cultural differences in the prevalence of adolescent difficulties led Mead to conclude that difficulties experienced while passing through adolescence cannot be considered a biological inevitability, but instead have cultural sources.

Over the twentieth century, evidence mounted against the universal storm and stress position, both cross-culturally (e.g., Condon, 1987) and within American society (e.g., Arnett, 1999; Offer & Offer, 1975; Steinberg, 2001). In spite of this evidence, the legacy of Hall's work lives on in the public mind— and in the mass media—to the extent that stereotypes have survived about "adolescent turmoil" and "raging hormones." A resurgence of the nature– nurture debate in the 1980s included a critique of Mead's work in Samoa (Freeman, 1983), a critique that in turn has been refuted (Côté, 1992, 1994; Shankman, 2009), culminating what has been called one of the ten "great feuds in science" (Hellman, 1998). In spite of this refutation, many contemporary nature advocates still use Freeman's erroneous critique of Mead's work as a basis for attacking "nurture assumptions" (cf. Shankman, 2009), showing how deep-seated these beliefs about the fundamental causes of human behavior can be. A reading is recommended at the end of this chapter that evaluates Mead's and Freeman's claims, and places the controversy in the wider context of the nature–nurture debate.

The nature–nurture debate is not over in the field of youth studies. The stereotypes formed by the early, erroneous constructions of reality by psychologists like Hall have taken on a life of their own. Although youth studies experts know that *universal* adolescent storm and stress is a myth, the public and media still tend to hold to the belief. Furthermore, following a set of iterations over the twentieth century, this prejudice against the functioning capacities of the young has recently resurfaced with the research about the "adolescent brain" (cf. Sercombe & Paus, 2009). Some researchers claim the "adolescent brain" is less developed than the "adult brain." For instance, Ortiz (2003) argues for a further suspension of the legal rights of young people, with the claim that "age 21 or 22 would be close to the 'biological' age of maturity" (Ortiz, 2003, Section 5, para 5). Ortiz (2003) claims that "there is now biological evidence that adolescents do not have the same ability to make sound decisions and to prevent impulsive behavior" (Section 5, para 4).

Although there may be some truth to the claim of adolescent–adult differences in brain functioning and psychological/behavioral characteristics, there are myriad problems with this claim that still need to be worked out scientifically and logically before a causal link between the two sets of phenomena can be determined scientifically. A leading researcher in the area of brain development points out that this field is still in its infancy and has yet to conduct the proper population level, controlled studies to draw causal conclusions on such matters (Paus, 2009). And, as noted in Chapter 2, it is now widely accepted that most behaviors involve "interactions" between nature and nurture influences (Lerner, 2002); in spite of this trend, interpretations of this brain research tend to be entirely biological, or "nature," especially those filtered by the mass media to the public.

When this area of research is finally put to serious empirical tests, it is likely that the plasticity of human brain development will be revealed, confirming that nurture influences are as important, if not more important than genetics, in determining the rate of certain forms of brain development during the youth period. An implication of the plasticity view is that by denying young people the choice to assume responsible roles, societies are actually inhibiting and slowing the development of brain structures associated with the reasoning abilities underlying decision-making processes. Paus (2009) expresses this view that biologically deterministic views are faulty as follows:

> [T]he common [biologically determinist] logic assumes that cognitive/executive control of behavior emerges only after the prefrontal cortex reaches an adult-like level of structural maturity. But given the role of experience in shaping the brain, it might also be that high demands on cognitive control faced, for example, by young adolescents assuming adult roles due to family circumstances may facilitate structural maturation of their prefrontal cortex. This scenario, if proven correct, will move us away from the "passive" view of brain development into one that emphasizes an active role of the individual and his/her environment in modulating the "biological" (e.g., hormonal) developmental processes. (p. 110)

In spite of its embryonic nature, this "brain research" currently enjoys a high profile among the stereotype-driven media and a gullible public. It is also telling that this belief has grown simultaneously with the lengthening of the transition to adulthood, providing yet another justification for socially controlling young people (Sercombe, 2010). Bessant (2008) has also examined this new line of research and is a recommended further reading, listed at the end of this chapter.

Thus, although most observers agree that behaviors are a complex mixture of the two influences, there are still those who vigorously raise the issue of the relative importance of genetics over life-experiences in shaping human development, in this case "the adolescent brain." In the case of the family, as we see below, Harris (2009) argues that the influence of parents over their children is *not* as important as their children's genetic makeup and the factors related to that makeup, like the peers with which they chose to associate.

At the same time, and in contrast, there appear to be some diehard nurture advocates in some disciplines, insisting that human development is totally determined by experiences during the person's lifetime. Many postmodernists appear to take this position as they apply, or rather overextend, social constructionism to that topic. This tendency is especially evident with their use of the concept of *essentialism*, as we see in Chapter 9 on identity formation. Among postmodernists, there is tendency to label anything that smacks of genetics, biology, or psychology as "essentialist." However, this word is rarely defined in this usage, so often the referent remains vague. Brock, Raby, and Thomas (2012) define essentialism as follows: "a position that assumes that human behaviors are rooted in some inherent, unchanging essence" (p. 354).

Unfortunately, Brock et al. do not specify what they mean by "essence," and a standard dictionary definition does not clarify what is wrong with speaking of something having an "essence." For example, "essence" is defined as "[1] the intrinsic nature or indispensable quality of something, esp. something abstract, that determines its character: *conflict is the essence of drama*; [2] Philosophy: a property or group of properties of something without which it would not exist or be what it is" (*New Oxford American Dictionary*, Word for Mac 2011). Given that it is mainly postmodernists who use this term, presumably the concern is that some position refers to "nature" influences rather than "nurture" influences; if so, postmodernists are taking an extreme nurture position that rejects nature influences—and even interactions between nature and nurture—as acceptable explanations for human behavior.

The problem with this charge of "essentialism" is that few social scientists endorse extreme nature explanations because there is little evidence for any single-cause phenomena. Consequently, most reputable academics have accepted "interactionist" positions: that nature and nurture interact to produce human behaviors and that human physiology and psychology are plastic (malleable to experiences over the lifetime; see Chapter 2). So, notwithstanding the more egregious examples of extreme nature claims like "universal storm and stress" and "the adolescent brain," if the intention in calling something "essentialist" is to claim that someone is making an extreme nature claim of behavioral causation, it may well be a fatuous charge. If it is intended as a "scare word" intended to discourage people from considering a matter more deeply, it amounts to an ideological gambit that discourages critical thinking.

Structure vs. agency: Causation

A second seminal dispute involves the extent to which people can resist, by exercising their own "free will," the influences of social structures and cultural institutions (including corporations). This debate involves the issue of how much free choice people are capable of exercising in their dealings with social structures, even in societies that are considered to be politically free, as in social and liberal democracies (cf. the early work on *pragmatism* by William James and its influence; Hewitt, 2003).

This debate has a relatively long history in sociology, and came to a head on the issue of the "oversocialized conception of man" among previous generations of sociologists, with Wrong (1961) criticizing structural functionalists for viewing people as not having the capacity (agency) to resist, or deviate from, social pressures, or to overcome structural obstacles.

In traditional, authoritarian societies with rigid hierarchical status systems, like caste systems or feudal systems, there is little question that social structures are all-determining, although there would be aspects of personal life that are open to some choice. Conversely, this debate emerged in Western sociology in attempts to understand how much individual choice and goal setting are possible in modern, ostensibly democratic, societies. Those who argue that structural obstacles based on social class, gender, race, and age are real and potent tend to downplay how much choice can be exercised in dealing with them. Others downplay the impact of those structural obstacles, especially poststructuralists who focus on individual adaptations to unstructured situations (e.g., Pakulski & Waters, 1996). This dispute is fundamental to the epistemological divide discussed above and is behind Furlong and Cartmel's (2007) notion of the *epistemological fallacy*.

The issues in this debate that are relevant to youth studies can be roughly characterized as follows:

- On the one hand, the social structures responsible for socializing youth can be quite imperceptible. Even when no physical coercion is used in enforcing these structures, a high degree of conformity can be found, as in the case of conventions of personal appearance, self-presentation styles, and consumer behaviors. This mass conformity raises several questions: Is the widespread in-group conformity in the way many young people dress and present themselves simply a matter of them not having the willpower to resist peer pressures? Or, is it a matter of most young people not being able to create their own truly unique behavior patterns? At the same time, structural obstacles can involve a type of portcullis that protects people of higher status or class, as in the historical cases of aristocracies using formal sanctions to block any mobility or change in material conditions among the peasantry, and later the working classes. These tendencies have modern equivalents in most Western countries, but tend to be more informal and behind the scenes, and therefore difficult to study.

- On the other hand, the issue of what constitutes agency and what might make people capable of it is still hotly contested, with the following questions still being explored: Is agency an inherent mental capacity; is it something that we learn; or is it a combination of both (nature–nurture interactions)? Is it a trait that varies among people, so that some people have more of it than others and are therefore more able to resist social pressures? Is it something that we use only when the opportunities arise? Or, is it exercised only when people are faced with a lack of guidance and structure from their culture, as in anomic, secular societies? The most recent thinking on this matter uses concepts such as individualization (e.g., Beck, 1992), "self-socialization" (Heinz, 2002), "intentional self-development" (Brandtstädter & Lerner, 1999), "self-efficacy" (Bandura, 1989), "identity capital" (Côté, 1997), and bounded agency (Evans, 2002) to account for how people in modern societies can manage their lives, in spite of multiple, contradictory, and incomplete influences, as well as structural obstacles.

This debate plays out in the field of youth studies in a number of ways, to be noted in the chapters that follow, but it is nicely illustrated in an exchange between Bynner and Arnett regarding the implications of the concept of "emerging adulthood." Here we see how a clash between a more conservative agenda (Arnett) and a more liberal agenda (Bynner) can play out in terms of the structure–agency debate.

Arnett has engineered a vigorous movement in adolescent psychology that is committed to insisting on an ontological divide of the youth period into two development stages: adolescence (10–17/18) and emerging adulthood (18–29) (Arnett, 2000). Rooted in adolescent psychology, Arnett's emerging adulthood model is decidedly based on the notion of "free choice," namely, that people choose their fates within certain "environmental" constraints (cf. Roberts, 2011). Hence, there is an understanding of the influence of social structure, but it is downplayed in preference for emphasizing the agentic potential of the individual. In his exchange with Bynner (2005), Arnett (2006) expresses this position as follows, in response to Bynner's criticism that his theory is "insufficiently attentive to structural factors":

> This is a criticism I have heard before from sociologists, who tend to place structural factors at the center of their interpretive frameworks—in contrast to developmental psychologists like me, who tend to view structural factors as one influence among many, with other important factors including personality, intelligence, and relationships with family and peers, among others. Developmental psychologists usually view the developing person as an active agent in the environment, whereas sociologists are more likely to view people as unwittingly subject to structural factors over which they have no control. Bynner accurately describes my view by stating that "In this theoretical framework, structural factors are seen more in terms of environmental influences and constraints in the way of life goals rather than as shaping, in a fundamental way, roles and identities to match modern conditions."
>
> (Arnett, 2006, p. 115)

Arnett therefore expresses in this quoted passage a boilerplate assumption in (adolescent) psychology regarding "agency" over "structure," and an unwillingness to consider a more structural position in determining human experience and behavior, or even structure–agency interactions. Indeed, it appears that this exchange between Bynner and Arnett did not alter Arnett's position concerning the role of economic structures in the prolongation of youth (e.g., Côté v. Arnett, 2005). Arnett claimed in a later exchange with Hendry and Kloep that the main influence of social class is merely to "shorten" the stage of emerging adulthood by "a year or two" (Arnett & Tanner, 2011, p. 49).

The structure–agency debate often implicitly informs many topical areas in youth studies, as we see in many of the chapters to follow, but it is especially relevant in considerations of identity. Hence, youth-identity theory and research are covered in two chapters below, the first focusing on more agentic aspects of identity and the second on the more structural aspects of identity.

Stage vs. status: Ontology revisited

At the time of Hall's (1904) writings, the industrial revolution and changes in agricultural society were displacing increasing proportions of young Americans from productive agrarian and household roles, leaving many idle in urban centers. As a result, they were increasingly seen as a threat to community tranquility and part of a social problem associated with increasing urban crime (cf. France, 2007, 2008). Hall put a name to why the young would be prone to this "problem" ("storm and stress"), while declaring adolescence to be a specific developmental stage of the life course rooted in human biological makeup. As we saw above, Hall's assumptions regarding storm and stress have been abandoned or modified, even among psychologists (Steinberg, 2001). However, many psychologists have retained the view that adolescence is a necessary stage of human development if the person is to follow a schedule of increasing complexity and maturity.

At the same time, more nuanced positions have merged from psychology regarding the nature of "stages." For instance, Snarey, Kohlberg, and Noam (1983) argued that adolescence should be classified as a "cultural age," not a developmental stage, because there is an emphasis "on quantitative changes in age, mastery, performance, knowledge, rights, and responsibilities" (p. 328). What many people consider developmental stages have a "structural" basis that involves qualitative changes in the structural arrangements of mental processes like cognitive structures or the ego. Moreover, "psychosocial stages" like those proposed by Erikson (e.g., the identity stage, as we see in Chapter 9) should be classified as "functional phases" because there is both a qualitative change in (identity) structure and a quantitative change in social status (from adolescence to adulthood) upon resolution of the stage (cf. Hendry & Kloep, 2010).

The choice of terminology and the vagaries of these assumptions constitute a major disciplinary fissure in youth studies between psychology and sociology. Sociologists tend to eschew the term "adolescence" because of what they see as "normative assumptions," and instead prefer the term "youth" to refer to this age-period as an age-status that is imposed by cultural expectations. This position is consistent with the above Snarey et al. (1983) classification of adolescence as culturally specific in its manifestations. In addition, rather than seeing young people who violate the norms of this age-status as somehow maladjusted, sociologists tend to see "youth deviance" as a form of resistance or reaction to oppressive or unreasonable cultural expectations. By and large, whereas psychologists tend to take an ontologically realist position that adolescence is a "stage," sociologists and anthropologists tend to take nominalist or pragmatic constructionist positions that "youth" is a socially constructed age-status (nominalism) that acts back on the person in "real" ways (pragmatic constructionism). From their ontological positions, sociologists and anthropologists object to developmental-stage characterizations, seeing them as errors of reification, namely, taking an abstract idea and considering it to "real" (Côté, 2010). Still, as noted in Chapter 2, it would be a mistake to assume that psychologists are uniform in their views about the ontological status of this age period.

Sociologists and anthropologists also see the strictly realist conception of adolescence as ethnocentric because of the evidence of extreme cultural variability. The inter-disciplinary research shows that although most cultures provide some sort of transitional period between childhood and adulthood, in most *premodern* societies this is a relatively short period, with puberty signaling that it is time for the person to take on the roles and responsibilities associated with adulthood in that culture. Beyond the near universality of the rites of passage and initiation ceremonies (like bar- and bat-mitzvahs, confirmations, and graduations) that institutionalize the passage out of childhood, Schlegel and Barry found evidence of a "social stage" of adolescence in virtually all of the 186 tribal societies they studied. In this research, they defined adolescence as "a period of social role learning and restructuring, away from the behavioral modes of childhood and toward adult modes" (1991, p. 8). Actually, this "social stage" is often as short as one year, especially for females. In most premodern societies, adolescence ends at age 16 for females and between 16 and 18 for males. It usually ends with marriage in a girl's teen years. For sociologists and anthropologists, then, youth is a "floating signifier" to the extent that the meanings of age differ according to cultural and normative contexts.

In light of these cross-cultural considerations, it is important for students and experts of youth studies to be mindful of variations in the ontological status of youth in a given society. What we now call this period of the life course did not exist for most of human history, and certain aspects of what is now found in Western societies characterizing this age period are not found in contemporary non-Western countries (e.g., expectations of teen rebellion and conflict with parents).

In fact, even today in the West, governments do not consistently recognize who belongs to this age status. To illustrate, in the United Kingdom, "youth" is officially limited to the 16 to 19 age period (Bynner et al., 2002), but in Norway and Finland it is defined to last until age 29 (Wolf et al., 2004; Ministry of Education, Finland, 2008). The reasons for these contrasting definitions are specific to the policy decisions taken in each country: to the extent that "youth" is defined as a period of semi-dependency financially, governments may be constitutionally responsible for providing entitlements to those under the age that defines the youth period there. Apparently, the UK government is less willing to provide financial entitlements to its young people to offset their economic disadvantages than is the Norwegian government (a common difference between liberal- and social-democratic countries).

Apropos to the discussion in Chapter 1 about ontological questions concerning the concept of "society," the former UK Prime Minister, Margaret Thatcher, in exposing one of the underlying neoliberal assumptions of today's liberal democracies, is famous for saying the following:

> I think we have gone through a period when too many children and people have been given to understand "I have a problem, it is the Government's job to cope with it!" or "I have a problem, I will go and get a grant to cope with it!" "I am homeless, the Government must house me!" and so they are casting their problems on society *and who is society? There is no such thing! There are individual men and women and there are families* and no government can do anything except through people and people look to themselves first.
>
> (emphasis added; Keay, 1987)

Does this mean that there are more "youth" in Norway or Finland than the United Kingdom? In a sense, yes, because as noted above, from a pragmatic constructionist perspective, to the extent that something is defined as real it can be real in its consequences. But to answer this question in a way that can bring youth studies experts to a consensus, a workable definition of "youth" is normally set against the concept of "adult." The adult is typically defined as someone who is financially self-sufficient and upholding family/community responsibilities, among other things, so we would need some way of comparing self-sufficiency in the United Kingdom with Nordic countries like Norway and Finland. However, the political differences between the two countries complicate this comparison because in the liberal-democratic United Kingdom, families are expected to provide for their members, even those in their twenties, as the above quote from Thatcher explains, whereas in the social-democratic Norway, the State assumes more of this responsibility.

We can take from this debate the caveat to watch out for reifications in our formulations. Stage concepts may work best as "heuristics," or what sociologists call ideal types. The concept of stages becomes less plausible when they are proposed as normative prescriptions. At the same time, age-statuses may have functional logics and not be entirely arbitrary impositions on people (e.g., as in the case of post-secondary students gaining meaningful credentials for complex professions). As with other concepts, the problem comes when ideas like stages are over-generalized, leading to homogenized concepts and normative expectations applying to the wrong segments of the population (e.g., assuming that the delay taken by post-secondary students in professional training should apply to all people of that age).

Critical vs. conservative politics: Agendas revisited

As argued in Chapter 1, all theories are infused with some sort of political agenda, ranging from conservative stances to preserving the status quo of societies, through liberal standpoints that seek to reform the status quo without substantially altering it, to radical positions that seek to replace the status quo in some way. This mixture of politics and science is something that is often an unspoken, yet fundamental, element of many debates in the social sciences and humanities.

Toward the conservative pole of political agendas, there tends to be a denial of this mix of values and logic, with claims of value-free science, while toward the radical end, there tends to be a celebration of the value priority of the theory. As it happens, some radical researchers appear to take the sharp-edged aspects of their theories as part of their identity as academics, sometimes lending an intense emotional component to their work. But at the same time, as noted, it is often difficult to draw lines among conservative, liberal, and radical approaches. In this section, we examine disputes among theorists—generally and in youth studies—that are political in nature, with this ambiguity in designation in mind.

A long-standing dispute in sociology has concerned the conservative implications of functionalism. Functionalism as a general approach, including its corresponding perspectives in anthropology, demography, and criminology, has been criticized from a number of perspectives for decades (e.g., Burrell & Morgan, 1979; see Mills, 1959, and Wrong, 1961, for specific critiques from an earlier generation of sociologists). Although functionalism and its counterparts provide useful descriptive information about societies in general, and specifically about youth, functionalists have been accused of making the logical error of making an "ought" from an "is;" that is, of making prescriptions out of descriptions. Consequently, functionalists have a tendency to assume that because some social arrangement or practice exists it is beneficial in some way, and therefore it *ought to* exist. This assumption thus bypasses the moral-ethical concerns of other sociologists who question the social justice aspects of certain social arrangements.

Critics also charge that functionalists assume too much inevitability in the social order and of evolutionary social change; that societies evolve naturally according to some quasi-biological logic rather than because of purposive human activity. These evolutionary-order assumptions seemed to work well when functionalism was applied to tribal and subsistence-type societies, as anthropologists did in the first part of the twentieth century. This was likely the case because these cultures seemed to need strict order/regulation to stave off serious material privations like starvation. In contrast, modern Western societies have clearly been more change oriented, with reforms and revolutions undertaken over the past few centuries through intentional human actions designed to equalize distributions of material resources to all members of society, away from the hoarding tendencies of (first) the aristocracies and (later and currently) the bourgeoisie (now, commonly called the "1%").

These intentional social justice initiatives were undertaken to correct inequalities in the distribution of resources and wealth, not only for the benefit of the less privileged in societies but because more equal societies are generally better for everyone in those societies (Wilkinson & Pickett, 2010). In the minds of many, more radically oriented, social scientists and humanists, this struggle for social justice is far from over. For them, functionalist theories have not been as useful as other theories in explaining these revolutionary changes or accounting for the actions of conflicting interests in societies that can lead to change.

In the preceding chapter, we saw that functionalist formulations normalize the current prolonged youth, seeing mostly benefits in it, even from an evolutionary standpoint. However, their conclusions are not based on the "hard" demographic data they normally produce, but on an interpretation of data that can be construed in other ways, as is done by the other youth researchers. Functionalists' interpretive processes are just as susceptible to biases, including political ones, so there is nothing in their otherwise scientific methodology verifying these conservative conclusions about social evolution.

A similar critique has been applied to adolescent psychology: because the discipline defines the teen years as constituting the period of adolescence, psychologists tend to automatically assume that the form of adolescence as now found in Western societies *ought to* exist (exceptions can be found to this tendency, of course, most notably with Epstein, 2007). When also based on the erroneous theory of adolescent storm and stress, there has been an expectation for teenagers to experience emotional turmoil, resulting in all sorts of behaviors among teens being seen in this negative light (e.g., Côté & Allahar, 1996, 2006). In point of fact, we can identify in the history of this field a tendency to medicalize and pathologize adolescence, and to even treat adolescence as if it is a disease or an epidemic (cf. Hill & Fortenberry, 1992). At the same time, as noted in the previous chapter, it would be a mistake to pigeonhole contemporary psychologists of adolescence as "all biology" or "all blame" regarding adolescents.

Still, this early conservative tendency in adolescent psychology may be partly responsible for the palpable "anti-psychology" among many radically minded postmodernists, an objection that seems to be based on a rejection of the entire discipline as *essentialist* (e.g., Rattansi & Phoenix, 2005). This previous tendency in psychology may also be partly responsible for the dismissal of adolescent psychology by some youth sociologists with more liberal or radical agendas (e.g., Wyn, 2012). A number of psychologists have responded to this critique (e.g., Chandler, 1995; Kroger, 2005), but given the prevalence of academic silos today, these responses are unlikely to have been read. It is quite possible, then, that much of the hostility toward psychology is based more on political grounds, along with an anti-realist nominalism in the case of youth studies (e.g., Payne, 2001), than a careful point-by-point critique.

The more radically oriented perspectives can also be critiqued in terms of their lack of clarity in their political agendas, even as these agendas affect the conclusions drawn from research.

For instance, political-economy-of-youth theories have been criticized in terms of their structural determinism and implicit functionalism, as we see in the chapters on education and work. These criticisms are debatable (Bowles & Gintis, 2003), but the over-extension of these theories is most obvious in the early claims of the revolutionary potential of youth (e.g., Rowntree & Rowntree, 1968) and the attempts to explain the youth period in terms of alienation and false consciousness. Although the youth segment of the 1960s appeared to have revolutionary potential at the time, the overthrow of capitalism did not occur, even if certain social justice changes did come about (e.g., the civil rights-, women's-, and green-movements). And, while alienation and false consciousness can be identified among certain segments of the youth population, their subjective experiences and potentials likely involve much more than this, including their agentic potentials.

An important complication of the political-economy perspective is that it is often difficult to provide neat packages of compelling proof to skeptics. Most social scientists are accustomed to evidence based on quantitative or qualitative models. However, the major events of interest to political economists occur in private for the very reason that they involve self-interested manipulations of policies and the non-democratic exercise of power. Documenting these events requires ethnographic analysis for which permission would rarely be given, or forms of investigative journalism (e.g., Schlosser, 2001). Political economists must therefore engage in careful critical analyses of historical, economic, and cultural factors. Even then critics often dismiss the products of these types of analyses as "conspiracy theories." In the above respects, though, without any assumptions of "conspiracies" against young people, youth exploitation can be identified as "business as usual" in contemporary neoliberal capitalist societies (Côté & Allahar, 2006; Côté, 2014b).

Although the late-modernist perspective was classified as a radical theory in Table 1.3, no radical agenda for late-modernism has been articulated for youth studies, although the call for the renewed recognition and eradication of structural barriers would certainly require significant changes to the status quo (e.g., Furlong & Cartmel, 2007, 2009). Still, a manifesto about how to eradicate structural barriers has not been offered, so the radical nature of this perspective remains implicit, and the perspective thus appears to be more liberal than radical in its influence. For example, Giddens proposed a liberal agenda based on his late-modernist social theory in his advocacy of the "third way," an approach that has influenced government policy in the United Kingdom (Giddens, 1994). Re-norming modern Western societies in ways that would make the individualization process a more benign influence for all people would largely be a cultural project beyond the purview of governments. In addition, efforts to block corporations from substituting individualistic consumerist norms for traditional cultural norms could be undertaken, or re-established, if a collective will and sense of moral outrage could be mobilized (Côté, 2000). But, these efforts would likely involve liberal reforms rather than revolutionary actions. Revolutions mounted in the name of combating "Western decadence" seem to be a thing of the past, although countries with fundamentalist religions around the world can apparently still garner support for protecting their traditional values from market forces.

Finally, turning to the postmodernist perspective, in Chapter 1 both conservative and radical strands of this approach were identified (Table 1.3). The problem is that much of this work is difficult to categorize paradigmatically because many postmodern writings have a "radical panache," yet do not advocate a change in the status quo, and some even seem to celebrate the current "status quo" calling for further "postmodernist" changes (cf. Hollinger, 1994). Gergen's (1991) psychological version of postmodernism has this celebratory quality, as does the post-subcultural approach in cultural studies, which argues that consumption provides creative resources for "youth identities," without questioning the overall capitalist context of this consumption (cf. France, 2007; see also Bennett, 2011).

As noted above, the distinguishing feature of critical perspectives is that they are not only critical of the status quo but advocate alternatives that would radically change the structure of the society. This requires more than simply pointing out power or status differences in societies, because some would argue that all societies will have these differences regardless of the outcome of any reform or revolution attempts (cf. Shackel, 2005). The definition used in this book is that radical agendas advocate significant changes to the status quo, whereas conservative positions affirm the status quo or call for minor reforms to it (in their liberal variants). Within this context, it is not clear how extensively certain self-identified postmodernist theorists are seeking to change the status quo as opposed to improving it, so that realities conform to ideals, as in the case of the ideal of modern Western civilization. Seidman (2004) notes this in his following conclusion about the influence of postmodernism on social theory:

> Postmodern thinkers would not merit serious attention if they were simply against the Enlightenment. Postmodern thinkers are heirs to the Enlightenment, but critical heirs. Their aim is to preserve the core ethical convictions or values of the Enlightenment and its hope for a better world but to offer different understandings of knowledge, social life, politics, the self, and social evolution. (p. 202)

In specific reference to youth studies, arguing from a late-modernist position, Furlong and Cartmel (2007) object to the claims of some postmodernists that structural factors like social class and gender have lost their relevance as life-course determinants. This form of "poststructuralism" can amount to a very conservative position. Furlong and Cartmel refer to the rejection of "structure" as the epistemological fallacy, where illusions of socio-economic equality fly in the face of these persisting old inequalities. They argue that in the current era many people in general, and some social scientists in particular, have been mistakenly convinced that these old forms of discrimination are no longer relevant to people's lives. A primary consequence of this at the level of the individual is that people who believe that these old barriers are no longer operant blame themselves for any personal disappointments or failure to reach certain goals in their own lives. This belief is consequently a powerful social control mechanism in perpetuating societies that deny the very barriers that make their social relations of production possible, as in the case of capitalism. In this way, the concept of the epistemological fallacy parallels the concept of false consciousness, highlighting how an ignorance of the importance of structural factors in one's life can lead to self-blame.

In a similar fashion, Côté and Allahar (2006) refer to this feature of late-modern societies as "the individualization contradiction" where "people are expected to be the architects of their own destinies, but for many the avenues do not exist to turn this expectation into a reality" (p. 78). Following Giddens, they argue that many of the supposed freedoms found in late-modern societies come more from the institutional voids created by institutional destructuring, and less from a decline in oppressive and exploitive structures. In a sense, then, these are "negative freedoms" that can be very difficult to take advantage of because there are few means and models for doing so.

In point of fact, postmodernists and late-modernists cover much of the same ground (e.g., fragmentations in self and society), but late-modernists do not generally make their case "in opposition"—that other perspectives are invalid—while postmodernists often begin their publications by rejecting all other attempts to understand a problem at hand. This "oppositional" nature of some postmodernist analysis may appear radical in identifying some unspecified "enemy" but may actually be a hindrance to the development of well-articulated theory; certainly, postulating well-articulated, logically based theories are in some ways antithetical to the oppositional and relativist nature of forms of postmodernism (cf. Shackel, 2005).

The implicit conservatism of postmodernist youth approaches has also been criticized on a number of substantive grounds. For instance, France (2007 p. 5) argues these "approaches are shown [in his analysis] to have weaknesses when it comes to explaining the wider influences that are at play within the 'market place'." This suggests an over-extension—or rubber sheeting—of postmodernist theory, for example, in trying to explain economic phenomena from a nominalist perspective. It also raises questions as to whom or what postmodernists identify as the "enemy." That is, some postmodernist approaches appear on the surface to be radical, but it is not clear what "status quo" is seen to be the problem: modernism, capitalism, quantitative methods, rationality, science, or some other unspoken convention or institution? This drawback is discussed further below in attempts to apply the perspective, especially in the two identity chapters and the youth culture chapter.

In youth studies, many publications are based implicitly or explicitly on postmodernist assumptions regarding the fragmentation of identities and problematic subjective experiences, with empirical work taking aggressively anti-realist nominalist stances (e.g., see McDonald's, 1999, application of Touraine's method of the "sociological intervention" to marginalized Australian youth). But, in this focus on subjectivities rather than material conditions, the issue of critical/conservative approach lands on the conservative side because there is little attention to the material world of life-chances and the distribution of wealth. Without specifying an "enemy," an approach may simply be a form of pseudo-radicalism obfuscated behind high-sounding prose (cf. Seidman, 2004).

Quantitative vs. qualitative: Methodologies

As is the case of the social sciences in general, a palpable division among youth-studies researchers involves the preference for one type of methodology over another. In point of fact, this differential methodological preference can be found throughout the history of the social sciences (e.g., see Blumer's, 1969, symbolic interactionist critique of "variable analysis"). From the point of view of a mature discipline, though, beliefs that qualitative and quantitative methods are mutually exclusive are false (Neuman, 2006). High-quality research projects can use both methodologies in a complementary fashion (Cahill, Fine, & Grant, 1995; Helve, 2005), a tradition that can be found in early social-scientific studies before the development of rigid disciplinary boundaries and the emergence of academic silos that characterize contemporary universities (e.g., Sherif, 1958; Hollingshead, 1949). As Neuman (2006) argues with respect to the social sciences in general, qualitative and quantitative methods differ in ways that are often complementary. Unfortunately, communication between researchers favoring each type is limited in part because "the languages and orientations of the styles are mutually intelligible" but many researchers do not take "the time and effort to understand both styles and to see how they can be complementary" (Neuman, 2006, p. 151). Likewise, as we have seen for the current phase of youth studies, methodological preferences generally follow the epistemological divide associated with the nominalism–realism dispute.

In general, those in the realist paradigms, especially adolescent psychologists and functionalists, tend to automatically adopt quantitative models, which require data points for all conclusions, even though their own theories are often laden with "unobservables," as in the case of evolutionary theories. However, the purely scientific model is best suited for artificial laboratory-type research; in contrast, social problems tend to be complex and changeable, making it impossible to gather data points in support of every conclusion. A problem with wanting "the data to speak for itself" is illustrated in the remarks of a sociologist who conducted an in-depth study of the consumption-based status relationships of American high-school students. Speaking to the issue of whether marketing to teens "works," he takes a "neutral" stance and simply says "there seems to be very little careful research on marketing to adolescents published in peer-reviewed journals or by academic presses," so he refuses to draw conclusions about the possible negative implications of marketing to teens (Milner, 2004, p. 158). He takes this position in spite of the mounds of data that he provides in his own book showing the corporate influence in the status-anxious lives of the high-school students he studied. The drawback with waiting for the scientific "evidence" to appear in academic journals and books is that many problems will not be defined as such in the first place "without the data." It is a more reasonable position to use statistical methods as only diagnostic tools, but to draw wider conclusions based on statistical results in terms of theoretical frames of reference.

At the other extreme are a number of postmodernists who explicitly endorse "anti-modernist" proclivities based on an anti-realist nominalism. Postmodernist formulations of youth remain controversial, though, even as they have a particular appeal among those who have an affinity with nominalism in general and social constructionism in particular, and especially among those who reject quantitative research methods and the scientific assumptions underlying those methods (e.g., Tilleczek, 2011). Actually, as with postmodernism in general, many postmodernist formulations found in youth studies publications appear to represent more of an "anti-modernism" than a "post-modernism" (cf. Côté & Levine, 2002; Hollinger, 1994; Kegan, 1994; Shackel, 2005). This hostility to realist ontologies seems to have widened the epistemological divide in youth studies as well—a chasm that is so difficult to bridge that many scholars on both sides of the divide apparently simply ignore each other's empirical work. Thus, while a postmodernist can feel justified in simply dismissing any research that is based on a quantitative method and/or realist assumptions because that method and ontology are viewed as invalid, in turn, others can dismiss postmodernist findings on a variety of grounds (e.g., questionable reasoning, ambiguous evidence).

Although postmodernism continues to seek adherents in youth studies (e.g., Lesko & Talburt, 2012), the strident views of certain postmodernist formulations can have a strong but contradictory ideological bent (cf. Hatcher, 1994) that make it difficult for many other youth-studies researchers to accept. For instance, postmodernist assertions have included the following contradictions: (a) claiming to having uncovered the relativity of knowledge in an absolute manner; (b) declaring the sovereignty of subjectivity over objectivity through recourse to (implicit) objective principles; and (c) claiming to undermine relative "truths" with their own absolute, but never articulated, "truths" (as in the case of proposing the meta-narrative [of postmodernism] to end all meta-narratives, thereby becoming a grand narrative itself; cf. Seidman, 1994).

Ironically, these formulations have a rather strong reliance on modernist (Enlightenment) forms of rationality and ideals of human liberation (cf. Seidman, 2004), especially those embedded in nominalism. But, nominalism does not require the boilerplate assumptions that many postmodernists have adopted, either against the critical-realist paradigm or even against the conservative-nominalist paradigm.

A recommended reading at the end of Chapter 1 (Unger, Draper, & Pendergrass, 1986) explored the reasons behind the appeal of opposing "personal epistemologies." Their study represents early work into tensions between personal beliefs in social constructionism vs. "logical positivism." Both sets of beliefs are defined as "covert causal assumptions about the relationship between the person and physical and social reality" (p. 67). Unger et al. proposed that the "side" chosen by a person in explaining causes of social behavior depends in part on the person's past experiences (e.g., those who favor social constructionism have felt discriminated against in the past). Their study presented a questionnaire designed to measure both sets of beliefs as contrasting "personal epistemologies."

Other than linking personal biases to academic perspectives, Unger et al.'s study is of interest because the research question in that study appears not to have led to much further research. This may be because they contrasted social constructionism with "positivism" rather than realism. The term "positivism" has become a disparaging epithet among many scholars who favor qualitative methods, but positivism and quantitative methods are not the same. For example, Halfpenny (1982) identified 12 forms of "positivism" involving various combinations and permutations of assumptions commonly attributed to "positivism." In effect, many people use the term positivism as if it simply refers to quantitative statistics (Turner, 2006), when in fact it does not; besides, the use of statistics is not incompatible with nominalism.

This false distinction between these two genres of methods can be easily avoided by using the terms "nominalism" and "realism," rather than constructionism and positivism because the former terms do not have the baggage that can bring productive discussions to a halt. At the same time, as noted above, the term postmodernism has been increasingly conflated with nominalism, when the two concepts are actually distinct. A postmodernist might prefer nominalist ontologies, but a nominalist does not have to accept any of the assumptions of postmodernism, in any of its forms (cf. see Hewitt, 2003, for a strong critique of postmodernism from a symbolic interactionist perspective).

Strictly speaking, a methodology is any system of guidelines for answering questions and solving problems. It does not have to involve numbers or interviews (Neuman, 2006). As noted in Chapter 1, critical thinking can constitute a methodology if it follows a systemic set of steps that allow others to understand how a conclusion is reached and to repeat the process. At the very least, a methodology should prevent a conclusion from being based solely on the "confirmation bias," the tendency to accept, with little proof, ideas, positions, or evidence that confirm a person's existing beliefs (e.g., Oswald & Grosjean 2004; see also Chapter 1). In the case of the social sciences, as noted in the preceding chapter, each theory is prone to errors created by an uncritical adherence to boilerplate assumptions.

Moreover, even when one or more of the established qualitative or quantitative methodologies is used, the results still have to be interpreted through some system of thought or mental operation and the best way to avoid the confirmation bias in interpreting these results is through careful, systematic critical thinking, as opposed to simply reaffirming boilerplate assumptions through ritualistic methodologies. In addition, being mindful of the theories of truth (discussed at the beginning of the present chapter) helps investigators avoid the hubris that accompanies some research endeavors that culminate in simply "preaching to the choir." The general lesson to be taken from this section is that the strength of an argument is proportionate to the extent that a "non-believer" will at least take notice of the conclusions, or at most, accept them.

This fracture in the social sciences and humanities can be understood in terms of different topical applications of the two methods. Both can sometimes be used together in mixed methods to triangulate on a research question sequentially or simultaneously, depending on the strength of each method for the topic at hand (Neuman, 2006, pp. 149–50). But, often a particular topic is best approached with qualitative methods, as in "documenting real events, recording what people say (with words, gestures, and tone), observing specific behaviors, studying written documents, or examining visual images" (Neuman, 2006, p. 157). Other topics are best approached with quantitative methods, as in examining the relationships between processes and structures that have variable qualities and pertain to large samples or populations. For example, understanding educational attainment can be enhanced by ethnographic studies of schools that examine the experiences of students and teachers as they are affected by school cultures (e.g., Milner, 2004; Willis, 1977), in conjunction with statistical studies of the relationship between parental education and affluence and the educational paths and occupational destinations of their children (e.g., Bowles & Gintis, 1976; Torche, 2011).

Finally, Neuman (2006) puts the false opposition between these methods in perspective as follows, noting that a more mature approach is to understand the merits of both methods as they are applied to the different topics for which each is best suited:

> Too often, adherents of one style of social research judge the other style on the basis of the assumptions and standards of their own style. The quantitative researcher demands to know the variables used and hypotheses tested. The qualitative researcher balks at the turning humanity into cold numbers. The well-versed, prudent social researcher understands and appreciates each style on its own terms and recognizes the strengths and limitations of each. The ultimate goal of developing a better understanding and explanation of the social world comes from an appreciation of what each has to offer. (p. 177)

Conclusion: The way forward—beyond academic silos

This chapter began with a discussion of ways in which to evaluate the merits of theories—on the one hand, in terms of the ways philosophers have evaluated them by triangulating on their validity in terms of correspondence, coherence, and consistency—and on the other hand, with respect to how psychologists have evaluated specific theories of human behavior and experience. These insights were offered to remind youth researchers that the "truth" can only ever be approximated and a goal of the social sciences and humanities is to find ways to improve those approximations. This goal is also the object of using critical thinking as a methodology.

When examined in terms of their boilerplate assumptions, it is easier to see how and why the various perspectives are popular in different ways. Generally, those endorsing particular perspectives on the key debates examined above have been socialized to do so through their higher-educational experiences, including their undergraduate careers. Those who have been through degree programs in psychology are obviously more likely to endorse the assumptions of adolescent psychology, while those with sociology degrees would be more likely to endorse those supportive of one of the perspectives that have emerged out of sociology. Also, there are likely selection factors leading people to major in psychology over sociology, for instance. Within sociology, there are differing influences, with some students taking courses advocating critical perspectives and others emphasizing conservative perspectives, depending on the department and university. There has been little research into what these selection factors might be.[1] However, if the field is to move forward, youth researchers need to be willing to question these formative disciplinary assumptions in terms of a boilerplate that might be impeding their continuing growth as academics. They should also take the time to read the work of those in competing disciplines when reviewing their positions on key debates. And, they must be willing to re-evaluate their previous assumptions in terms of how useful each perspective is in explaining phenomena in different topic areas. The topical chapters in Parts II and III illustrate some ways in which this might be accomplished.

Recommended readings

Judith Bessant (2008). Hard wired for risk: Neurological science, "the adolescent brain" and developmental theory. *Journal of Youth Studies*, 11, 347–60.

> This article is a sociological critique of the emerging neurological field of research on the adolescent brain development.

James E. Côté (1992). Was Mead wrong about coming of age in Samoa?: An analysis of the Mead/Freeman controversy for scholars of adolescence and human development. *Journal of Youth and Adolescence*, 21, 499–527.

> This article examines the controversy that developed in the 1980s over the validity of Mead's 1920s research contesting Hall's storm and stress thesis. Among other things, an undercurrent of this controversy is the nature–nurture debate, with Mead's critics largely being nature advocates who bear grudges against the ground gained by nurture advocates over the twentieth century.

Leo B. Hendry & Marion Kloep (2010). How universal is emerging adulthood? An empirical example. *Journal of Youth Studies*, 13, 169–79.

This qualitative study illustrates alternative ways of classifying young people during the transition to adulthood that do not require the "free-choice" model adopted by Arnett.

Monica Payne (2001). Limitations unlimited: Interrogating some finer points of the "scientific study" of adolescence. *Journal of Youth Studies*, 4, 175–94.

This paper is a scathing critique of the tendency of adolescent psychology to publish low-quality quantitative studies, calling for more politically informed and methodologically diverse approaches to be taken in the adjudication of studies by academic journals.

Jonathan H. Turner (2006). Explaining the social world: Historicism versus positivism. *The Sociological Quarterly*, 47, 451–63.

This essay examines opposing qualitative–quantitative methodologies, exposing myths about the nature and impact of "positivism."

Part II

The Socio-Economic Influences Structuring the Youth Period

This part of the book examines the antecedent or causal factors that have shaped the youth period, as it is currently found in most Western countries. Within the current historical period, the social and economic influences are examined that define and affect the portion of the population that on the one hand is biologically mature (i.e., post-pubertal), but on the other hand is not fully included in the productive functions of society. This is the age-period that is the focus of contemporary (Western) youth studies.

As noted above, the youth period can be found to range from ages 14 to 30, depending on the culture in question, with a lower boundary more relevant in traditional societies and an upper margin more common in contemporary Western societies. In distinguishing this age-period from the earlier and later periods of childhood and adulthood, the word "youthhood" would be appropriate. In fact, this word was first used in the English language several centuries ago (Jones, 2009; *Oxford English Dictionary*, 1921/2012), and after a long hiatus, was reintroduced by Mørch (1995) and Côté (2000). Nevertheless, the term "youth" is in current use, so will be used throughout this book.

In many ways, then, the chapters in this book examine the prolonged transition to adulthood, or delays in attaining full community membership and "economic maturity," as well as disputes about (a) why this transition has become prolonged and (b) the implications of this prolongation. With this focus on the prolonged transition in Western societies, the content of these chapters does not include much of what psychologists study as early adolescence. Also, by implication, it touches on the changing nature of adulthood, especially early adulthood.

Each chapter examines key issues associated with the emerging and changing structuring of the youth period. For every chapter, at least one exemplary issue, debate, or controversy is identified and briefly discussed. These exemplars are analyzed using the fundamental assumptions discussed in Chapter 1 that underly opposing interpretations of the meaning and relevance of these structural influences (i.e., ontology, political agenda, and value priority). Further readings are then recommended to encourage additional explorations of these key disputes.

When possible, each chapter focuses on those authors who identify opposing perspectives in their publications, especially if they claim to have a better perspective than do their opponents.

Education and the Youth Period

4

Mass educational systems from the primary to the tertiary levels have been growing in most countries around the world to the point where it is common for secondary systems to be "universally" attended. That is, all young people up to a certain age (e.g., 18) are strongly pressured to attend, and in many cases are legally required to do so until age 16. Although the extent of participation in tertiary systems by youth populations varies widely around the world, there is a global trend led by the West for countries to institute universal post-secondary systems. Much of the growth in colleges and universities has been driven by beliefs about the economic value and societal benefits of certain forms of learning, types of skill-acquisition, and patterns of behavior as preparations for contemporary labor forces. These beliefs are now strongly held by policy-makers and publics around the globe, a major change from even a half-century ago (e.g., Bowles & Gintis, 1976; Collins, 1979; Davies, 2005). For example, according to Livingstone and Hart (2005), in Canada, there was a doubling of public support for post-secondary education between the 1970s and the 1990s as measured by parental beliefs in the necessity of this level of education for their own children.

In addition, critics are increasingly pointing to the mounting evidence that mass systems are experiencing multiple crises in many countries, especially at the secondary and tertiary levels. These systems are suffering from underfunding, overcrowding, declining standards, and a delegitimation among students compelled to attend such systems because of a lack of alternatives in the labor market. Consequently, university systems in many countries appear to be "devolving" into hitherto secondary-type systems, under pressure to provide more time and space for students to socialize with their peers in place of full-time academic studies, raising questions about the fundamental missions or *raison d'être* of non-vocational programs (Côté & Allahar, 2011).

One explanation for this crisis is that this growth of mass systems has taken place under the hegemony of neoliberalism, which shifted fiscal responsibilities from governments and the wealthy to individuals and their families. Accordingly, at the same time that young people from all socio-economic backgrounds have been pressured to go further in school, governments in many countries have dramatically reduced their financial support of higher-education systems, in part because of the unwillingness of the wealthy to pay income taxes at a rate necessary to fund quality educational systems (Lasch, 1995; Steger & Roy, 2010). In the face of these competing pressures of *credentialism* and underfunding, some critics are revisiting the older claims regarding the latent functions, hidden curriculum, and indoctrination associated with mass education (Bowles & Gintis, 1976/2011). They are doing so especially in light of the evidence of the widespread *under*employment among the most educated segments of youth in developed countries (Kalleberg, 2007) as well as the *un*employment in developing and developed countries hit hard by the global crisis of capitalism that began in 2008 (International Labour Office, 2012, 2013).

These developments have important implications for young people in those countries most affected by mass expansions of upper secondary and tertiary systems because advanced educational credentials are becoming minimal requirements for labor force entry in all but the lowest skilled jobs. These requirements force a delay of financial independence and a prolongation of various forms of dependencies (e.g., on the family and the State) that result when people (of any age) are not able to earn a living wage. Although family dependency is not always a problem, especially in those cultures with a history of co-residence of young people with their parents, in some cultures and contexts it can pose a serious problem for the young person who can become caught in a socio-economic "limbo."

In this chapter, we examine the debate that has been ongoing for some time between those (conservative) functionalists who subscribe to "human capital theory" and those who follow a (critical) Marxist-based political-economy theory. In this debate, the conservative view tends to see forms of extended education and credential acquisition as a social and individual advantage. In contrast, the critical view questions the need for prolonged types of formal credential-based education, arguing instead that the real purposes include a reproduction of existing social class structures, the preservation of an army of cheap surplus labor, and opportunities for amassing wealth by Capital.

This debate hence becomes one of whether education in general, but especially higher education, is the "great equalizer" that publics believe, or instead is a form of ideological indoctrination into the capitalist ethos. As we see, regardless of the conclusions one draws about this debate, one effect of extending educational requirements is to prolong the youth period, and this can have a ripple effect to other youth experiences and outcomes. With the extended youth period becoming increasingly correlated with educational requirements for employment, this issue is central to youth studies. It can be argued that "youth" has become a new "filter" of social reproduction, with credential attainment acting as a smokescreen, obscuring structural obstacles by attributing success and failure to specific attributes of the individual in making youth transitions. If this is the case, many young people are being warehoused in schools and enticed by arbitrary credential acquisition, until employers need them, with their labor power exploited along the way (in the low-paying jobs available to students and younger workers) as well as upon graduation.

Although much of this literature comes from the United States, raising questions about its applicability in other countries, there is strong evidence that many countries around the world are in the process of "Americanizing" their educational systems (Roberts, 2009), so the American example may be a foretoken for those countries. Further research in countries that have resisted the Americanization process will shed light on the global pervasiveness of these processes, especially countries that have managed to maintain viable dual systems with apprenticeship tracks leading more directly to full employment at a younger age. For a particularly provocative critique of the UK university system from a social-justice perspective, see Furlong and Cartmel (2009). For critiques of the neoliberal transformations of the UK system, see Hayes and Wynyard (2002) and Molesworth, Scullion, and Nixon (2011).

After critically analyzing the conservative and critical theories, we examine ways of synthesizing these theories to help us understand more clearly the circumstances currently facing young people in mass educational systems.

Functionalism: The great equalizer?

In the educational debate, functionalists fall clearly on the "equalizing" side. Functionalists argue that schools perform five "manifest functions": (1) occupational training and socialization; (2) the identification and certification of abilities and talent (providing social mobility on the basis of merit); (3) the production of "good democratic citizens"; (4) the creation and maintenance of a common cultural identity; and (5) the nurturance of intellectual and personality growth (e.g., Lennards, 1983).

It is a boilerplate assumption of functionalism that the expansion of higher education into mass systems is an inevitable part of a larger social-evolutionary process of institutional differentiation, whereby universities have emerged to perform a socially necessary function in complex societies, a function that could not be performed by other, or less differentiated, institutions (e.g., Parsons, 1959; Parsons & Platt, 1973). Thus, mass participation in universities is viewed as necessary in economically developed societies, which are also postulated to be "knowledge societies" where technological knowledge and other forms of applied science are new forms of "capital" that can wed science and industry to produce high levels of economic growth (e.g., Becker, 1964; Florida, 2012; Lockhart, 1971). Although many academic theories have little uptake among those who determine social and economic policies, policy-makers in most governments around the world have apparently found the reasoning behind this theory very appealing because most of them subscribe to some version of it, and have thus taken steps over the past half-century to expand their university systems.

A popular educational version of functionalist theory was proposed by Trow to characterize developments in the American university system over the twentieth century. Based on the American system, he argued that higher-educational systems expand through three stages (as did secondary systems), from élite, through mass, to universal, and at each stage standards change/drop to accommodate the increasing diversity of students. According to Trow, élite university systems can handle up to 15 per cent of a country's youth population; mass systems are necessary when up to 30 per cent of the population in the normal student age range is involved; and universal systems emerge when proportions of the youth population exceed 30 per cent (Trow, 2010, p. 571). As university systems grow, Trow argues, the student base becomes more diverse demographically as well as in terms of abilities and motivation, with the latter changes requiring a lowering of standards and more "progressive" forms of student-centered teaching.

The human capital theory developed by some economists (e.g., Becker, 1964) complements current functionalist formulations. Human capital theory provides the most commonly referenced concepts and evidence used by governments to justify the expansion of universities. This theory supports the largely unquestioned belief that universities inculcate the skills and knowledge necessary to fuel and advance capitalist economic development. The concept of "human capital" that is much bandied about refers to the skills possessed by workers that can be converted into profit for the worker and the employer. The empirical evidence for this theory is based merely on correlations between years of schools and wages. With this meager evidence, it is argued that most of the skills cultivated in schools are convertible into wages in the workplace. The theory thus justifies the mass expansions of school systems by governments as part of labor market policies that focus on the "supply side" in the belief that schools will supply workers with greater skills than otherwise (cf. Kalleberg, 2007).

Political economy: Social reproduction and indoctrination?

From a functionalist perspective, the university system is a meritocracy that permits social mobility because of ability and achievement; therefore, it corrects to a degree preexisting inequalities of opportunity by equipping graduates with the human capital skills that are needed and used by the labor market. However, political economists question the extent to which social mobility actually takes place for students as a result of the educational/university experiences in capitalist societies (e.g., Bowles & Gintis, 1976/2011). Instead, these theorists posit that educational systems have the "latent functions" of legitimating capitalism and reinforcing the interests and power of the élite stewards of capitalism: the extremely wealthy owners of the means of production and the handsomely salaried top-level managers of their business enterprises and supporting institutions.

The specific point of contention for political economists such as Bowles and Gintis is the claim that education systems in general, and universities in particular, are the "great levelers" of society. Governments typically justify the expansion of university systems based on the opinion that they provide meritocratic structures of "contest mobility," whereby the economic benefits of capitalism are shared among the classes through an educational "refereeing" of the abilities and efforts of each individual student/worker. In contrast, Bowles and Gintis argue that these educational systems are more likely instruments of "sponsored mobility" (reproducing of social classes), while at the same time sites of indoctrination into capitalist ideologies. Consequently, on the one hand, the children of more affluent parents are favored by schools in multiple ways, while on the other hand, the children of the less affluent are prepared to accept lower paid, alienated labor. The compliance of the less affluent is orchestrated largely through authoritarian rule structures that favor and inculcate specific conformist behavioral traits, as well as the *false consciousness* that reflects the eventual destinations of the lower social classes in the workplace (see also Henslin, Henslin, & Keiser, 1976).[1]

Those students who accept these alienating arrangements tend to do best in these school systems and have the best educational and occupational outcomes, while those who "resist" are eliminated from the system at lower levels. Bowles and Gintis (1976) proposed the "correspondence principle" to explain why the social organization of schools corresponds to that of the workplace, while producing different occupational outcomes:

> The rule orientation of high schools reflects the close supervision of low-level workers; the internalization of norms and freedom from continual supervision in élite colleges reflect the social relations of upper-level white-collar work. Most state universities and community colleges, which fall in between, conform to the behavioral requisites of low-level technical, service, and supervisory personnel. (p. 12)

Of particular interest here is the political-economy interpretation of recent mass expansions of university systems. These expansions have created surpluses of white-collar workers who conform within work conditions of relative autonomy, but who still hold false-conscious beliefs (so will not be quick to unionize). In turn, these surpluses create reserve armies of white-collar labor that must compete with each other for jobs, so wages are kept down. An important implication of this is that the widespread underemployment among post-secondary graduates that is becoming obvious in many countries is an intrinsic feature of mass higher-educational expansions. As we see below, large percentages of university graduates are underemployed, and this has been a "dirty little secret" of higher education for decades. Underemployment is thus structural and not simply due to poor individual planning or institutional mismatches with the workplace. When viewed in political-economy terms, post-secondary systems are uniquely valuable to the capitalist economy for the above "hidden" reasons, so graduate underemployment is not a transitory aberration that can be remedied by policy reform (Bowles & Gintis, 1976).

More generally, mass educational systems operate to weed out and sort out students, especially those from less affluent backgrounds, who are deemed as not suited for the more financially and psychologically rewarding occupations that allow workers to be autonomous and self-managing. The weeded out students are then "cooled-out" (e.g., Clark, 1961; Henslin, Henslin, & Keiser, 1976) by secondary and tertiary systems and pressured to blame themselves for not "making it" (cf. Furlong & Cartmel's, 2007, concept of the epistemological fallacy). These weeded- and cooled-out individuals must then settle for poorly paid jobs that require accepting alienating industrial-type conditions, or equally alienating service-sector circumstances requiring ingratiating self-supervision and self-discipline. If they do not accept these alienating contexts, they face unemployment and/or precarious employment (i.e., social exclusion).

In turn, the surplus of university-educated white-collar-job incumbents allows employers to maintain control over the workplace in terms of limiting solidarity and wages among these workers. This control is possible because this oversupply of university graduates produces the situation where university-educated workers are forced to compete with each other for jobs by merit of their sheer numbers. Financially insecure workers, in turn, are less likely to unionize or to ask for higher pay. These workers are thus controlled psychologically by a "divide and conquer" strategy as they fight among themselves for the low wages offered by employers: their focus is on competing with each other for scarce resources rather than on those in control who are amassing and hoarding those resources for themselves.

Labor surpluses are to the advantage of employers because they produce a "buyer's market" of jobs. This situation puts a downward pressure on wages. In contrast, a "seller's market," which occurs when there is a shortage of labor, raising wages because workers have more options to take other jobs and thus have more bargaining power. It is therefore in the interests of Capital to maintain a buyer's market, and in the interest of Labor to have a seller's market, but capitalist conditions in general, and neoliberal conditions in particular, pressure governments to maintain buyer's markets to maximize profits through high levels of surplus value on labor.

Bowles and Gintis's (1976) theory of "the emerging white-collar proletariat" posits that higher-educational system in the United States accommodated the mass influx of students from the 1950s on by moving away from the traditional, high-standard, four-year liberal arts and research-university models for educating élite (high-ability) students toward more general/vocational, lower-standard models, including community colleges. The liberal model of education would not have been suitable for a radicalized mass of minority and working-class students destined for alienated labor. In their words: "The educational processes best suited to training an élite are less successful in fostering quiescence among followers" (Bowles & Gintis, 1976, p. 203) because the followers would learn too much about how the economic system really operates and would be equipped with the intellectual tools to challenge a socio-economic system that the élites do not want changed. This downgrading of educational standards that reduces the information available to the masses also deals with the potentially volatile mismatch between the number of mass student aspirants of higher credentials and the limited number of high-status jobs available to them.

Which theory is right?

This debate over the role played by university systems in capitalist societies provides a good example of how critical thinking can help sort out the issues, but only if one is willing to question one's preconceptions and ideological biases. The first step in this critical analysis involves an acknowledgment that the question in the above heading is not the best way to phrase the matter. Instead, as discussed in Chapter 3, the question is more appropriately worded, "which theory is most *useful*, in which contexts and with which issues?" The second step is to sort through the evidence for each claim to discern the focus and range of convenience for each theory. (Note that both theories share realist ontologies, but differ in political agendas and value priorities.)

Mass educational systems arose and spread in many societies around the world through the secondary level in the first part of the twentieth century, and to the post-secondary level in the latter part of the twentieth century. Based largely on beliefs associated with functionalism and human capital theory, as of the early twenty-first century, many governments had as a policy goal the inclusion of 50 per cent of young people in university-type educations and the remainder of youth in other forms of post-secondary education (e.g., Wolf, 2002). The belief derived from human capital theory is that this intensity of extended mass education—sometimes called universal education—is necessary to meet labor market demands and stimulate economic growth. The veracity of this belief is arguable and is critiqued below. However, regardless of one's political agenda or value priority, it is clearly desirable that *high-quality* educational systems at the secondary or post-secondary levels link graduates with networks of productive roles of mutual benefit to the individual and society (i.e., all types of societies require this for optimal functioning, not just capitalist ones). We are thus left with questions about how much the professed ideals of mass/universal educational systems are actually met, and, if not, what these systems actually accomplish.

These questions are important to address because requiring an extended education of the vast majority of young people not only has implications for national economies, but also for the life courses of people who have their period of financial dependency extended well into their legal adulthood.

If the human capital-based beliefs about the benefits of extended education do not apply to all types of education (e.g., to non-instrumental academic and liberal-arts streams) and the ideals are illusory, then contemporary societies are potentially producing life-course problems for many of their citizens.

Indeed, if the political economists are correct, the transition to economic self-sufficiency is currently unduly prolonged and precarious. Consequently, many young people are being held in schools merely until they are needed by employers, while their labor is exploited along the way (in the low-paying jobs available to students and younger workers) as well as upon graduation. Moreover, university educations are expensive, even in countries where tuition is free, and this expense is mostly borne by students—the prospective workers—not the employers that will benefit from their more highly credentialed labor. That is, even in countries where tuition is free there are living costs that must be met while enrolled, but there are also opportunity costs, namely, the foregone wages from the employment opportunities that are given up while pursuing educational opportunities. The children of the wealthy have little need to bear debts if their parents pay their way, but those from less affluent backgrounds typically take on debt because their parents are unable to provide them financial assistance. Besides, if employers, especially corporations, need university-educated workers, it is a fair question to ask why they should not bear the costs of that education and training.

Human capital theory critically examined

Human capital theory can be taken to task on both empirical and theoretical grounds:

- Empirically, there are evidential problems with the equation of human capital acquisition with *any type* of education. It is unclear how academically oriented mass educational expansions could both drive economic development and solve employment policy issues in complex contexts.
- Theoretically, the original "human capital theory" was not really a theory at all, with a closely knit set of interrelated hypotheses, but rather a concept around which vague hypotheses have been generated, only some of which have been empirically verified.

If these critiques are valid, many proponents of this "theory" have been overconfident in their attempts to generalize and apply it to complex life-course outcomes. This is the "rubber sheeting" problem of theories referred to in Chapter 3. If both critiques have validity, governments around the world in both developing and developed countries have been misled about how "investments in human capital" pay off, especially in terms of the belief that all types of educational credentials create their own demand.

Empirical critique: Why educational credentials do not always represent exchangeable skills

Empirical evidence contradicting the basic tenets of human capital theory has been mounting for years. Even a casual look at mass educational systems around the globe suggests that something is wrong. Although mass secondary education has been in place for several generations now, there is still an extremely high level of youth unemployment in many developing countries, along with low levels of youth participation in the paid labor force (e.g., Côté, 1994; International Labour Office, 2004, 2012).

If human capital, in the form of *any* educational credentials, improved economic prospects to the extent claimed by human capital theorists and believed by policy-makers, these countries should now have far better employment opportunities. Instead, youth unemployment has increased over the same time that mass educational systems have expanded. These problems have been greatly exacerbated during the so-called Great Recession that began in 2008, a term that is euphemistic when applied to developed countries such as Spain where youth unemployment exceeds 50 per cent, up from under 20 per cent in 2007 (International Labour Office, 2013). Fewer young people in both developed and developing countries worldwide are participating in the paid labor force, and those who do participate face increased unemployment rates, with possible long-term scarring effects of lower earnings during later careers similar to those who entered the labor force during the recession of the early 1980s.

In developed countries, where educational systems are more extensively attended through the tertiary level, there are high rates of university-graduate *under*employment, especially among graduates of the liberal and general programs. As discussed in the next chapter, university graduates have faced high levels of underemployment for some time, as high as 50 per cent initially and 30 per cent chronically (Betts, Ferrall, & Finnie, 2000; Côté & Allahar, 2006, 2007; Frenette, 2000; Kalleberg, 2007; Pryor & Schaffer, 1999). And, as noted in the preceding section, some political economists provide compelling evidence that underemployment has been an inherent feature of the mass higher-educational system from the beginning because it serves the economic élites by providing a surplus of white-collar workers who can be more easily controlled politically and exploited economically.

If marketable skills closely adhered to any type of education, years of schooling would predict earnings and outcomes independent of whether a credential is attained, but this appears not to be the case. Instead, there appears to be a "sheepskin" effect of credential attainment, where the payoff of an undergraduate education is realized only if the student receives a degree and not in relation to the amount of time spent in university (i.e., if students do not complete a degree there is little payoff, even with several years of university-level learning). Pascarella and Terenzini (2005, p. 448) conclude that on whole the evidence suggests that graduate employment outcomes are affected about as much by the sheepskin effect as by the acquisition of marketable human capital skills, but that neither effect provides "a completely satisfactory explanation" of occupational status and earnings advantages. See Walters (2004) and Ferrer and Riddell (2002) for similar conclusions.

The difficulty in *finding a place* of full employment in the labor market points directly to a consequence of university-graduate underemployment, namely, the "downward cascading effect of credentials" (Côté & Allahar, 2006; Pryor & Schaffer, 1999, refer to this as the displacement or bumping effect). That is, university graduates who cannot find employment commensurate with their credentials are forced to take jobs that would have gone to those with lower levels of education. This creates problems for those with these lower levels of education, in terms of both their employment rates and level of remuneration (Vedder, Denhart, & Robe, 2013).

As we also see in the next chapter, in countries like Canada and the United States, the so-called "college premium" (the wage advantage of having a university degree over a high-school diploma) is largely due to a massive wage decline since the 1980s among those with lower levels of education. It is not due to in any real increase in the value of post-secondary education. Thus, while there is macro-economic evidence from many countries that university graduates *as a group* do better in terms of income and occupational status, subgroups of graduates clearly invest in more education than they can use in anything other than a status-competition manner, displacing others of lower status. In light of these problems, some observers have argued that credentials should no longer be taken as uncontaminated indicators of skills, but rather as a type of "passport" that signals something about the status of the person holding those credentials (e.g., Wolf, 2002) and therefore places them in the "labor queue" (e.g., Van de Werfhorst & Andersen, 2005).

Theoretical critique: A "rubber band" concept

The above empirical deficiencies of human capital theory can be traced to ambiguities in the development of the theory. If we turn to the original definitions of human capital, we find much more circumscribed designations than those that currently inform academic researchers and government policy-makers. For instance, Walsh (1935) argued that only investments in training for a profession would constitute "a capital investment made in a profit-seeking, equalizing market, in response to the same motives which lead to the creation of factories, machinery, and the like" (p. 256). Walsh did not recognize non-vocational forms of education as involving this type of profit-producing investment motivation.

Following Walsh's logic, education at the primary and secondary levels does not require students to engage in instrument profit-seeking calculations. Furthermore, most of primary education is not chiefly intended to directly develop vocational skills; neither are many secondary systems that follow the American model where the teaching of non-technical subjects is the norm. As Walsh argued:

> Rather it is the intent of the parents and the state to promote the education of citizens. The purpose is to provide political and cultural education in the widest sense. And although abilities which have their economic significance are developed as a part of the process of training an intelligent electorate, these abilities are by no means the preconceived object of the training. Their appearance is incidental to the major purpose.
>
> (1935, p. 256)

However, economists such as Becker (1964) who made the concept of human capital attractive to policy-makers shifted the concept away from these earlier assumptions, stretching its assumptions of student instrumentalism to include secondary educations in "academic" streams, as well as liberal arts programs at universities, both of which are now uncritically assumed to constitute forms of rational human capital investments. Unfortunately, the bulk of the empirical evidence simply does not support this rational-investment assumption, as we saw above with respect to the sheepskin effect.

But, most damning is the evidence that the skill requirements of most jobs in the labor force do *not* now require more skills than before the mass educational expansions (e.g., Kalleberg, 2007). The sectors that have increased in skill requirements are the vocational and professional sectors that require university-level credentials, but these actually constitute a minority of jobs in the overall labor force (e.g., Côté & Allahar, 2007; Kalleberg, 2007; Rifkin, 1995). Accordingly, the human capital assumption that increasing levels of *all forms of education* are highly correlated with increasing levels of marketable job skills is not empirically supported (Vedder, Denhart, & Robe, 2013). Instead, as we saw in the preceding section, human capital theory begins to fail empirically in its explanatory power precisely at the point where other theories (e.g., political economy) or explanations (e.g., the sheepskin effect) become useful.

If we accept that the human capital theory has been stretched too far beyond its focus of convenience, and thus begins to fail empirically, the next step is to identify theories that might better explain why contemporary societies require prolonged forms of education. When this is done, different implications emerge of the relevance of education for the well-being of the young.

Political-economy theory critically examined

In most countries, the mass expansions of educational systems constitute politically liberal reforms ostensibly intended to create greater social equality by providing more education for the masses. Nonetheless, these reform efforts have been criticized from the Right- and Left-wing since their inception. From the Right came the concern that academic standards were being sacrificed to unrealistic social experiments. For example, Murray (2008a, 2008b) argues that these expansions are a result of "educational romanticism," the belief that all people are capable of becoming proficient at anything, so long as they receive the proper instruction. From the Left was the boilerplate criticism that capitalism is inherently based on the inequalities created by the extraction of surplus value from wage labor, coupled with the tendency for self-preservation by capitalist élites of the underlying social class structure (i.e., the wealthy want to maintain or improve their wealth and pass it on to *their* children). Bowles and Gintis's *Schooling in capitalist America: Educational reform and the contradictions of economic life* (1976) was a critique of these liberal reform efforts. They argued that because of the basic structure of capitalism, economic inequalities were not created by education alone, so educational reform efforts will fail to reduce economic inequalities in capitalist economies.

Bowles and Gintis's book *Schooling* stands as the most influential work documenting the nature of educational systems in capitalist economies (e.g., Swartz, 2003), so will be the focus of this section. Fortunately, the book was reissued in 2011 with an updated introduction by the authors. In this updated release of the book, Bowles and Gintis provide reflections regarding how well their original formulations have stood the test of time. In this update, they report being distressed by the continuing failure of the American educational system to contribute to "a flourishing life for all people and to the more equal sharing of its benefits" (2011, p. ix). The failure of mass education to provide widely shared benefits inspired the writing of the book in the first place, and the persistence of this failure prompted their reprinting of the original work, not coincidentally perhaps during the most recent crisis of capitalism.

The three basic propositions of Bowles and Gintis's book can be summarized as follows:

- Human development. Based on their correspondence principle—that the reward structure of American schools is modeled after the capitalist workplace—they provided econometric evidence that the inculcation of certain personality characteristics through the daily disciplinary practices of schools is more important than the development of cognitive skills in terms of students' success in schools and ultimate attainments in the workplace.
- Inequality. They showed statistically, using standardized tests, that the social class and economic status of students' parents is far more important than cognitive skills for student success in schools and the workplace.
- Educational change. They provided historical evidence that the evolution of the American school system was driven more by the interests of Capital (and the actions of specific capitalists and their agents) in transforming the workplace than by any democratic or pedagogical ideals.

In Bowles and Gintis's opinion, "the statistical claims of [their] book have held up remarkably well" (2011, p. x), and have been supported in the analysis of more recent economic data with more sophisticated statistical techniques. In particular, they stand by their conclusions regarding

> high levels of intergenerational persistence of economic status, the unimportance of heritability of IQ in this process, and the fact that the contribution of schooling to cognitive development plays but a modest part in explaining why those with more schooling have higher earnings.
>
> (*ibid.*, pp. x–xi)

They admit to having underestimated "the value of [certain forms of] schooling in contributing to productive employment" (*ibid.*, p. xi), as well as failing to consider what schools could be, rather than what they are (i.e., they were more descriptive than prescriptive). Nor did they explore how schools in non-capitalistic countries might achieve democratic and humanistic goals of education that benefit all in the society. They thus admit to having provided little practical advice for educators and policy-makers in reforming educational systems. Still, they believe that their political-economy approach embeds "the analysis of education in the evolving structure of the economy and the polity ... giving attention to the noncognitive as well as conventional effects of education" (*ibid.*, p. xii). Clearly, Bowles and Gintis's self-reflexive analysis is an exemplary addition to the debate on the role of education in capitalist societies. (Recall that a central tenet of the present book is that the social scientists need to engage in more give and take with their own theories and their mutual boilerplate positions.)

The exchange between Bowles and Gintis and their critics is not limited to this one source. Swartz (2003) provided a useful summary and extension of the various criticisms directed at Bowles and Gintis's work. He identified a number of perceived shortcomings of the book, *Schooling*. In addition to ignoring gender and race, not providing sufficient theorizing about social change, and lacking an account of "cultural reproduction." Swartz also contended that *Schooling* constitutes a form of "neo-Marxist functionalism" because it posits a form of socialization in the links between education and the workplace. As a functionalist analysis, Swartz argued that Bowles and Gintis's work has many of the same problems that plague the more conservative, functionalist approaches to education, being "too structural, too determinative, too mechanical, giving insufficient attention to processes of resistance, contradiction, and contestation. Working-class youth are portrayed as passive victims of the selecting and sorting action of schools" (Swartz, 2003, p. 173).

In their response to Swartz's critique, Bowles and Gintis were remarkably non-defensive, admitting that their "macro-social research strategy did not allow [them] to shed much light inside the black box of how what goes on in the classroom accounts for the role of schooling in the reproduction of the social order" (Bowles & Gintis, 2003, p. 343). They did take issue with the claim that theirs is a functionalist analysis, arguing that they were at pains in three chapters of their book to document historically how individual (wealthy) actors played causal roles in the creation of the American school structure.

Bowles and Gintis went on to explain that they have revised their position based on their experiences over the years. They have concluded that while "Marx had accurately captured the centrality of conflict in the process" (*ibid.*, p. 345), their more recent work "embraces institutions favored by liberals—private property and markets—while advocating policies that would radically redistribute wealth and power, objectives commonly associated with the Marxian tradition" (*ibid.*, p. 346). Appropriately, Bowles and Gintis shifted from a more radical Marxist position to a more social-democratic one that might currently be found in countries with advanced, consensus-seeking political systems that are committed to reducing economic inequalities (as in the Nordic countries), where

> private property and markets are indispensable components of good economic governance, but their contribution to efficiency, democracy, human dignity, and fairness depends on the distribution of wealth. Egalitarian wealth distributions can harness markets and private property to these time-honored ends of democratic and egalitarian social movements. A school system that teaches all children well without labeling the white, or the rich, or the male, or the American as more deserving of subsequent economic privilege is an essential component of such an egalitarian wealth redistribution, now even more than when *Schooling* was written.
>
> (*ibid.*, p. 347)

The handling of criticisms of their work by Bowles and Gintis, along with their willingness to amend their positions, stands as an exemplar for how the social sciences can develop and mature. Bowles and Gintis did not insist on the Marxist boilerplate assumptions that informed their early work and have gone on to help the social scientific community develop a much better understanding of the political economy of mass education. They also acknowledge that further improvements to this field are necessary.

Next, we extrapolate from the debates examined here, in light of recent evidence about the crises universities around the world are currently facing, to draw conclusions about how the expansions of mass higher-educational systems have affected the youth period and the prospects of the young.

Synthesis: Zombie educational systems and the prolongation of youth

How are these theories, and the debates about them, relevant to the current youth period and the educational experiences of young people affected by mass higher education? To answer this question, it is most useful to identify what each theory seems best at explaining and to use these insights to better understand the multifaceted nature of current mass educational systems. When this is done, we can then consider the ways in which educational theories can be modified to better capture the issues relevant to youth studies.

To begin, the focus of convenience of human capital theory needs to be recognized, as do its limitations. As noted above, human capital theory best explains the value of vocational and professional training in terms of workplace integration. Other forms of education, including the general education associated with the liberal arts and sciences, are only indirectly relevant to the workplace. Clearly, basic literacy and numeracy are essential features of most jobs in the modern workplace, assets in other jobs, and necessary to participate as consumers in the global economy; nevertheless, specialized, technical knowledge is essential for only a minority of jobs, even in so-called knowledge societies (e.g., Kalleberg, 2007). As recently as a century ago, rudimentary literacy and numeracy were the goals of primary education, which was considered sufficient preparation for basic functional participation in the economy. However, with the credential inflation that accompanies mass education, in many countries this goal was pushed to the secondary level, with recent signs that even post-secondary educations do not guarantee these basic abilities to process written information (e.g., Côté & Allahar, 2007).

This does not mean that a general education is not useful in the lives of most young people or later in their lives. In fact, there are marked economic-developmental differences between societies with universal and free primary schools systems and those without these systems. At the level of the individual, there is much for students to learn about coping in the modern economic and social worlds, both in terms of "hard skills" as found in mathematics and "soft skills," some of which include self-discipline (a point made by Bowles and Gintis in their critique of the American system). Regrettably, as argued, human-capital logics have shifted public attitudes to equate all forms of schooling with job training, with some rather unfortunate consequences. One of these consequences is that many students have become more instrumentally job oriented in their approach to their education. In these cases, it becomes more difficult to teach general subjects to students who do not appreciate their relevance to personal and intellectual development because they feel the subject material will not help them to "get a job." Consequently, non-vocational secondary and tertiary systems have experienced a decline in the legitimacy of their curriculum from the student perspective at the same time that there has been an increased demand for these credentials from the perspective of employers (Côté & Allahar, 2007, 2011).

This undermining of personally enriching learning has grown as employers have increasingly used these credentials as sorting mechanisms. The more that these credentials have been used to sort job candidates, the more credential inflation has taken place; as this has happened, human capital theory has lost even more explanatory power because of the increased disconnect between the length of schooling and the skill-demands of jobs. In many countries, large percentages of mass higher-educational graduates have found themselves

in low-skilled jobs that they have obtained by merit of their higher credentials merely putting them ahead in the job queue. And, as one problem can
beget other problems, the potentials for deep learning suffer (cf. Willingham,
2009). For instance, perfunctory attendance will not help students learn how
to critically analyze information that might help them to recognize their own
false consciousness and alienation. So, as the quality of the general education
declines, employers look for those with higher credentials and it becomes "normal" for them, say, to require an undergraduate degree to qualify for only
low-level service or clerical work. Yet, with this decline in standards at the tertiary level, it becomes more difficult to argue that post-secondary graduates are
"underemployed" if they possess less "human capital" than did graduates from
past cohorts.

In place of the investment in mass education producing schools that lead to
"a flourishing life for all people and to the more equal sharing of its benefits"
(Bowles & Gintis, 1976, p. ix), an instrumentalism has taken over, turning
many educational systems into "zombie" organizations where students and
teachers are often simply going through the motions (cf. Whelan, Walker, &
Moore, 2013). In the extreme, some would argue that "students pretend to
learn and teachers pretend to teach." Strong evidence of this shift comes from
Arum and Roksa (2011), who found that some 40 per cent of American university students showed no increase in knowledge or critical-thinking abilities even
after four years of university, mainly because of a lack of effort on their part
and the failure of their schools to require much effort or learning of students.
Indeed, the accumulating evidence shows that more than a few students are
disinterested in the subjects they feel forced to take, but they attend simply to
collect the credential at the end of each program of study (e.g., Brotheridge &
Lee, 2005). And, as this mindset has taken root, many teachers become frustrated and give up trying to challenge students to engage in deep learning.
As this problem permeates educational systems, the promise of a liberal education diminishes, and these liberal programs become mere shells of their former
selves. To the extent that university systems ever produced a critical consciousness in their graduates, their current mass forms seem to have "killed the goose
that laid the golden egg" (cf. Vedder, Denhart, & Robe, 2013).

This problem of ineffectual educational systems has been well publicized at
the secondary level, especially in American schools. But, more recently, as a
general malaise has set in, a problem of student disengagement has emerged
in many colleges and universities in countries embracing mass higher education. This malaise has potentially serious consequences for the large numbers
of young people in these systems, whether it is those who have a real desire to
learn but go unchallenged, or those who feel forced to enroll because of poor
job prospects if they do not acquire the credentials. With these educational systems adrift in terms of their own missions, it should come as no surprise that
many young people enrolled in them also find themselves adrift, dissatisfied,
and frustrated.

Thus, while human capital theory does help identify some of the skills necessary for advanced economies, the overproduction of credentials because of

government policies and student status-competitions has left many young people unmotivated in schools. In addition to casting doubts on the explanatory utility of human capital theory, this widespread student apathy and alienation toward deep learning suggests that political-economy theory is also limited in terms of its claims about the correspondence between school and of the labor force. As noted above, Willis (1977) pointed out a similar problem in terms of the resistance of working-class "lads" in the United Kingdom. Now, regardless of class, student disengagement in general can be viewed as a general form of resistance to the pressures to stay in schools for such a long time simply to compete for low-level jobs at the end of that time. Those students who do not value learning and therefore do not study much will be relatively unaffected by any curriculum, hidden or otherwise (cf. Arum & Roksa, 2011).

Bowles and Gintis (2011) admitted in response to criticisms that they did not sufficiently analyze the internal structures of schools, so in building on their perspective there is a need to examine the internal structures of post-secondary institutions. As discussed above, Bowles and Gintis did argue that part of the social-reproduction process involves weeding out those from lower class levels in terms of educational progression, but in many countries larger percentages of working-class and lower middle-class youth are now attending tertiary institutions. Moreover, they did directly link alienation with academic disengagement by making specific reference to student alienation from the process and product of learning (Bowles & Gintis, 1988). They argued that those who are most accepting of the alienating conditions are also most likely to continue to the university level, where the emphasis is on the internalization of norms and internalized standards of control. They also charge that the over-supply of graduates is a normal aspect of universities in capitalist societies, providing employers with prospective employees who have little bargaining power as proletarianized white-collar workers.

In linking the literature on credentialism with Bowles and Gintis's work, it can be argued that a consequence of the credential inflation is that many universities, especially undergraduate programs, have become "proletarianized." For a variety of reasons examined above, many mass universities are overcrowded, especially with students who have been pushed to attend when they would prefer to do something else. To manage these students, many universities are becoming rule-bound, monitoring more closely student behaviors. This authoritarianism discourages the internalization of norms and the forms of autonomy previously fostered by universities at the undergraduate level, contrary to Bowles and Gintis's depiction of the early phase of mass higher education. This spreading credentialism and its consequences thus require a revision of Bowles and Gintis's theory. When we do so, we discover the possibility that social reproduction has shifted from the undergraduate to graduate level (Torche, 2011), with affluent students obtaining proportionately more graduate/professional degrees and earning higher salaries from these degrees. If this is the case, graduate degrees may now be replacing undergraduate degrees as the gateways of social reproduction (cf. Côté, 2014b).

Bowles and Gintis's amended perspective helps to account for this zombie-like nature of mass higher-educational systems under neoliberal capitalist conditions. It also explains the widespread denial or ignorance of the myriad problems with these systems. In capitalist systems in general, but especially during the current neoliberal era, governments serve dominant economic interests generally and corporations specifically. If individual governments were to challenge neoliberal goals, international pressures would be brought to bear on them and their national economies would suffer. Even so, it is rare to find open opposition to neoliberalism because most politicians governing developed countries are from an economic élite, so they are actually looking after their own interests and those of their reference group (cf. Giroux, 2012).

As a first principle of political-economics, lower wages allow for the owners of the means of production to make more profits because they can extract more surplus value from workers. As a matter of fact, dominant economic interest groups need an over-supply of all forms of labor to keep wages down. At the same time, economic élites have little incentive to provide a high-quality education to the masses because this might empower the masses to seek to change the system. Besides, the financing for improving mass educational systems would likely come from higher taxes on the wealthy and corporations, and this taxation of wealth is precisely what neoliberal initiatives have targeted for elimination (Steger & Roy, 2010; cf. Lasch, 1995).

Bowles and Gintis provided strong empirical support for these claims in their original work (1976), and argued that more recent analyses with more sophisticated techniques support these original claims (Bowles & Gintis, 2011). If these claims have even some validity, it is little wonder, then, that in mass higher-educational systems many students and teachers are just going through the motions, figuratively like zombies. If true, these systems pretend to provide academic "excellence" when they are often just "warehousing" most young people until they are needed in the labor force. Meanwhile, this warehousing provides the means for the manufacture of consent and false consciousness in the production of compliant white-collar workers headed for proletarianized, alienated labor.

In sum, a strong case can be made that the youth period has become increasingly prolonged as a result of the spread of mass-secondary and mass-tertiary educational systems that have absorbed surplus labor and neutralized its potentially destabilizing effects on the capitalist system. With the poor job prospects created by neoliberal policies, and the transfer of entry-level jobs to developing countries where labor is cheaper, it has been necessary to institutionally contain young people, while convincing them that it is justified that they must wait for an indefinite period before they might find meaningful employment that provides a living wage. To sustain this arrangement, governments adopting mass-educational policies make the promise that higher education is the route to economic security.

However, government promises that this educational route is the "great equalizer" are often empty: social class reproduction has been largely preserved by these mass-educational systems; the most recent adaptation of intergenerational status and wealth transmission is to use postgraduate credentials as the necessary level of educational attainment to escape most forms of proletarianized labor. This credentialism not only unduly extends the youth period, but also in many countries drives young people from less affluent backgrounds into debt in the process. Consequently, the zombie mass-educational systems in various cultures and contexts often serve to keep a large segment of young people in a socio-economic "limbo." Just what can be done about this "new normal" is beyond the purview of this book, but see Côté and Allahar (2011) for suggestions about restoring quality to (mass) higher-educational systems.

Conclusion: Educational policies, credentialism, and the prolongation of youth

The problems of credentialism and underemployment have been with us at least since the early 1970s (e.g., Berg, 1970; Lockhart, 1971; Vedder, Denhart, & Robe, 2013); regrettably, the stewards of mass educational systems in governments and educational administrations have rarely openly acknowledged these problems. Although these problems are continually "rediscovered" (e.g., Kalleberg, 2007), the most common response is to deny them and hide them behind statistics linking educational attainment and university-graduate access/employment/earnings. These statistics are problematic in a number of ways. They tend to gloss over the fact that mass systems are not always of "excellent" quality. They also disguise the much more complex situation concerning the relationships among social class, educational attainment, and occupational destination, as we see in the next chapter. In order to justify mass-educational policies based on the faulty premises noted above, governments have needed to manufacture the consensus that these systems are rational, coherent, and democratic and thus are in the best interests of the public.

The mass educational systems in most countries are now clearly driven by governments that do not have youth-labor-market *demand* policies; instead, they rely on labor *supply* policies that play directly into corporate–capitalist interests in producing reserve armies of surplus white-collar labor. Although it is more difficult to show that the policies are driven by economic élites, it is easier to show how they are complementary to élite interests, especially those policies that underfund mass education while giving tax relief to the wealthy and corporations. Still, most politicians in most countries are from the economic élites that benefit from these policies, so it is likely not a coincidence that the masses derive far fewer benefits from mass education than do the élites and their children from their more exclusive and targeted education.

Of course, certain forms of schooling can have benefits for specific people in specific contexts, and there is evidence of upward mobility for some people from the masses in some countries, at least for the past few generations.

However, the better-quality higher education traditionally given to the children of the élites—a good liberal education in Anglo-American countries—is not to be found in mass systems. Mass higher education has come to take on other meanings, becoming more of social than an academic experience, especially providing a perfunctory rite of passage for affluent students and a chance for some working-class youth to learn middle-class mores and folkways. But in so doing, these systems have altered the life course for the masses, often with consequences that are far different from what the public has been led to believe. The realization of the disconnect between belief and reality has led many people to ask just what the purpose of higher education really is now, and as the missions of universities drift, to question who in the future should assume the role of stewardship of university systems. There is now strong evidence that under the stewardship of the self-interested wealthy, the benefits to the masses have been far less than would otherwise be the case.

Recommended readings

Philip Babcock & Mindy Marks (2010). *The falling time cost of college: Evidence from half a century of time use data.* Working Paper 15954, National Bureau of Economic Research, Cambridge, MA. Retrieved from http://www.nber.org/papers/w15954

This study shows how universities in the United States have become less demanding of high standards as the process of massification spread. Before massification, university students were expected to give their full attention to their studies. Over time, this expectation has been reduced so that "full-time" studies are now a part-time activity for most students.

Michael Burawoy (2011). *Redefining the public university: Developing an analytical framework.* Retrieved from http://publicsphere.ssrc.org/burawoy-redefining-the-public-university/

Burawoy discusses the worldwide crisis facing universities in the face of different forms of political interference and control.

Charles Murray (2008). Are too many people going to college? *The American: A Magazine of Ideas*, Monday, 8 September 2008. Retrieved from http://www.american.com/archive/2008/september-october-magazine/are-too-many-people-going-to-college

Murray takes the American higher-educational system to task for sustaining the illusion that élite standards still prevail in its universities after decades of massification. He calls for a re-assessment of the education-to-work transition that is more in line with the interests and abilities of all students, not just the academically inclined.

David Walters (2004). The relationship between postsecondary education and skill: Comparing credentialism with human capital theory. *Canadian Journal of Higher Education*, 34, 97–124.

This study provides a useful empirical assessment of the competing explanations of the value of postsecondary education: that it is now a credential machine vs. a means of inculcating marketable skills for graduates.

Work and Changing Employment Opportunities

5

The preceding chapter on education pointed to serious disjunctures between educational systems and the labor forces of many contemporary Western societies. The nature of work has changed dramatically over the past century in these societies, and so too has the nature of access to the labor forces of these societies. Gone are the days when young people simply assumed the same occupations as their parents, learned work skills as part of household production, or assumed an apprenticeship in the case of males (Bowles & Gintis, 1976).

In Western capitalist societies, most of the population now sells its labor and, to be part of a labor market that is dominated by major transnational corporations and government bureaucracies, people need certain credentials and certificates to prove their skill sets. This has been the case for some time, but over the past few decades, as we saw in the education chapter, a labor queue has formed for most jobs and professions. This bottleneck of employment opportunities requires workers to compete with each other on the basis of their credentials, resulting in an oversupply of many post-secondary credentials and thus in credential inflation as employers require even higher credentials as a basis for sorting large pools of applicants. Consequently, the time taken to assume full-time work roles providing a living wage is now longer in most countries, and the process of qualifying for these work roles requires remaining in educational systems to ever-higher levels for increasing portions of the population.

With these historical developments in mind, the present chapter focuses on the various explanations that have been offered for these declining employment opportunities for the youth segment and the implications of the resulting delay of their functional independence. This thread follows from the previous chapter, tracking how educational credentials have become necessary for workplace entry, delaying that entry as people make their way through the labor queue. We saw that the more conservative approaches posit that the delay is functional and necessary, given the putative complexity of contemporary occupations and careers. In contrast, the more radical political-economy perspective sees the delay in functional independence as a consequence of the sorting of

99

proletarianized labor and ratcheting up of educational requirements to "re-set" social class reproduction. This upward ratcheting of educational requirements accomplishes two things: it satisfies the demands from the masses for greater educational opportunity, and it preserves the élites' intergenerational hold on power. This is the case because the affluent simply have to finance their children's educations to levels higher than those obtained by the masses, which in many cases now means obtaining professional and graduate degrees.

In the context of the "work-side" of the education-to-work equation, we can identify similar positions, but in this case the positions taken are more internal to youth studies than is the case with the "education-side" of the equation because of the more explicit government-policy involvement in educational systems. The involvement of governments' *supply-side* youth labor policies has brought educational sociologists and economists into this aspect of youth studies (partly as a result of the extensive funding of educational research), whereas the neglect of many governments in formulating youth-labor *demand-side* policies has left the youth work and employment field more open (and more neglected in terms of research funding, resulting in a less-studied field).

Thus, in this chapter, we turn to more internal youth-studies issues and debates, which are generally informed by the functionalism vs. political-economy debate in the education area, but more focused on the implications of employment prospects during the youth period among recent cohorts. In addition, the equivalent positions in youth studies to the conservative functionalist positions in the education field can be more appropriately termed "liberal" in this area. The "liberal" designation is appropriate because, although these generally include the functionalist assumption that more education is necessary to fix youth-labor-market problems, these positions also acknowledge the problems youth encounter in converting educational credentials into jobs and they advocate for youth in a number of ways.

In contrast, the political-economy perspective maintains many of the same assumptions that are applied to the role of education in social reproduction, but follows through to point out ways in which social reproduction is accomplished in the workplace; it also calls for remedies to the exploitive nature of youth work. At the same time, it should be noted that the political-economy perspective in this field is rather inchoate and does not have well-known advocates, like Bowles and Gintis in the case of the education field. In fact, most of the political-economy arguments and evidence come from economists, not sociologists, and within youth studies the neo-Marxist version currently has few representatives.

My own efforts to bring the political-economy perspective to the fore began a couple of decades ago (e.g., Allahar & Côté, 1998; Côté, 2000; Côté & Allahar, 1996, 2006), but as we see below, more liberal positions have dominated the youth-studies examination of youth-employment problems and prospects. However, a strong case can be made that the overall understanding of the youth question remains incomplete without a recognition of the changing material conditions associated with the youth period; the liberal positions are useful in understanding some of the consequences of these changing material conditions, but are of limited use in coming to grips with their causes.

Declining employment: Critical vs. liberal perspectives

Of all the topics covered in this book, the topic of youth work and employment opportunities most clearly illustrates the changing material conditions associated with the youth period and thus how the fortunes of the youth segment have changed over the past century, especially in the last three decades.

The political-economy perspective identifies the relentless proletarianization of the young—from marginalization from the labor force for the majority of youth to social exclusion altogether for a minority of youth. This economic disenfranchisement has been traced empirically over the past half century or so (e.g., Côté & Allahar, 1996, 2006), and the roots of ideological support for this process have been dated back to the support for negative stereotypes created by academic psychology a century ago with Hall's (1904) popularization of the adolescent storm-and-stress thesis (see Chapters 2 and 3). The proletarianization argument posits that these negative stereotypes have left young people politically disempowered and thus vulnerable to corporations and other employers who have sought to extract more profit from wage earners.

Also, the technological advances that have continually displaced human labor throughout the history of industrial capitalism have more recently displaced many entry-level jobs. And, during the more recent period of corporate capitalism, as a result of the trade agreements associated with globalization, many lower-level jobs have been "outsourced" from richer to poorer countries where labor is extremely cheap. At the same time, the labor practices used to produce consumer items for Western countries are exploitative of the most vulnerable in poorer countries; accordingly, class relations have taken on international proportions in this globalized economy, so that even the working class in developed countries gains from the exploitation of workers in these developing countries (e.g., Beck, 2007).

As a result of these technological and global-labor changes, in many Western countries the service sectors have become the predominant employers. But, as the service sector grew during the twentieth century, young workers became the preferred workers for (proletarianized) subordinate-service positions, presumably because of their lack of bargaining power with respect to wages and benefits. Without this vulnerable group of wage laborers, it is doubtful that the service sector would have grown as it did in many countries, especially the fast-food industry. For evidence of this, see Schlosser (2001), an investigative journalist who published an exposé of how corporate lobbying by corporations like McDonald's redirected American government youth labor policies, including keeping the minimum age low. Moreover, as we saw in the last chapter, educational credentials have increasingly been replacing entry-level on-the-job training, thereby relieving employers of much of the expense of training their workers and sidelining surplus workers in educational institutions.

In contrast, liberal perspectives commonly present the assumption that the declining fortunes of the young are unfortunate in some ways, yet were unavoidable because of inevitable economic transformations. Liberal perspectives do not recognize the proletarianization of the youth labor market, or the age-based redistribution of wealth. The task for policy-makers, then, is to provide supports and compensations for the regrettable features of the current youth period, through more education, compensatory instruction, and specialized training programs, all of which are designed to help young people fit themselves into the current capitalist workforce.

As we see below, a variety of liberal positions share these assumptions. Before discussing them, it is useful to summarize the main points of the political-economy critique:

- Liberal approaches do not get to the origins or roots of certain problems of material existence.
- The focus on "subjectivities" or "psychological states" normalizes exploitive situations, while mislabeling coping behaviors among the exploited.
- Advocacy positions based on the belief that the young person "can do no wrong" can be misguided in seeking solutions to their problems.
- Recommending that solutions to youth problems lie with transforming the young person into an "adult" too readily accepts the class containment of youth (cf. Côté, 2014b; Rowntree & Rowntree, 1968).

Following the data: The decline in youth wages

Before presenting the political-economy critique of specific liberal positions concerning youth employment, it is instructive to first examine some data that help us to view the situation historically. With one particular data set from the United States, we can gain a perspective concerning the labor conditions of the youth segment before the current neoliberal era of corporate capitalism, and what young people's earning power might now have been had historical forces played out differently over the last 40 years.

It is fortunate that the U.S. Census Bureau has been collecting data over the past 40 years that allows for this historical tracking. In the 1960s, the Census Bureau began recording median weekly salaries of all full-time workers, and reporting it by age categories and gender (e.g., U.S. Census Bureau, 2011). This allows us to see in the changing wage structure of the American labor force evidence that a redistribution of wealth that has taken place there, with age as a principal axis. A virtually identical trend appears to have taken place in Canada (Côté & Allahar, 1996, 2006; Myles, Picot, & Wannell, 1988; Picot, 1998). Blanchflower (1999a, 1999b) reports this downward trend in a number of OECD countries as occurring from the 1970s through the 1990s, including the United Kingdom. Readers are invited to examine these trends in their own countries if similar census data sets are available.

Sum and McLaughlin (2011; Sum et al., 2011) use this U.S. census data, which began in the late 1960s. They found that males aged 16 to 24 working full-time earned about three-quarters that of males 25 years and older, while young women earned 90 per cent that of older women. However, youth wages declined steadily relative to older workers, especially for young males. Twenty years later, young men in this age group were making about half that of older men. Another decline occurred in 2008, which appears to be continuing. Meanwhile relative earnings of young females have been steadily declining over the entire period. As of 2010, their earnings were about 60 per cent those of older females. In constant 2010 dollars, the decline in earning power for young American males was 30 per cent over this period. The comparable decline for young females was just over 10 per cent.

In understanding these trends, it must be remembered that in the United States and most other countries the wages of females of all ages are lower than those of males. A consequence of this has been a convergence in the earnings of young males and young females, but mainly because of the decline of the wages of young males and not an increase in the wages of young females (Allahar & Côté, 1998). In this data set, males earned about 30 per cent more than females in 1973, but this difference dropped to about 5 per cent by 2010. Thus, gender differences in the earning power are now minimal (in the United States), but not because an improvement in female wages; rather both young males and females have suffered a decline in earning power.

What is perhaps most scandalous about this proletarianization of young workers is that had youth wages increased to the present by even only about 1 per cent per year, their earning power would be radically different than it is now. According to Sum and McLaughlin (2011), young male workers would now be making over twice their current wages, instead of 30 per cent less ($1014 per week vs. their current $443). This converts to $571 per week per full-time worker. As Sum and McLaughlin (2011) conclude: "What a radically different economic world these young workers would have faced in recent years!" (p. 3).

Political economists would be quick to point out that this is a lot of *additional* surplus value on youth wages! When we look into how many young male workers this involves (U.S. Census Bureau, 2011), we find that in 2010 there were about seven million full-time male workers aged 16 to 24. Doing the math, this equates to four billion dollars per week in additional surplus value, or $200 billion per year. If we include young male and female workers worldwide, the additional wealth that is being extracted annually from young workers amounts to trillions of dollars!

This evidence points to a massive age-based redistribution of wealth that has taken place with little public awareness or discussion. We know who suffers from it, but who has benefited from this surplus wealth extraction from youth labor? One answer comes from an examination of the segment of the population that experienced dramatic increases in earning power and wealth since the 1980s. This segment includes the "captains of capitalism," especially the now-called "1%," or the bourgeoisie (ruling class). The increased wealth of this small segment of the population is staggering, especially when contrasted with declining youth wealth.

The easiest way to track this group is through the magazine/website Forbes (www.forbes.com/billionaires/), which has been tracking the exponential growth of billionaires worldwide. According to Forbes, this group has grown as follows: The billionaire was a rare breed before the 1980s; in the early 1980s, there were a "handful"; by the late 1980s there were 52 billionaires worldwide; just ten years later there were ten times as many (535 in 2001); and by 2013 there were three times as many again (1,426). The net worth of this small group of people is $5.4 trillion.

Is this ballooning of wealth among the bourgeoisie coincidental to the decline in youth wages and the economic disenfranchisement of youth since the 1980s, the era of neoliberalism? It is certainly an interesting correlation (cf. Côté, 2014b; McQuaig & Brook, 2011).[1]

Employment prospects: Stopgap work vs. youth as worker

Tannock picks up on the story of the proletarianization of youth labor, focusing on the ways in which the young workers have been viewed by most youth researchers. He argues that the dominant view involves the "pathway model," namely, that researchers typically focus on "the trajectories of youths from school...to career" and "little on what youths are actually doing in any particular job during their transition from school to career, and more on where youths are initially coming from...and where they are eventually going" (2001, p. 23). Tannock argues that these approaches ignore how young people are "positioned in the workplace as workers" and what might be done to improve "the generally poor conditions of youth work" (*ibid.*, p. 23). In doing so, he argues, youth researchers give short shrift to the issues of youth-worker exploitation and how the nature of jobs available to young people might be improved. Consequently, policy recommendations from the youth-studies field usually involve ways in which young workers can be helped to move on to better, "adult" jobs, rather than improving the actual jobs available to them. For Tannock, such recommendations will not improve service-sector jobs, nor do they deal with "whether there will ever be enough good 'adult' jobs for all youths to move up into" (*ibid.*, p. 24).

The pathway models that Tannock critiques tend to view the jobs available to young workers as "stop gap" jobs that are suited to them in terms of their life circumstances. In addition to ignoring the "bad jobs" that are given to young workers, little consideration is given to the possibility that many young people are not interested in a trajectory to something else, but would like to earn a living wage in a good job "now." Tannock identifies four versions of the pathway model that share these shortcomings:

- Youth-labor-market theory: This theory sees young workers as passing through a "secondary labor market" (dead-end jobs with poor wages and benefits) on their way to a "primary labor market" (stable, career-oriented jobs) without experiencing a "scarring" from these experiences. These jobs constitute a "functional match" with the young because of their ostensible immaturity and desire to explore and experiment rather than commit themselves (e.g., Osterman, 1980). Influenced by adolescent psychology, this approach sees the youth labor market "as a natural and functional adaption of economic structures" to the (temporary) developmental needs of young people (Tannock, 2001, p. 27).
- School-to-work theory: This perspective recognizes the problems with the youth labor market for those not in the post-secondary educational system, focusing on the floundering that takes place there. The source of the floundering is identified to be a result of the exploitive practices of employers, and not some inherent instability on the part of youth (e.g., William T. Grant Foundation, 1988). Unfortunately, as Tannock submits, the solution offered "does not fit the problem:" bridging programs designed to lift youth out of their exploitive situations do nothing to change those exploitive jobs for other youth, which will likely come to be occupied by the most disadvantaged segments of the youth population, such as immigrant youth.
- Student-worker theory: This model emerged out of the socialization field, positing teenage work experiences to be a beneficial part of the socialization process in terms of developing the traits necessary for eventual entry into full-time jobs after schooling is complete (e.g., Fine, Mortimer, & Roberts, 1990). A debate emerged in this area, with Greenberger and Steinberg (1986) questioning the socialization potential of many of the mindless jobs available to teenagers, and worrying that working too much while in school had demonstrably harmful effects. The thrust of this perspective has been to recommend limiting the work undertaken by young people in school, and thus focuses on them as students rather than workers. Tannock argues that this middle-class bias paints all young people as bound for post-secondary studies, needing only extra money for discretionary spending because their parents will subsidize them. To the contrary, young people from disadvantaged backgrounds, especially early school leavers who will not go on to a post-secondary education, need to make a living wage in the present, not the future, either to support themselves or to help their impoverished family.
- Social-reproduction theory: Tannock is critical of these theories (examined in the education chapter; e.g., Bowles & Gintis, 1976) because, although they recognize the exploitation of youth, especially through school systems, they have little to offer in terms of concrete remedies. Instead, they adopt the pathway focus of examining where young people begin and end their

passage to the adult workplace, but not on what happens in between. Thus, Tannock argues that their concern with permanent labor-market stratification does not account for the temporary stratification that is the mark of the contemporary youth period.

The alternative that Tannock advocates to all of these pathway models is the "stopgap worker model," which looks at

> youths as *workers*: with the work they do, the workplaces in which they work, the employers who hire and manage them, the ways they are positioned as workers in the workplace and labor market, and the possibilities for improving their working conditions.
>
> (Tannock, 2001, p. 38)

Although he does not use the term, Tannock is essentially concerned with how the age of "economic maturity" has risen (e.g., Torche, 2011), marginalizing those under this age into exploitive sectors of the labor force. With an underpinning of prejudices and stereotypes against the young, few people see this as exploitation; instead, an ideology based on these stereotypes has emerged to legitimize the exploitation. He implores youth researchers "to develop parallel research and theory on youths as (stopgap) workers" that "engages with the interests, experiences, and demands of youth workers" (Tannock, 2001, p. 39). His ethnographic research, based on the political-economy perspective, is exemplary of the direction that a more comprehensive youth-studies field could follow. Unfortunately, as we see in the next three sections, his pleas to the youth-studies community appear not to have been heard.

Three liberal positions

Prolonged workplace marginalization as functional

As we saw in Chapter 2, functionalists tend to see the prolonged youth period as a social-evolutionary development. One version of this position is that an extended youth period is part of the "second demographic transition" (Beaujot & Kerr, 2007). This view grew out of the most conservative theories in sociology, and in the case to be examined in this section, out of the demographic sub-discipline of sociology, which itself has been heavily influenced by functionalism. To account for the extended youth period, along with its workplace marginalization, Beaujot and Kerr (2007) cite changing norms allowing for greater choice, such as easier entry and exit into relationships, including marriage and divorce, along with greater acceptability of premarital sex and cohabitation. Their position with respect to workplace opportunities also follows a "free-choice" assumption, namely, that young people can now choose to delay entry into the labor force. The argument is that they do so in part because they are not normatively pressured to take up marriage and family roles. This is viewed as a rational decision in taking advantage of a period of semi-autonomy afforded by parental support, especially in extending or renewing intergenerational cohabitation.

Absent from this type of analysis is a serious consideration of structural obstacles, especially those related to socio-economic disadvantage. Beaujot and Kerr (2007) attempt an imagined rebuttal to critics who might point this out:

> From the political economy perspective, the main reason for late transitions must be that youth lack opportunities. Yet this view is undermined by the observation that some population groups that also lack opportunities react by rushing rather than delaying these same transitions. (p. 25)

However, the reasoning of this account has it wrong. Those who "rush" the transition—the so-called "fast track" transitions—may not want anything to do with a period of semi-autonomy, and instead want their full citizenship rights, which include full employment (Bynner, 2001). If there were workplace opportunities to support the assumption of work roles at an earlier age, there would be no notion of "rushing" to apply to this situation. At the same time, this theory puts "the cart before the horse" for those who delay marriage and family formation precisely because those young people cannot afford these options as a result of their poor workplace opportunities.

Clearly, certain forms of "delayed transitions" are useful in terms of gaining knowledge and skills, as well as for developing psychosocially, as in the so-called "slow track" transitions (Bynner, 2001), but this is not the point in contention. What is contended is that many young people are denied their rights of citizenship to workplace opportunities (which in most countries legally begin at age 18); instead, they are exploited, marginalized, and excluded because of practices imposed by merit of their age. If there were no such obstacles blocking these opportunities, the functionalist claim of free choice would be more convincing.

Emerging adulthood and the choice to experience an economic hiatus

Arnett's (2000) emerging adulthood model is also based on assumptions of "free choice"—that people choose their fates within certain "environmental" constraints. While there is an understanding of the influence of social structure, these influences are downplayed in preference for a focus on the agentic potential of the individual. In Chapter 3, we reviewed an exchange in which Bynner (2005) criticized Arnett's theory as "insufficiently attentive to structural factors," with Arnett (2006) responding that as a psychologist he sees structural factors "more in terms of environmental influences and constraints in the way of life goals rather than as shaping, in a fundamental way, roles and identities to match modern conditions" (p. 155).

Arnett thus expresses a boilerplate assumption from psychology regarding "agency" over "structure." In his exchange with Bynner, Arnett insisted "emerging adults [desire] to try different possible educational and occupational paths until they find the one that provides the right identity match" (Arnett, 2006, p. 118). He also asserted that the young have the collective power to change their circumstances themselves, claiming "they will seek to change educational and occupational paths to match their identity needs, and they will press their school officials and governments to allow them to do so" (*ibid.*). However, Arnett does not provide evidence for this assertion of the dominance of agency over structure.

This psychological model is the equivalent of both a functionalist theory in sociology and a pathway model identified by Tannock (2001). Accordingly, there is a lack of attention (a) to the exploitative nature of the youth labor market and (b) to the nature of the work performed by the young in his contention that this period is dominated by "identity explorations" with various types of jobs rather than coping with exploitive job situations. Arnett (2004, p. 373) admits that for many young people identity exploration "is a bit too lofty a word to describe their work history." He goes on to admit that these work experiences are often "not nearly as systematic, organized, and focused as 'exploration' implies. 'Meandering' might be a more accurate word, or maybe 'drifting' or 'bouncing around'." Still, Arnett has never investigated the causes for these "pathway" variations.

The pathway assumptions of Arnett's model are clearly stated in the following passage:

> Adolescents tend to view their jobs not as occupational preparation but as a way to obtain the money that will support an active leisure life—paying for compact discs, concerts, restaurant meals, clothes, cars, travel, and so forth.... [In contrast] in emerging adulthood, work experiences become more focused on preparation for adult work roles. Emerging adults begin to consider how their work experiences will lay the groundwork for the jobs they may have through adulthood. In exploring various work possibilities, they explore identity issues as well: What kind of work am I good at? What kind of work would I find satisfying for the long term? What are my chances of getting a job in the field that seems to suit me best?
>
> (Arnett, 2000, pp. 473–4)

Tannock identifies Arnett's model as one of several theories that normalize the degraded status of young people in the neoliberal political economy. In doing so, Tannock argues, Arnett's model therefore potentially exacerbates the deleterious conditions of this age period by "recommending" emerging adulthood to the public and policy-makers

> as the category of youth is extended upward into adulthood, the childlike characteristics of adults are emphasized: adults as youth (emerging adults)

are constructed as immature, still in development, not yet fully "grown up," and consequently, may be said to be less entitled to make claims on such things as a family wage job, career stability or the means to live independently. Indeed, the promotion of emerging adulthood as a normal stage of development, that is argued to be healthy for society and positively experienced by most individuals in their late teens and 20s (e.g. Arnett...), works directly to normalize the erosion of social and economic standards of living that has taken place for large segments of younger generations under conditions of neoliberal restructuring.

(Sukarieh & Tannock, 2011, pp. 683–4)

Vanguard generations

A debate between Wyn and Woodman (2006, 2007) and Roberts (2007) reveals a key fissure that has developed among youth sociologists. The issue pertains to whether the "transitional approach" in youth studies is valid or whether it should be replaced by a "generational approach." Wyn's concern in this debate overlaps Tannock's, with Wyn critiquing "transitions" approaches and Tannock critiquing the similarly conceptualized "pathway" approaches. However, it would appear that the reasons for their objections to these approaches differ in terms of value priorities: Wyn and Woodman tend to take an advocacy approach whereas Tannock's approach resembles a critical emancipation one.

Wyn has championed this generational approach in various works (e.g., Andres & Wyn, 2010), but it does not appear to be widely shared. Wyn's approach to the debates about the nature of the employment opportunities available to young people is relevant in three ways: (1) her position regarding why youth employment opportunities have deteriorated in the last few decades; (2) her account of why other youth scholars might have missed the story she tells about the "vanguard generation" she claims has emerged since the 1970s; and (3) her advocacy position regarding current youth cohorts.

Employment opportunities: Wyn acknowledges that youth employment opportunities have deteriorated, but there no macro analysis of how or why this happened. Unfortunately, there is little sense that these material conditions have seriously affected young people's well-being or instilled a sense of false consciousness. To the contrary, she has gone to great lengths to valorize the young for adapting to these conditions; furthermore, she claims they have positive-minded "subjectivities" that are proof they should be considered a "vanguard generation," presumably a model for future generations. How is this logic to be understood? An examination of the other two assumptions helps us understand this reasoning better.

Vanguard generation: In her various writings, Wyn repeatedly takes youth-studies scholars to task, claiming they hold negative views of young people (e.g., Wyn & Woodman, 2006, p. 498). She associates these negative views with the "transitions approach," which she claims is predicated on the experiences of the Baby Boomer generation. Her reasoning is that because many youth-studies scholars are Baby Boomers, the transitions approach is the product of these Baby Boomers projecting their own biased expectations into their academic work (i.e., they are supposedly biased by their own coming of age experiences that involved early passage of the social markers leading to adulthood). This ad hominem argument includes the claim that Baby Boomers negatively view later transitions, and since recent generations cannot measure up to the early transitions of the Baby Boomer generation, Baby Boomer transitions scholars see these later transitions as having "failed" in someway in becoming fully functioning adults.

Unfortunately, this characterization of the so-called "transitions literature" appears to be a caricature. A different reading of this diverse literature is that prolonged transitions have been imposed on the young through no fault of their own. Delays in transitions such as school to work are most plausibly economic in origin and arguably a product of neoliberalism; to identify root causes of their employment problems is not to "blame" the young for those problems.

The second part of this assumption of bias is that Baby Boomer youth researchers have supposedly missed the real story about contemporary youth, which she calls a "vanguard" generation that has created a "new adulthood," as follows:

> The concept of a new adulthood assumes a generational framework. It signals the emergence of significant new priorities and subjectivities that are anchored in the political and material conditions of young people's lives. It is suggested that these subjectivities are not simply "transitional" (or "age effects"), and implies that a generational shift had occurred. Changes in labor markets, in the relationship between education and employment and in workplace relations, and in the actions of the state, have altered the significance of the traditional "markers" of adult status in industrialised countries. These changes have had effects across the generations, but with specific effects for the post-1970 generation because of their particular positioning in the network of social relations and because they have known no other world.
>
> (Wyn & Woodman, 2006, p. 500)

Wyn is not the first scholar to suggest that adulthood has changed (see, e.g., Côté, 2000), but her identification of the beginning of this change in the nature of adulthood is questionable, and seems conveniently linked to the age of the Australian sample that she studied over 14 years who left secondary school in 1991 at about the age of 18 years (Andres & Wyn, 2010). The idea of a vanguard generation forging a new adulthood "is described in many of the writings to emerge from the Life-Patterns study, and most recently in Research Report 27" (Wyn & Woodman, 2006, p. 500). However, it turns out that this study is based on a sample of a very narrow age range (1 to 2 years) born in the early 1970s, raising questions about how generalizations can be made about an entire generation. This type of theory should be based on a much larger spread in birth years to qualify as a "generational analysis." Besides, as we saw earlier in this chapter, there is evidence that the decreasing earning power of young workers began with Baby Boomers, not those born in the early 1970s, so this essential tenet of Wyn's position is based on a questionable assumption, at least as pertains to most developed countries (Blanchflower, 1999a, 1999b).

Alas, as with liberal approaches in general, Wyn's generational formulations can have the effect of normalizing the coping responses of "post-70s" generations to these neoliberal conditions. Instead of looking at the impact of exploitation (e.g., alienation, false consciousness, etc.), Wyn's formulations seem to constitute an apology for this very exploitive era of capitalism. In this respect, her position sends a message to policy-makers, which is similar to Arnett's position: little needs to be done about the fundamental conditions of young people's employment opportunities, other than for those who experience adjustment problems.

Advocacy position: The puzzle of Wyn's position regarding critiques of other youth researchers in her apparent defense of young people becomes clearer when we examine her third assumption. Wyn takes an advocacy position regarding current youth cohorts, seemingly needing to defend them against perceived negative stereotypes. In doing so, she makes reference to youth "subjectivities," thereby setting materialist concerns aside and looking at symbolic ones (i.e., moving from what people do to what they think about; e.g., Wyn & Woodman, 2006, p. 507).

Sukarieh and Tannock (2011) comment on this sort of admonishing advocacy approach, contending that these sorts of "positivity" advocacy positions feed into the neoliberal domination of the youth period, as in the case of the obsessive attempt to view all young people (and all of their actions) in a positive light. This type of bias downplays the role of neoliberalism in creating current conceptions of "youth" and how corporations benefit from the prolongation of youth in the creation of a cheaper labor force and a large consumer market. Sukarieh and Tannock argue, "it is not just negative stereotypes of youth that need to be critically interrogated, but positive stereotypes as well" (p. 675).

They claim that the "positivity imperative" in youth studies is "closely tied to a larger neoliberal project of further vocationalizing education, promoting close business–education partnerships, and reshaping schools and other institutions working with youth along corporate, business and market lines" (Sukarieh & Tannock, 2011, p. 680). This positive emphasis is also implicated in "opening up the spheres of education and youth development to market forces and business interests, promoting the ideology of neoliberalism among the young and undermining the traditional entitlements of welfare state provision" (*ibid.*, p. 682).

Sukarieh and Tannock (2011) lay down the following challenge for youth-studies scholars to recognize how their biases are shaped by and support neoliberalism:

The challenge for critical analysis is not simply to replace negative stereotypes of youth with positive ones (or vice versa). It is, rather, to understand how and why particular kinds of positive and negative stereotypes of youth—or, indeed, invocations of the youth label in the first place—are mobilized by different groups in changing social and economic contexts over time. In this way, the field of youth studies and organizing can follow similar movements in women's, ethnic and race studies and organizing, to go beyond simply inverting stereotypes to critically interrogating the material and social conditions of the construction of these broad categories of identity. (pp. 688–9)

The three articles in the Wyn/Woodman–Roberts debate are suggested as recommended readings at the end of this chapter to give readers an appreciation of the finer points of this dispute.

Conclusion: Labor exploitation, neoliberalism, and the prolongation of youth

This chapter counterposed the political-economy perspective against other perspectives with respect to their fundamental assumptions concerning work conditions and employment opportunities for young people in their teens and twenties. Based on a review of how the assumptions of the political-economy perspective challenge liberal assumptions about the structure of the current youth period, an examination was provided of data from the United States documenting the decline in youth wages during the neoliberal era. In addition, based on Tannock's exposé of the exploitation of young workers, several positions were critiqued and found wanting. When the integrity of youth labor is taken seriously as recommended by Tannock, a political-economy position corrects deficiencies in these liberal approaches by highlighting several things. First, workplace marginalization and exploitation are imposed on young people as a cohort—these problems are not merely individual-level or restricted to the lower social classes. Second, the capitalist economy creates conditions that delay financial independence, so this delay is not merely a result of youth cohorts "choosing" to delay earning a living wage. And, third, neoliberal conditions have produced a youth labor market that needs to be rectified, and not accepted as a situation to which recent cohorts have cheerfully adapted.

Recommended readings

James E. Côté & John Bynner (2008). Changes in the transition to adulthood in the UK and Canada: The role of structure and agency in emerging adulthood. *Journal of Youth Studies*, 11, 251–68.
    This article provides a sociological critique of Arnett's model of emerging adulthood, noting among other things that it is not the name coined for this period that is

problematic, but several unsubstantiated assumptions that Arnett insists characterize this period.

International Labour Office (2013). *Global employment trends for youth 2012: A generation at risk [Executive summary]*. Geneva: Author. http://www.ilo.org/global/research/global-reports/global-employment-trends/youth/2013/WCMS_212899/lang—en/index.htm

This international organization discusses, in its annual report on youth employment, the growing challenges facing young people around the world in gaining access to the labor force and retaining jobs that pay a living wage.

Steven Roberts (2011). Beyond "NEET" and "tidy" pathways: Considering the "missing middle" of youth transition studies. *Journal of Youth Studies*, 14, 21–39.

This qualitative study examines the experiences of 24 young British males working in lower-level retail positions, whom Roberts calls the "missing middle" because these types of young workers do not normally attract the attention of (sociologically oriented) youth researchers, whom he argues are more interested in "slow track" vs. "fast track" trajectories.

Andrew Sum, Ishwar Khatiwada, Joseph McLaughlin & Sheila Palma (2011). No country for young men: Deteriorating labor market prospects for low-skilled men in the United States. *The ANNALS of the American Academy of Political and Social Science*, 635, 24–55. DOI: 10.1177/0002716210393694

This article analyzes in depth the census data discussed in this chapter revealing the deterioration in wages over the past several decades among young American men and the implications of this deterioration for their opportunities—as young people—with respect to family and marriage transitions and risks of incarceration.

1. Johanna Wyn & Dan Woodman (2006). Generation, youth and social change in Australia. *Journal of Youth Studies*, 9, 495–514.
2. Ken Roberts (2007). Youth transitions and generations: A response to Wyn and Woodman. *Journal of Youth Studies*, 10, 263–69.
3. Johanna Wyn & Dan Woodman (2007). Researching youth in a context of social change: A reply to Roberts. *Journal of Youth Studies*, 10, 373–81.

Picking up on the discussion in this chapter of a recent debate, these three articles show the lively dialogue regarding the conceptualizations of young people in "generational" vs. "transitional" terms.

Family Life and Parental Influence

6

It is commonly assumed by the public and social scientists alike that family background and parental behaviors have significant determining effects on how children turn out as adults, both in terms of their life chances and personal development. However, in a provocative book, Harris (2009) charged that these beliefs are largely untrue, and that influences outside parents' control are more determining, especially during adolescence and youth. Harris also argues that genetic factors—obviously beyond the control of parents—are more determining of how children turn out than are parenting techniques (recall the nature–nurture debate discussed in Chapter 3).

Still, research examining these assumptions about parental influence has continued, with a number of investigators claiming that they have clear evidence of the enduring effects of family life and parenting styles. Unlike the previous two chapters, though, there are not major disagreements among different paradigms in youth studies, but rather disputes within paradigms over the specific relevance of findings. Thus, there tends not to be ontological, political agenda, or value-priority disputes in this area, but rather empirically focused disputes on the reliability and validity of findings.

The absence of debate on other grounds is rather remarkable in a field replete with disputes. In sociology and cultural studies, there appears to be a preference for "sexier" or more politically charged topics. But, what we find by the end of this chapter is a pressing need to know more about what parents might be able to do to prepare their children for youth transitions and adulthood outcomes. This need is especially urgent for those from less affluent backgrounds who might be able to "inoculate" their children from the corrosive influences of Western societies as well as to give them the resources needed to surmount the obstacles laying in wait for them if they attempt to become upwardly mobile.

In point of fact, this is an extremely important area in which answers to important questions are needed; much is riding on the answers to those questions, especially in terms of the assumptions politicians adopt in framing social policies affecting families, children, adolescents, and youth. If their assumptions are faulty, there may be inadequate financial support available through some policies as well as inappropriate policies in terms of how young people are treated outside the family sphere.

Here is a partial list of the questions that need to be answered concerning how much control parents have over the fates of their children as they make their way to adult roles in society, particularly in capitalist societies with wide (and widening) economic inequalities, a situation exacerbated by the late-modern tendency toward normative ambiguity:

- Can parents prepare their children early in life for the vicissitudes of neoliberal, late-modern societies?
- Do certain childrearing techniques studied as "parenting styles" prepare young people in ways that help them to traverse the multiple risks of these types of societies?
- Do some parenting styles disadvantage young people in their ability to navigate the jeopardies in neoliberal societies, as in the disjunctive and individualized transitions through educational systems into the labor force?
- Do parenting styles work in the same way for minorities, and those from less affluent backgrounds, as they do for those from affluent, majority groups?
- Can parents from disadvantaged backgrounds provide their children with the agentic resources to overcome their economic and social disadvantages simply by employing certain parenting styles?
- And, how much is known with certainty based on this empirical research—is there enough certainty to be taken seriously by policy-makers?

We explore these questions in this chapter through the lens of "parent styles:" one model from psychology and the other from sociology. In both cases, we find internal debates about their utility. At the end of this chapter, we review the above questions to see if they have been adequately answered and what further study might be required.

Parenting styles: Psychological models

In his 2000 Presidential Address to the Society for Research on Adolescence, Steinberg made a passionate plea

> to institute a systematic, large-scale, multifaceted, and ongoing public health campaign to educate parents about adolescence, one that draws on the collective resources and expertise of health-care professionals, scientists, governmental agencies, community organizations, schools, religious institutions, and the mass media.
>
> (2001, p. 1)

The basis for this dramatic claim is his assumption, based on his 20 years of researching the topic, that "there is enough evidence to conclude that adolescents benefit from having parents who are authoritative: warm, firm, and accepting of their needs for psychological autonomy" (Steinberg, 2001, p. 1). He argues that there is now enough solid evidence for policy-makers to launch a "public health campaign...to educate parents of teenagers [in the same fashion as] past efforts to educate parents of infants" (*ibid.*, p. 16).

Undeniably, research into parent–adolescent relationships has become a minor industry in adolescent psychology. By Steinberg's estimate, in the last decade of the twentieth century, about one-third of publications in child- and adolescent-psychology journals focused on these relationships. Much of this research concentrated on parenting practices and styles, and moved from an earlier focus on conflict, based on storm-and-stress assumptions, to one based on close, communicative relationships involving a give and take between the needs of both adolescents and parents. Rather than viewing all adolescents as troubled and their relationships with parents and authority figures as rebellious, accumulating evidence suggested that these negative experiences characterized only about a quarter of adolescents and their families, with the remainder being happy and enjoying relatively harmonious relationships.

Steinberg's involvement in this renaissance in adolescent psychology lead him and others to focus on the extent to which parents can grant "psychological autonomy" to their adolescent offspring, namely, helping them to think for themselves and explore their potentials and social opportunities. Steinberg (2001) and others now are certain that adolescents who are granted more psychological autonomy, but who abide by parental guidance, tend to show the best outcomes in many areas of functioning.

The framework identifying authoritative parenting also identifies three other parenting styles based on two underlying dimensions: demandingness and responsiveness (Baumrind, 1968; Maccoby & Martin, 1983). Demandingness refers to parents' expectations about their children's maturity and compliance with their wishes. Responsiveness involves the parents' sensitivity to their children's behavioral cues, interpersonal needs, and psychological states.

Cross-tabulating the two dimensions identifies the following typology of styles:

- The *authoritative* style is high on both responsiveness and demandingness, which set the stage for the effective granting of psychological autonomy.
- The *authoritarian* style exhibits high demandingness but low responsiveness.
- The *indulgent* style, in contrast, is low on demandingness but high on responsiveness.
- The *indifferent* style is low on both responsiveness and demandingness. (The last two styles constitute what is commonly referred to as "permissive parenting.")

Steinberg appears to be correct that the published research on parenting effects consistently finds that authoritative parenting produces better developmental outcomes. These outcomes include fewer problems with depression and anxiety

(Steinberg, 2001), as well as higher levels of self-esteem (Dusek & McIntrye, 2003), self-efficacy (Schunk & Meece, 2006), moral development (Walker & Henning, 1999), and proactive identity formation (Berzonsky, 2004). Young people with authoritative parents also do better in high school (higher GPA and academic engagement; Darling & Steinberg, 1993; Steinberg, 1996) and university (Turner, Chandler, & Heffer, 2009), in part because authoritative parents monitor their children's school activities more closely, guide them more in their courses, and involve themselves in school functions (Darling & Steinberg, 1993).

The explanation for these positive effects, especially with respect to nurturing agency, is that authoritative parenting encourages independent problem solving and critical thinking among progeny, and this practice provides opportunities for young people to engage in the proactive exploration of ideas. Those raised by authoritative parents are more likely to employ adaptive, task-oriented strategies that are associated with prosocial identity formation (Aunola, Stattin, & Nurmi, 2000).

In contrast, over- and under-controlled adolescents appear to engage in more task-irrelevant or passive behaviors that characterize inactive identity formation (see Chapter 9 for a discussion of types of identity formation). Indeed, the literature suggests that young people raised by parents employing either of the permissive styles develop less self-regulation, greater impulsivity, and lower self-reliance and orientation to work (Lamborn, Mounts, Steinberg, & Dornbusch, 1991).

Finally, authoritarian parents can discourage the proactive exploration of ideas and independent problem solving, and instead encourage an unquestioning dependence upon their control and guidance (Hess & McDevitt, 1984).

Parental authoritativeness has also been found to have a cumulative effect. It is better to have one authoritative parent than none. Research shows that the authoritatively inclined tend to marry each other, resulting in mothers and fathers being in agreement about 75 per cent of the time concerning authoritative issues (Steinberg, 2001). The benefits of authoritativeness also seem to expand beyond the family—adolescents also profit from having authoritative vs. authoritarian teachers, school principals, coaches, and bosses; in addition, a critical mass of authoritative parents in a given neighborhood can have additional positive effects on resident adolescents through contact with neighboring peers and parents (Steinberg, 1996).

Steinberg (2001) argues that authoritative parenting has benefits that cross the boundaries of ethnicity, socio-economic status (SES), and household composition. He contends that regardless of racial or social-class background, or family composition, adolescents have more positive outcomes when exposed to authoritative parenting. Moreover, research carried out in countries representing a range of value systems (China, Pakistan, Hong Kong, Scotland, Australia, and Argentina) supports the cross-cultural validity of the beneficial impact of authoritative parenting, although it may take different forms in non-Western cultures (Arnett, 2001).

As good as all this sounds, there is far from a consensus among psychologists concerning the validity of this parenting-style typology, or about Steinberg's enthusiasm for taking the authoritative style to the public through policy initiatives. Objections can be found on a number of grounds, especially the normative assumptions about what constitutes "good parenting," but also how evenly distributed the styles are among different ethnic and income groups, and how easy it is to put the principles of authoritativeness into practice.

Even if authoritative parenting has similar effects across social structural categories such as class and ethnicity, as the research apparently shows, this does not mean that the parenting styles are evenly distributed across these categories. Certainly, a repeated criticism of this approach is that the authoritative style reflects White, American "middle-class" parenting preferences. Studies do find positive correlations between authoritative parenting and SES, along with negative correlations of SES with authoritarian and indifferent styles (Spera, 2005; Steinberg, 1996), but these SES measures do not differentiate discretely among social classes (e.g., differentiating categories of working class with middle class). Furthermore, even if lower SES and ethnic minority parents may want to be more authoritative, they may be hindered by a lack of time to monitor their children's social and school activities because of work demands (Spera, 2005). They may also be hindered by a lack of educational resources, because they did not go far in school themselves, so do not have the wherewithal to advise and guide their children through higher-educational levels.

Likewise, there appears to be more of a reciprocal effect between the parent and the adolescent than this model implies. Some studies show how young people can shape their relationship with their parents, and have their own ways of responding to outside influences from their peers, the school, and the mass media (Kuczynski, Marshall, & Schell, 1997). Sometimes adolescents bring issues into interactions with their parents that can make authoritative parenting quite difficult. To cite an extreme example, trying to authoritatively reason with a person who (temporarily or persistently) is stubborn, aggressive, or withdrawn may be fruitless simply because that young person may not be open to reasoning and discussion and cannot handle psychological autonomy (Adams, Côté, & Marshall, 2001). At the same time, the parents themselves may not have the upbringing or character associated with making reasoned exchanges, or do not believe in the values underlying this form of democratic parenting.

In point of fact, there is a lively debate among adolescent psychologists regarding the importance of these parenting *styles* vs. parenting *practices* (e.g., Spera, 2005) as well as how to characterize the give and take in parent–adolescent relationships. More than a few developmental psychologists have been skeptical about this model and the nature of the effects of authoritative parenting. As noted above, Harris (2009) argues that genetics has a stronger effect on children's personality than parenting styles. Part of this effect, she argues, is that genetics affect children's personalities (e.g., how affable vs. disagreeable they are). She further argues that parenting-style researchers have not taken these influences into account, and mistake the nature of the correlations found in their research. Harris argues that the direction is not from parent to child, but the other way, such that children with difficult personalities require more authoritarian styles to achieve compliance, and children with pleasant personalities invite authoritative styles. Perhaps most serious in undermining the research model is Harris's claim that the research methods used by this line of research are not capable of detecting these influences because researchers typically have adolescents fill out the surveys about their own behaviors as well as those of their parents, producing a "shared method variance" error (Harris, 2009, p. 300). For instance, adolescents with obstinate temperaments may perceive their parents as more discipline oriented and they may admit to more wrongdoing, while adolescents (with the same parents) with more affable temperaments may tend to see their parents as more reasonable and be less likely to admit to any wrongdoing.

Those who argue that the styles do not take into sufficient account how adolescents affect their parents also argue that the parent–child relationship changes over time as both parent and offspring adjust to their respective roles. Moreover, these roles can change over time in terms of dependency, self-regulation (psychological vs. behavioral control), and disclosure in various domains (e.g., Barber, Stolz, & Olsen, 2005; Kerr & Stattin, 2000; Marshall, Tilton-Weaver, & Bosdet, 2005; Rubab, Marshall, & Shapka, 2010; Smetana & Asquith, 1994; Smetana et al., 2006; Stattin & Kerr, 2000).

Stepping back from this bountiful research to look at its underlying assumptions, we can clearly see its paradigmatic origins in conservative realism, along with a value-priority position based on the belief that young people need (benign) facilitation–guidance from adults. For all its value, the coverage of the factors that affect the influence of parents on their young offspring reveals a limitation of the psychological approach where "social context" is most often treated as a control variable (e.g., SES) rather than a primary variable to be thoroughly explored, either as a cause or outcome (i.e., as an important independent or dependent variable, namely, how social class reproduces parenting styles or how parenting styles reproduce social class). Likewise, it is easier for researchers to treat young people as *tabula rasa* to be shaped by parental practices, both theoretically and methodologically because bi-directionality is far more difficult to deal with using quantitative techniques, the preferred method among psychologists over qualitative techniques (cf. Marshall, Young, & Tilton-Weaver, 2008).

Two additional limitations of this literature are evident when we place it in the context of the field of youth studies.

First, the lack of attention to the long-term effects of parenting is surprising, especially in terms of how young people make the transition to adulthood in their passages through educational systems and into the labor force. Some young people appear to have a good start in the educational system, but does that advantage carry through in the real world of adulthood, including helping young people from less affluent backgrounds overcome social-class obstacles? It appears to be a matter of faith that authoritative parenting has an inoculation effect like this, and there is no published longitudinal research, although the cross-sectional research is relatively consistent that student perceptions of (past) authoritative parenting are related to better academic adjustment and achievement among college and university students from a variety of ethnic groups and cultures (Abar, Carter, & Winsler, 2009; Akinsola, 2011; Ejei, Lavasani, Malahmadi, & Khezri, 2011; Hickman & Crossland, 2004; Liu, Qian, & Huang, 2004; Wintre & Yaffe, 2000).

Second, there appear to have been no efforts to link these psychological models of parenting with sociological models, a linkage that might correct the biases introduced by the psychological boilerplate governing this research tradition.

In the next section, we examine the sociological equivalent of this psychological research tradition.

Parenting styles: Sociological models

The issue of how parenting affects the development and life chances of offspring has been approached from a different angle in sociology, influenced by its distinctive disciplinary tradition of concentrating on the effects of social class on life chances (e.g., Blau & Duncan, 1967). Lareau (2003, 2011) has focused on this issue for the past 25 years, producing a rare longitudinal ethnographic study. Her work is based on the theoretical perspective developed by Bourdieu (1973, 1977; Bourdieu & Passeron, 1977) in the mobilization of class-based "capital," as well as in the empirical works of Bernstein (1975) and Kohn (1977) that draw stark contrasts between middle-class and working-class families.[1]

Bernstein (1975) focused on the effects of two "linguistic codes" used by parents (in the United Kingdom) in influencing the societal orientations of their offspring. He found that middle-class parents were more likely to use *elaborated codes* of language that were more complex and universalistic in their reach, while working-class parents were more likely to use *restricted codes* that were more particularistic and in-group oriented. Similarly, Kohn (1977) contrasted "self-direction" vs. "conformity to authority," respectively, in comparing middle- and working-class parental directives to their children (Weininger & Lareau, 2009).

Following these dichotomous models, Lareau proposed that two distinct parenting styles characterize social-class influences: "accomplishment of natural growth" and "concerted cultivation." She argued that these contrasting styles produce distinctive results in educational attainment, with (lower-income) working-class parents assuming that their children will find their destiny, as opposed to (upper-income) middle-class parents impressing upon their children that they have to make their own destiny through effort and self-assertion.

More specifically, parents who adopt the accomplishment-of-natural-growth style believe that providing for basic physical and emotional needs is sufficient for the offspring to grow and thrive. They do not see the need to organize their offspring's activities, but they are more controlling of certain aspects of their children's behavior, enforcing conformity through punishments.

In contrast, the concerted-cultivation style entails parents providing highly structured activities for their children and closely monitoring their activities to ensure that they are developing certain life skills, including specific linguistic and cognitive abilities (Lareau, 2002).

Lareau's ethnographic, longitudinal project involved 88 American families from three "classes": middle, working, and poor, each equally represented by Blacks and Whites. Social class was operationalized as follows:

- Middle-class families had at least one parent employed in a higher managerial position or in a career requiring at least university-level credentials.
- Working-class families were defined as having neither parent qualifying for the above middle-class criteria, but working in blue-collar or lower white-collar occupations.
- Poor families had parents who were recipients of social assistance or neither parent had regular employment.

Her primary findings with respect to the transition to adulthood were entirely predictable from a social-reproduction perspective: most middle-class parents were able to guide their children through a high-quality high school and into good college/university settings with relative ease. In contrast, the case was bleak for poor families: only one graduated from (a low quality) high school and none went onto college/university. Most working-class children graduated from high school (that were of poor quality), but few graduated college/university (Lareau, 2011). For obvious reasons, then, the poor and working-class children were on a "fast track" to adulthood, taking jobs and responsibilities, as well as facing a variety of struggles in gaining independence, earlier than their more affluent cohorts, who were taking the "slow track" (cf. Bynner, 2001, regarding these tracks in the United Kingdom). Lareau also concluded that the distribution of styles and their outcomes did not vary between White and Black families. These findings are independently supported by numerous studies from various countries. Parent's education and income has been found in most countries to be the strongest predictors of their children's level of educational attainment. In some countries, such as Canada, parent's education is more important than income as well as all other variables investigated in those studies (e.g., Finnie, Lascelles, & Sweetman, 2005).

Lareau's interview techniques allowed her to investigate the reasons for these class differences on a case-by-case basis, compiling and comparing the case outcomes. Middle-class young people had the continuing advantage of parents who had the informal knowledge and the "cultural repertoires" concerning how the educational system works and how to overcome its many obstacles and penetrate its structures (e.g., college admissions requirements). In contrast, higher education was "foreign" to those brought up by poor or working-class parents. Middle-class parents intervened when necessary to provide financial and emotional support at critical junctures, while poor and working-class parents generally left such interventions to educational professionals. When their children left the school system, working-class parents welcomed them as autonomous adults, happy for them to enter the labor force in their late teens or early twenties. In contrast, middle-class young people were still being "treated as children" by their parents in their late teens or early twenties as they made their way through college/university.

How well has Lareau's research been received and evaluated? As with the psychological version of parenting styles, the reception and subsequent empirical tests have been generally positive, but some mixed findings and interpretations have emerged.

For instance, using large population-representative longitudinal surveys, several researchers evaluated Lareau's claims regarding the importance of concerted cultivation for school success using advanced quantitative methods (the accomplishment-of-natural-growth style has not been studied, presumably because it is more difficult to operationalize for survey research). These studies are part of an important emerging literature, revealing that Lareau's qualitative approach is a good example of how ideas that emerge out of qualitative investigations can be (subsequently) assessed quantitatively for their external validity (i.e., their generalizability to larger populations). Moreover, because Lareau made no anti-realist claims, and the quantitative researchers made no anti-nominalist objections, there is no epistemological divide to be bridged here. Instead, we find here an excellent example of collaborative efforts to push the boundaries of knowledge through the use of the best tools available, both qualitative and quantitative, nominalist and realist. Lareau herself (2011) undertook some quantitative analyses based on nationally representative samples, finding support for her qualitative findings where variables from survey questions could be used to represent the features she explored qualitatively. In some cases, she found that it was not possible to quantify things like "linguistic interactions," even with proxy variables (p. 341).

This emerging literature supports Lareau's model in certain ways, but not in others. In doing so, the parenting style approach is now expanding in sociology, but appears to be a couple of decades behind the literature in psychology in the complexities that have been investigated. Nevertheless, this expanding literature is furthering our understanding of family influences, specifying issues that require further theorizing, clarification, and empirical testing.

There appears to be a consensus that concerted cultivation can be measured as a reliable construct (construct validity) and is generalizable in a number of respects (external validity) (Bodovski & Farkas, 2008; Cheadle, 2008, 2009; Cheadle & Amato, 2011; Roksa & Potter, 2011). In these studies, concerted cultivation was operationalized on the basis of questions administered to parents concerning their active involvement in their children's schooling, parental perceptions of responsibilities (to teach their children certain things), children's involvement in extracurricular activities, and the number of books the child had at home. SES was generally measured as a composite variable based on parental education, income, and occupational prestige. The conclusions regarding generalizability of Lareau's findings tend to vary by the sample of interest.

Cheadle (2008, 2009) found that concerted cultivation has a strong effect on children's knowledge of the world in kindergarten, but not afterward when they are in the regular school system. In addition, he found that SES explains about half of the variance in concerted cultivation, but race operates more independently of SES than Lareau found. Along with Black families, Cheadle also included Hispanic and Asian families, finding that concerted cultivation is more commonly employed by White, English-speaking parents (compare the findings reported above in the psychological literature that authoritative parenting is also more common among this cultural group of parents). Cheadle and Amato (2011) concluded, "concerted cultivation appears to be circumscribed by cultural as well as class boundaries ... [and may even be] a particularly U.S.-based parenting strategy" (pp. 669–70). Cheadle also expanded Lareau's model, finding that factors other than SES also influence the use of concerted cultivation, including the gender of the child (it was used more with daughters), mother's age and work status (older women who were not employed full time were more likely to engage in this style), and family type (step-parent and single-parent families engaged in this style less often).

Bodovski and Farkas (2008) also found a strong association between parental SES and use of the cultivation style, but that the style played a rather modest role in children's academic achievement in their first grade of primary school. In a subsequent article, following the same children to their fifth grade, Bodovski (2010) again found a strong positive association between SES and concerted cultivation, but replicating Cheadle's studies, discovered that Black parents engaged in this parenting style significantly less than did White parents, even when controlling for SES. Bodovski also found an interaction with gender: White girls were the objects of the most concerted cultivation, while Black females were the objects of the least amount. In other words, White parents seemed to favor their daughters more, while Black parents seemed to favor their sons more in terms of this type of parental oversight.

Unfortunately, none of the above quantitative studies extended their analysis to the adolescent or youth periods, so much research remains to be conducted to confirm if and how parenting styles during childhood have the assumed deep-seated effects necessary to affect the transition to adulthood.

Compared to the psychological literature, there have been surprisingly few independent studies of these parenting styles, or of alternative models proposed and investigated. This is in striking contrast to the field of adolescent psychology where one-third of publications in journals in that field have focused on these issues, as noted above.[2] At the same time, there have been criticisms of Lareau's operationalization and characterization of "class" as being too narrow and therefore overlooking attitudinal variances among parents and behavioral dissimilarities among children within each class designation.

To more closely examine class differences, Irwin and Elley (2011) employed strategic sampling to arrange interviews of parents in the United Kingdom from three social-class designations. They did so guided by the attitudes these parents had expressed toward education in a larger population-based survey. Focusing on these attitudes, they found a variety of parental orientations toward their children's educations among both middle- and working-class families. In light of this attitudinal variation, Irwin and Elley were critical of "a tendency towards overstating the internal homogeneity of middle-class and working-class experiences" in Lareau's model and more generally in other sociological analyses. In contrast, they found "diverse parental orientations to their children's education within, as well as across, classes" (Irwin & Elley, 2011, p. 480)

Chin and Phillips (2004) also reported greater within-class variation than did Lareau. They likewise used a categorical approach to class, but included more ethnic diversity in their class groupings. Their ethnographic methodology found that more affluent American parents had an easier time engaging in concerted cultivation because they had more time, resources, and latitude in their parenting behaviors, but the effect of these efforts depended on the characteristics of the child in question. Child compliance and motivation to respond to parental cultivation efforts mitigated both middle- and working-class parental efforts, such that motivated working-class children could compensate for the parents' lack of resources if they had the wherewithal, whereas unmotivated middle-class children could undermine their parents' efforts. Based on their qualitative findings, they rejected Lareau's class-based cultural logics of child rearing as too simplistic, especially when greater ethnic diversity is considered. Similarly, Siraj-Blatchford (2010) reported in a review of research focusing on ethnic groups in the United Kingdom that "disadvantaged families often have high aspirations for their children and provide significant educational support through 'concerted cultivation'" (p. 463).

These criticisms concerning the operationalization of the "middle class," especially as it is set against "working class," appear to have merit. As noted above, Lareau selected families for each of the classes based on exclusive criteria to ensure minimal overlap, contrasting more highly skilled managerial and professional careers with lower skilled, manual/service jobs. In doing so, however, she seems to have selected upper-middle-class professional positions in a way that accentuated the advantages of the knowledge sector of the economy— what has been called the "creative class" (Florida, 2012)—and downplayed the variation in the working class.

Not only might her middle-class sub-sample be more financially (tangibly) resourced than the typical "middle-class" family—especially as the public thinks of this class—but the people included might also have more "soft skills," intangible resources, such as achievement motivation, intellectual abilities, and the like. Indeed, when compared to the Gilbert-Kahn (Gilbert, 2003) model of the American class structure, Lareau's middle-class group seems to correspond to the upper middle class. This group constitutes 14 per cent of the population, and is just under the capitalist class—the top 1 per cent (which together make up the top 15% of the wealthy in the United States).

In contrast, her working-class sub-sample is two classes down the Gilbert-Kahn model, below the middle class (30%), and among the bottom half of the population. Moreover, Lareau's working-class families may be less resourced both tangibly and intangibly than the typical family that the public would consider "working class," because it did not include the more highly skilled trades-workers and blue-collar owners of small businesses (often called contractors).

By and large, Lareau may have eliminated the rich variation in both classes and selected families to exaggerate so-called middle-class advantages and working-class disadvantages, inadvertently feeding negative stereotypes about the more "manual" occupations and positive stereotypes about more "mental" occupations. In fact, Lareau (2011) reports that some of those portrayed in her first book (Lareau, 2003) felt betrayed and misused when they discovered what she wrote, with one working-class parent objecting that she felt like she was portrayed as "poor white trash" (p. 312).[3] Additionally, although the quantitative studies reviewed above did find that concerted cultivation is associated with higher SES, these studies operationalized "class" as an interval scale, rather than categorically.

Lareau (2011) rightly observes that social class is very difficult to define and acknowledges other problems with her methodology, but does she admit to all problems sufficiently? A consideration of this issue and a comparison of its implications with the psychological approach raise some interesting questions.

As an example, how much did Lareau's approach to the research question of class differences in parenting emerge from her own *habitus*, or general outlook, expectations, and belief system? That is, did she introduce biases into her methodology based on her socialization as a sociologist with a special affinity for Bourdieu's and Kohn's work, leading her to look for stark social-class contrasts; and thus looking, found those differences (cf. the confirmation bias discussed in Chapter 1)?

Before readers claim that it is unfair to raise this question, we can ask the same of psychologists such as Steinberg, who may have projected their American, upper-middle-class preferences and values onto this model of parenting styles. Certainly, as we saw above, there is evidence that both authoritative parenting and concerted cultivation are more commonly found among White, American parents who are more affluent.

Perhaps a more interesting question—one that raises the issue of paradigm contrasts—is how can psychologists "see" four parenting styles across all social classes, while sociologists "see" only two parenting styles, in the latter case styles that are so starkly contrasted by social class? There has been no active debate between psychologists and sociologists on this matter—certainly no studies appear to have been published that applied both models of parenting styles to the same sample. There seems to be a rather obvious homology between concerted cultivation and authoritative parenting awaiting empirical investigation, because both involve closely monitoring children's school activities and academic progress as well as participating in school functions, yet nothing has been published to date.

Accordingly, this appears to be a classic case of paradigmatic differences in the construction of reality; at the very least, it appears to be a clear example of how people's preconceptions can lead them to "see" or "construct" different realities. This case of paradigmatic differences demonstrates the value of recognizing the nominalist ontology as a threshold meta-concept, in this case showing how social scientists' interpretation of social realities can constitute a sort of Rorschach test, made famous by early psychoanalysts who studied how people's individual reality constructions can be projected on to patterns, revealing their preconceptions. Of course, it is possible that psychologists and sociologists are looking at different things, but without thorough empirical comparisons, it is conjectural to draw such a conclusion.

Finally, how should we position Lareau's work in terms of its critical/conservative implications? One way to do this is to place it within the larger context of capitalism. Does Lareau see these class differences as a result of the social relations of production, and therefore amenable to change? Or, does she see these differences as the inevitable result of status competitions that would be found in any society, even communist ones? She is not clear on this issue, although she mentions the implications of Bourdieu's work, which she adopts as a background theory. Lareau acknowledges that Bourdieu's "model suggests that inequality is a perpetual characteristic of social groups" (2011, p 363). Consequently, any attempt by the masses to gain advantages by replicating élite practices would simply lead to "the practice being devalued and replaced by a different sorting mechanism" (*ibid.*, p. 363).

If these class differences are viewed as intractable, then she would be located on the liberal side of the conservative political position, which would take the position that these class differences are a lamentable product of human nature in terms of how we organize ourselves, but we should do what we can to mitigate their negative aspects. In contrast, a critical position would view these differences as historically specific manifestations of oppressive social relations that advantage those who are most necessary in the perpetuation of capitalism at the administrative levels, but disadvantage to those whose labor can be the object of exploitation. There is no value to the bourgeoisie in empowering the working class to function any higher than necessary because this would threaten the extraction of surplus value from their wages. In this respect, conformity to authority is a highly complementary way to socialize prospective wageworkers to ensure their compliance in the labor force, including selling their labor cheaply.

This more critical approach to class relations was highlighted in the education and work chapters above with the examination of political-economy models. It is worth noting in this regard that Bowles and Gintis, who modified Kohn's model, asserted that the so-called middle class "self-direction" is more likely a "supersocialization" in terms of "internalized norms" of capitalist social relations. In this way, "workers in higher levels of the hierarchy of production... internalize authority and act without direct and continuous supervision to implement goals and objectives relatively alienated from their own personal needs" (Bowles & Gintis, 1976, p. 145). Bowles and Gintis agreed with Kohn's characterization of conformity among lower-level workers, but felt that the alienation among higher-level workers needs to be recognized "to avoid the error of attributing 'superior' values and behavior traits to higher status in the capitalist division of labor" (*ibid.*). They also noted that the internalized-norms orientation is the one favored by schools (teachers prefer students who are more self-motivated and self-regulating), giving children raised with this orientation an advantage in the school system and consequently contributing to social-class reproduction through families and schools.

Conclusion: Parenting for risk societies

A variety of questions in need of answering were presented in the introduction to this chapter. Based on the review of the various forms of evidence in this chapter, including the debates among various researchers, what can we conclude in terms of how far researchers have progressed in providing reasonably definitive answers?

Speculating upon what researchers like Steinberg and Lareau would likely argue from their own findings as well as the findings of critics who have expanded their models, the following answers can be tentatively offered:

- Parents can prepare their children early in life, and guide them later, by adopting an authoritative style that *cultivates* certain behavioral and altitudinal attributes that are rewarded in the schools and the workplace they will transit on their way to adulthood (in late-modern, neoliberal societies).
- The authoritative/concerted cultivation styles can likely "inoculate" some young people in relation to subsequent risks, but the characteristics of the children play a key role: if their children do not comply with the inoculation, there is little else that many parents can do to help them.
- Some parenting styles appear to disadvantage some young people in their ability to navigate the risks in the transition through educational systems and into the labor force, but the agentic potentials of some young people can compensate later for the deficiencies of those styles that do not nurture the rewarded behavioral and attitudinal attributes.
- The advantageous parenting styles (authoritative/concerted cultivation) do seem to work in the same way for minorities and those from less affluent backgrounds, but it is often much more difficult for them to employ those styles because of the fewer economic and social resources available to these parents.
- Not enough is yet known as to whether parents from disadvantaged backgrounds can employ certain parenting styles that would provide their

children with the agentic resources to overcome their disadvantages. It would appear that certain combinations of parental and child attributes are necessary to accomplish this, but these are not necessarily under individual control.
- There does not yet seem to be sufficient certainty based on the empirical foundation of research undertaken in either the psychological or sociological fields to convince policy-makers that progressive measures can be taken by them, in part because of the lack of sufficiently broad, longitudinal interdisciplinary research projects.

Apart from adolescent psychology (and anthropology), the field of youth studies has generally ignored parental influences at the micro level, as in the case of childrearing styles and their potential importance in human development. With the evidence of increasing economic disenfranchisement and social marginalization of youth and the associated dependencies of those in their late teens and twenties on parents in most Western countries (noted in the education and work chapters), there appears to be a resurgent interest in the family among sociologically oriented youth researchers (Jones, 2009). It has as a result become more important than ever to understand the role played by the family and parents in relation to young people making transitions to financial independence. As we saw in this chapter, this topic is ripe for investigation, and from a number of perspectives there are far more questions than answers.

Recommended readings

Tiffani Chin & Meredith Phillips (2004). Social reproduction and child-rearing practices: Social class, children's agency, and the summer activity gap. *Sociology of Education*, 77, 185–210.

This article is one of the early critiques of Lareau's model. Also based on qualitative methods, these authors argue that apparent social-class differences are better conceptualized as differences in the personal and economic resources of parents that enable them to adopt one style over another. The apparent effects of social class are also contingent upon the agentic characteristics of their children.

Judith R. Harris (1998). *The nurture assumption: Why children turn out the way they do, New York Times on the web.* Retrieved from http://www.nytimes.com/books/first/h/harris-nurture.html?_r=2&scp=3&sq=socialization%20of%20children&st=cse&oref=slogin

A reprint of the first chapter of the original edition of Harris's book questioning the validity of research that assumes that parents can control their children's destinations through "proper" parenting techniques. She argues that genetics have a stronger effect on children's personality than parenting styles, and in turn children's personalities (e.g., affable vs. willful) affect the style that parents use to raise them.

Annette Lareau & Elliot B. Weininger (2007). *Class, culture and child rearing: The transition to college.* Retrieved from http://www.hks.harvard.edu/inequality/Seminar/Papers/Lareau07.pdf

This "open-source" article is the draft for a chapter in the book *Social class: How does it work?* Edited by Annette Lareau and Dalton Conley (The Russell Sage Foundation, 2008) and for material that was published in Lareau's 2011 book. It provides the qualitative details of how young people from different class origins coped with their education-to-work transitions.

Laurence Steinberg (2001). We know some things: Parent-adolescent relationships in retrospect and prospect. *Journal of Research on Adolescence*, 11, 1–19.

This article presents Steinberg's 2000 Presidential Address to the Society for Research on Adolescence in which he makes his case for the certainty of psychologists knowledge about the benefits of the authoritative parenting style, and thus why policy-makers should use it to help parents raise their adolescent children.

The Mediated World and Technological Influences

7

This chapter lays the groundwork somewhat for the youth-culture chapter, which follows next. As we see, the youth-culture topic involves numerous issues that have been contested for decades. However, the sides have not been clearly drawn in the present topic, with the exception of the "digital native" debate. There is likely a reticence to take too firm of a stand on many issues in this topic area because mediated technology-use and its effects is a fast-changing area, and the evidence is still coming in with respect to many aspects of the use and impact of the new technologies, including those that provide new forms of mass-media delivery. Generally, though, youth researchers welcome new technology use with open arms and are advocates of the use made of new technologies by young people, seeing many positive benefits (e.g., Colin & Burns, 2009; Kelly, 2006; Merchant, 2005; White, Wyn, & Albanese, 2011).

At the same time, cautionary voices are emerging from other fields, particularly computer science and media studies, and from freelance journalists (e.g., Lanier, 2010; Morozov, 2013; Rushkoff, 2013), but these viewpoints have yet to be incorporated into youth studies. For instance, as with the impact of "old technologies" (especially television), issues linger regarding just how much young people are the primary agents in their use of technologies, as opposed to being exploited by other interests: the manufacturers of the technological devices and software; those who utilize the personal information that is now commonly published online and culled from people's Internet use; or more generally in the manufacture of consent and the encouragement of mass conformity to conditions complementary to corporate–consumer capitalism.

To put the issues concerning new technology-use in context, it is useful to first review debates about the old mediated technologies.

From old to new technology use: Predatorial marketing vs. agentic consumption

From the beginnings of the mass media, issues of the effects of what were then "new technologies" have been paramount. Obviously, by their very nature it is only through technologies that messages can be distributed on a mass basis. The printing press is a prime historical example, with the Catholic Church opposing printed books because of its fear that mass literacy would diminish the power of priests in interpreting the bible for the faithful (e.g., Erikson, 1958). As things turned out with the Protestant Reformation, those concerns were apparently justified from the point of view of the interests of the Catholic Church, but not in terms of other interests. This example provides a classic case of the tensions among conservatism (opposing books), liberalism (accepting books), and radicalism (using books to foment radical change), a tension that has been influenced by technological innovation throughout human history.

Many of the current political-economy concerns about media consumption originate with earlier twentieth-century views about the uses made of the mass media in the United States by politically conservative and dominant economic interests in the manufacture of consent (see Herman & Chomsky's, 1988, classic in the political economy of the mass media). The conservative interests first identified as engaging in this practice of deliberate mass influence were the governments that found they needed to engage in mass persuasion after the spread of the voting franchise in the early 1900s. With the entire adult population finally politically franchised (and not just White, male, property owners), the political élites needed to convince the masses to vote in favor of issues favoring dominant interest groups, such as industrial manufacturers (e.g., Caldicott, 1992). More recently, corporations' strategies of mass influence have been identified in their mass marketing to young people (see Nader & Coco, 1999, for the identification of predatorial marketing; see also, Bakan, 2004; Frank, 1997a, 1997b; Klein, 2000; Linn, 2004; Schor, 2004).

It is important to note that in the literature relevant to youth studies, it was not the technologies themselves that have been of concern to political economists and like-minded observers, but rather the uses made of them. In other words, for example, the concern was not with the existence of electronic technologies, principally radios and televisions, but rather the use made of them in content delivery by dominant political and economic interests. Similarly, the concern was not with the motives of journalists or actors themselves but with the roles they were forced to play and content they were expected to produce in supporting dominant interests. Currently, the political-economy concern is not with the new digital technologies themselves, but with the uses made of them, by both producers and consumers.

In the mid to latter part of the twentieth century, television was the main medium by which marketers reached their intended audiences, but as of the early twenty-first century, the Internet and the new digital technologies were quickly adding to the influence of first-generation electronic technologies. Based on the research concerning the psychological influence of analogue technologies along with the early digital technologies, Strasburger and Donnerstein (1999, p. 129) argued that "an increasing number of studies document that a serious problem exists" with respect to "children, adolescents, and the media." Part of their concern at the time was with the expansion of the media into video games and DVDs. When the time spent with these media was added to that of television, some teens spent as much as 55 hours per week in front of a TV or computer screen. More recent evidence finds that this trend continues (Bauerlein, 2008). A 2005 American study of 3rd- to 12th-grade students, using diaries and questionnaires, found that on average these children and adolescents spent over six hours per day of "screen time," using some form of media, mainly TV, the Internet, and video games. When media multitasking was considered (e.g., listening to an iPod while surfing the Internet), exposure to media content was about eight and a half hours a day—more than a full-time job.

A number of potential problems have been identified with high levels of technology usage. Foremost is that they can exert a behavioral and subjective "displacement effect." Behaviorally, the time spent watching television displaces other activities, especially physical exercise, reading books, and face-to-face interaction with other people. Subjectively, the *content* can affect the "consciousness" of the viewer—with consciousness referring to those thoughts that occupy people's minds and to which they have ready recall—and the younger the viewer, the greater the effect that has been found empirically. As the research on the manufacture of consent has revealed, the more people are exposed to certain ideas, or ways of thinking, the more likely these are to affect choices made and beliefs held by them, displacing other choices and beliefs; when the influence is on a mass level, the values and norms of society are affected and pushed in certain directions (e.g., Caldicott, 1992).

The displacement effect can involve a decline in cultural literacy, where the young person has little knowledge of the world outside of youth-mediated culture (Bauerlein, 2008), as well as "pathological Internet usage," estimated to now affect some 20 per cent of young people (Small & Vorgan, 2008). Excessive Internet use apparently interferes with important socialization processes derived from face-to-face interactions, including learning how to read people's non-verbal communications and how to interact with non-peers and adults. It has also been associated with lower school achievement (e.g., Kirschner & Karpinski, 2010). Obsessive technology use can also be a source of stress and many self-reflective young people are concerned about this influence in their own lives. To illustrate, a recent study of 18- to 29-year-old Americans found that although about half felt they relied on support from family and friends "through email, texting, and social networking activities," many also thought they sometimes "spend too much time on social networking websites" (54% of those 18–21, 48% of those 22–25, and 39% of those 26–29) (Arnett & Schwab, 2012, p. 17).

There is now clear evidence that attempts have been made to exploit all of these technologies in one way or another as part of the attempt to make profits by selling products and convincing people of certain ways of thinking. The effectiveness of these persuasion techniques has improved as technologies have become more sophisticated and miniaturized (e.g., witness what can now be done with smart phones and the various tablet devices). Given the 24/7 delivery-potential of these technologies into every aspect of people's lives—if people allow it—the potentials for marketing and consent manufacturing are amplified (e.g., Morozov, 2013; Rushkoff, 2013; Rushkoff & Purvis, 2011).

At the same time, it is important to note that the concern is not that all young people mindlessly buy into the marketing messages that are bombarding them—social scientific models are far more sophisticated than this. People, indeed many young people, are able to resist these messages if they are so motivated. However, marketers have learned how to feed off forms of consumer resistance, especially from young people, in the various youth-oriented industries that emerged in the latter half of the twentieth century.

As a result of the marketing mechanisms developed in the late twentieth century, many symbols of youth resistance to mainstream society and market forces have been commodified and sold to younger cohorts so they too can feel "hip" or "cool" as an integral part of their sense of identity. Frank (1997a) documented these marketing tricks and showed ironically how marketers have used the concepts of "cool" and "hip" to trick mass consumers into believing that they can show others how unique they are by wearing, using, driving, or consuming something that has been mass marketed. This practice is now so widespread that the term "cool hunting" has entered our vocabulary (e.g., Klein, 2000; Rushkoff, 2001).

Marketing strategies now also involve multimedia penetrations of consumers' lives (e.g., product placements in movies, music videos, television programs, the Internet, and magazine articles). They also include more direct peer-to-peer marketing and viral marketing. In peer-to-peer marketing, "trendsetters" are hired to encourage friends or strangers (depending on the venue in which the marketing takes place) to try a new product (Schor, 2004; Quart, 2002). Youth-culture "spies"—young people at the ready at their computers to give over-night feedback on corporate pitches for new products—are even employed to report to marketing firms when corporations want "intelligence reports" about the latest trends. In the 1990s, Frank contended that the attempts to appropriate youth culture have been highly successful, noting that contemporary "youth culture is liberation marketing's native tongue" (1997b, p. 45), a trend that has apparently accelerated since.

If these influences are as effective and extensive as the research suggests, we are perhaps witnessing the largest and most successful experiment in mass conformity that does not use physical force, in human history.[1] As we see in the next chapter on youth culture, many youth-studies researchers are not concerned about this influence; indeed, some celebrate certain forms of new technology use as liberating—empowering and transformative (e.g., Collin & Burns, 2009). But, as with most things, technologies are not all good or all bad; rather they have both benefits and pitfalls. For instance, as we see in the chapter on politics, there appears to be promise for the new technologies with respect to nurturing new forms of political engagement that would act against the attempts of vested interests to manufacture consent.

From personal lives to school settings

As the discussion in the previous section suggests, there are a variety of specific issues that could be taken up in the evaluations of debates concerning the impact of various media and technologies on young people's lives. In order to keep this chapter focused, and to select an area in which a critical mass of publications defining a debate is available, much of the emphasis for the remainder of this chapter is on the more extreme debate between those who see young people as a new societal force to be reckoned with because they are armed with the "power of the Internet" and those who see this imagined future role of young people as not in their interests in terms of long-term opportunities (cf. Morozov, 2013). This debate is most lively in the area of educational applications of digital technologies to current cohorts, who are imagined as "digital natives" by "technology advocates." We see here how various media and technologies are expanding their influence on the personal lives of young people, encroaching on their educational experiences, a realm previously protected from mass culture.

In order to evaluate the "digital native" claim, it is useful to first examine the oft-stated assumption that young people *as a generation* stand out for their "tech-savviness." It is important to establish some common ground in this respect so that we can identify any stereotypes that might skew positions in that debate. Recall that in Chapter 5 we reviewed an instance of a use made of the concept of "generation," noting that a major drawback in generational analyses is the hazard of over-generalization that creates stereotypes.

New technology use: The generational divide claim

A number of ardent new technology advocates, such as Prensky (2001), Palfrey and Gasser (2008), Gomez (2007), and Tapscott (2009), claim that those brought up in the "digital era" from the 1980s on have advantages over those who adopted these technologies later in life (born before the 1980s). This amounts to a claim that a specially endowed "net generation" or generation of "digital natives" has made, or is now making, the transition to adulthood. From a youth-advocacy point of view, this claim can be appealing, but just how much evidence is there for it?

Generational homogeneity

Contrary to certain claims, the evidence is clearly showing that not all people born after the early 1980s are "tech-savvy." Although the younger age

groups may currently be more likely to be early adopters of some technologies, even in affluent countries, some young people do not even own
a computer, and others do not know how to navigate through even basic
word-processing programs, including the widely used *Word*. In these societies, there is still an economic "digital divide" that is largely socio-economic,
but there is also a "second digital divide" within all age groups comprising those who are not comfortable with computers and related technologies even if they could afford them; many of these young people grew up
with technologies and are studying in today's schools (cf. Vaidhyanathan,
2008).

To illustrate, a study from South Africa found that age was not the relevant factor in ICT sophistication in that country; rather, experience was key,
as made possible by access and opportunity. Moreover, this study could clas-
sify only 14 per cent of a large sample of South African university students
as "tech-savvy," and most were from middle or upper socio-economic groups,
spoke English or Afrikaans, and had easy home access to the technologies. The
authors of that study refer to this as "digital apartheid" (Brown & Czerniewicz,
2010). More globally, there is clear evidence of a "global digital divide." Currently, less than one-third of the world's population has access to and is using
the Internet. Access and usage ranges from a low of 11 per cent in Africa to
77 per cent in North America, with Europe coming in at 58 per cent (Internet
World Stats, 2010).

The generational stereotype was also investigated in an Australian study
(Kennedy, Dalgarno, & Waycott, 2010), which uncovered a similar typology based on the usage patterns of over 2000 university-student ICT users
born after 1980. The most "savvy" group, which they termed "power users,"
constituted only 14 per cent of the sample (this group used a wide range of
technologies and did so very frequently, including web 2.0 usage such as Web
publishing and file sharing). They called the second most "savvy" group "ordinary users," who made up 27 per cent of the sample (characterized by web
and mobile phone use, but the infrequent use of games and web 2.0). Both of
these groups had more males than females. Some 60 per cent of the sample was
either "irregular users" (14%) or "basic users" (45%). These latter two groups
had more females than males.

Others have made note of similar deficiencies in the claims of the generational homogeneity.

Again in Australia, Bennett, Maton, and Kervin (2008) estimated that at
best 20–25 per cent of the university students could be considered tech-savvy
in terms of their usage of technologies. On the basis of these and other findings,
Bennett et al. concluded: "Our analysis of the digital native literature demonstrates a clear mismatch between the confidence with which claims are made
and the evidence for such claims." They continue by noting that with respect to
calls to transform educational systems to accommodate new digital technologies, educators "have every right to demand evidence and to expect that calls
for change be based on well founded and supported arguments," but "many of

the arguments made to date about digital natives currently lack that support" (2008, p. 782).

In sum, even with the global digital-divide aside, even in the developed countries studied, there is little evidence for the existence of a distinctive generation defined principally by their relationship with technologies. Technology advocates seem to have been engaging in "generational myth-making," misappropriating a sociological concept without exercising due caution. The advocates of the digital native claim have been committing a common error made by those who adopt a generational approach in attempting to explain and predict social trends. This is the "error of homogenization," whereby all members of a given birth cohort are assumed to have the same psychological and behavioral traits. Unfortunately, this conceptual error can lead to further errors: over-generalization, exaggeration, and the selective use of evidence (cf. Bennett et al., 2008), as in the case of the claim of sharp differences in the usage patterns between generations, to which we now turn.

Generational usage patterns

Like the above "within" generational claim, the empirical evidence does not confirm the claim of sharp "between" generational differences in usage, especially the claim hinging on the concepts of "digital natives" vs. "digital immigrants," as Prensky (2001, 2006) frames it.

As a matter of fact, studies are finding that the generational differences in Internet use are small. In Canada, as of 2007, 85 per cent of those 45 to 54 years of age regularly used the Internet, compared to 94 per cent of those 15 to 24 (Veenhof & Timusk, 2009). A 9 per cent difference is far from a sharp contrast between so-called "immigrants" and "natives" to the digital world.

Furthermore, when the actual quality of usage of the Internet is examined, the older "immigrant" person appears to be using the Internet in a more sophisticated manner. Another Canadian study of Internet users found that the younger users employed the Internet almost entirely for leisure and entertainment, while older users managed their finances with it and employed it more for informal learning—self-education and information gathering (Ipsos-Reid, 2008). This study also found that the younger users sensed this, with only 28 per cent of teens considering themselves "very skilled" in Internet use. In fact, the teens in this random population-based sample spent only 13 hours per week on the Internet compared to 19 hours for adults, and only 37 per cent of teens rated Internet use as an important part of their day, compared to 51 per cent of adults in the sample. Comparable findings have been reported in the United States (Wells Fargo, 2010) and United Kingdom (Helsper & Eynon, 2010).

As it happens, contrary to the digital native vs. immigrant claim, the accumulating evidence from population surveys comparing generations is clearly showing that the most sophisticated ICT age-demographic groups were *not* reared on these technologies. These studies of usage patterns suggest that many young people are using ICTs in pre-programed ways that take up enormous amounts of leisure time. Some observers argue that large numbers of young people actually seem more "slavish" to the technologies than "savvy" about them, feeling insecure when they do not have them within arm's reach. Given the six to eight hours per day now taken up by them (mainly for entertainment and social networking), an obvious question is whether this is really a "savvy" way to spend one's time, especially if healthful, intellectually stimulating, and pro-social activities are displaced (cf. Bauerlein, 2008; Lanier, 2010; Morozov, 2013; Rushkoff, 2001, 2013).

In general, studies conducted in educational settings suggest that, rather than being led into the digital age by their students, educators should be doing more to teach current students how to use these technologies in a more sophisticated manner so they can benefit from them in broader and deeper ways (Duke & Asher, 2012). This applies even when the computer skill levels and usage patterns of the most educated among the younger cohorts are examined—namely, university students (Grant, Malloy, & Murphy, 2009; Duke & Asher, 2012; Kirschner & Karpinski, 2010). In this respect, the digital native stereotype seems to be doing students a disservice, and is especially obscuring serious skills deficits that might be interfering with full functioning in higher-educational systems and the workplace, where computer literacy is often taken for granted by the very teachers and employers who are dismissed by technology advocates as "digital immigrants" or worse, Luddites (cf. Kolikant, 2010).

Technologies in whose interests: Corporations or educators?

With these generational stereotypes put in context, we can step back to critically analyze the big picture of the political economy in terms of who benefits the most from the digital age and the massive adoption of new technologies by people of all ages. When we do so, the utopian visions of a technologically mediated future take on more of a balanced view. Morozov (2013) discusses current trends and possible futures and is concerned about a number of issues, especially the way solutions to economic, social, and political problems are framed in terms of what he calls "Internet solutionism," the belief that the Internet and various related technologies can cure all ills. In this section, the focus is on current trends and possible futures of educational systems.

As is widely known, neoliberal governments around the world are looking for ways to finance their mass educational systems more cheaply. What is less widely recognized is that the digital native stereotype is increasingly being used as a justification for imposing online education in mass-educational systems. Regrettably, these initiatives are based on faulty assumptions; consequently, it should come as no surprise that they cannot live up to their promises.

In actuality, as we have seen, these policies are often at odds with the available peer-reviewed published evidence, especially policies based on the claim that new technologies save money while meeting high educational standards. The research published thus far in reputable journals with respect to the use of new technologies at the university level reports they have numerous limitations, pedagogically and financially, as follows:

- classroom use of laptops and tablets do not universally engage students or increase students achievement (they can actually have the opposite effect);
- the effectiveness of "clickers" (audience response systems where students can electronically register multiple-choice responses to instructor queries) depends on why they are used and on the motivations of the teachers and students using them;
- audio or video "podcasts" can reinforce lectures, but they can be expensive to produce and do not interest all students;
- and online courses do not offer a financial savings or pedagogical advantage over classroom-based course of the same size and academic standards (Côté & Allahar, 2011).

Why then does the digital native stereotype persist in the case of educational policies? Several explanations for this persistence have been offered.

Borrowing from Cohen's (1973) concept of the *moral panic*, Bennett et al. (2008) argue that technology utopians have created this form of panic by evoking a media-driven sense of urgency claiming the need for immediate changes in education systems. More recently, Bennett and Maton (2010) offered two additional explanations for why the current discussion has been resistant to "the intellectual rigour it requires and deserves: 'historical amnesia' and the 'certainty–complacency spiral' " (p. 328). Historical amnesia involves the "forgetting" of past claims about how "new" technologies would revolutionize education (e.g., the over-estimated impact of television on education in the 1950s and 1960s), while the certainty–complacency spiral involves the repetition of an idea so often that it is taken to be self-evident. With respect to the digital native concept, they describe this as follows:

> Belief replaces considered debate, and echoing common-sense perceptions of fundamental change and citations of similar claims made by other authors substitutes for research evidence. Each proclamation of the existence and needs of "digital natives" thereby iteratively amplifies and reinforces the sense of certainty and encourages intellectual complacency. Rather than representing bold conjectures to be tested, claims become unquestioningly repeated as if established facts, restricting the possibility of open, rational debate. Intellectual complacency over the veracity of claims (whether digital natives exist, whether they take the form ascribed and whether education needs changing in the ways called for) is masked by the urgency and stridency with which calls for change are made. (p. 328)

It can hardly be coincidental that this sense of urgency to reform education is strongly supported by the economic interests that stand to profit from a massive takeover of higher-educational systems worldwide. Indeed, as we saw in the education chapter, there are strong reasons to believe that certain interest groups have agendas that have nothing to do with the desire to deliver high-quality educations to students in mass-educational systems, and everything to do with the marketization of education defined by the hegemonic discourses of neoliberalism (cf. Levidow, 2002). Countries that currently face huge cuts to educational budgets—because of the hegemony of neoliberalism itself—may be particularly vulnerable to these promises of simple solutions, especially if politicians and policy-makers are naïve enough to accept the claim that current students prefer online course delivery, especially when the accumulating evidence suggests otherwise (Jaggars, 2013). Indeed, if the rhetoric is uncritically accepted at the national policy level, countries risk handing over control of their educational systems to the corporations that control these technologies and their delivery (Giroux, 2012).

If countries do this, they not only risk allowing these corporations to define pedagogies, but they might also allow these corporations to delegitimize university autonomy in defining academic standards and learning outcomes, especially for the liberal education, which will likely not survive if the university system is redefined as a virtual marketplace. Moreover, if universities are left to "sink or swim" in unregulated marketplaces, countries may find themselves in a situation that characterizes the current "Wild West" situation in the United States with respect to online schools such as Kaplan University and the University of Phoenix where economically disadvantaged students have been driven into debt pursuing degrees of dubious value (e.g., Blumenstyk, 2010; Durrance, Maggio, & Smith, 2010).

Players in this for-profit marketplace have made it clear that they intend to de-legitimize traditional education and replace it with their own delivery formats and curricula. If politicians are naïve enough to go for these quick-fix solutions, we may witness something like "hostile takeovers" where corporations buy their competitors and then shut them down, closing up shop and firing now-redundant employees, as has been happening in the United States in the for-profit university sector (Durrance, Maggio, & Smith, 2010, recommended documentary viewing, listed at the end of this chapter). If this spreads to other countries, university systems around the world might become financially dependent on multinational corporations, which in turn will control curriculum based on profitability and the manufacture of consent in favor of consumer–corporate capitalist values and norms. These corporations will then be free to produce various curricula promoting their (neoliberal) interests. We are already seeing early warning signs of this. For instance, Rivard (2013) reports a growing concern over "intellectual neo-colonialism" associated with the Internet in general, but specifically with respect to online courses, which favor native English speakers and are based on the American model of emotional distance between few professors and many students in large classes, along with the requirement that students be self-motived, capable of self-teaching, and able to work in ambiguous contexts.

On top of a loss of the university as a place for free enquiry unfettered by means-ends logic, this would be disastrous for many students, especially those from disadvantaged backgrounds whose labor-market vulnerability will be further exploited. This is bad news for teachers, whose role will be delegitimized. Individually, teachers forced to teach online courses will likely face further wage exploitation, and reduced career security and benefits. Professors forced to turn their lectures into podcasts and courses into online packages would lose their intellectual property rights. Collectively, the teaching profession could experience a further proletarianization characterized by technological labor-displacement and a loss of collective bargaining.

Is it really prudent to hand over control of national education systems to corporations? In this worst-case scenario, the digital native rhetoric is merely a Trojan Horse that gets corporations into schools and allows them to take them over, sacking them first.

Toward a political economy of the digital revolution

Given the above links drawn between corporate interests and the digital revolution that has swept into the lives of youth people, it is appropriate to offer further suggestions about the utility of the political-economy position, anticipating its application to youth culture in the next chapter.

Before considering these inferences, readers are reminded of the wisdom that, as with most things, the digital revolution has its benefits and drawbacks. In terms of benefits, at a micro level, people have greater access to information and consumer services on the Internet. Various types of financial transactions and interpersonal interactions are far easier than they were in the past via computers and various hand-held gadgets. Many people can now work from home rather than commuting every day or even living in the same country of their employers. By and large, the Internet has radically improved many people's lives in conjunction with the new technologies tethered to it.

Additionally, though, there are discernible drawbacks in people's lives. We examined above concerns about overuse and even addictions to the Internet and attention-displacing digital gadgets among young people. Furthermore, younger and older workers alike are increasingly expected to be "on the job" 24/7 in responding to emails and text messages from their employer and clients. The possibilities for surveillance of citizens' activities have increased exponentially, which in some countries may seem benign in the name of "national security" but in others can lead to imprisonment. Surveillance opportunities for corporations have also increased dramatically, from marketing surveys to monitoring keystroke activities and search patterns on computers owned, or given access to, by these businesses. All the while, giant conglomerates have emerged to monetize online activity, developing huge data bases on individual spending habits, tastes, and opinions that are sold to other corporations or used by politicians to mange public opinion and election campaigns. Yes, the potential for increased "democratic participation" is enhanced by the Internet in creating and spreading information among individual citizens, but how much is this actually practiced and what impacts does it actually have at the macro level (we return to this point in Chapter 11).

The above points are increasingly being discussed and debated, but one has to look mainly to old print media to find these conversations (e.g., Bauerlein, 2008; Lanier, 2010, 2013; Morozov, 2013; Rushkoff, 2010, 2013), and one is hard pressed to find much critique in the mainstream media or on the Internet itself (which is often touted as the repository of all available information, an obviously fatuous claim). These media multinationals are owned and controlled by a few enormous multinational conglomerates (to the point of micro-management in many cases; Herman & Chomsky, 1988), so one is unlikely to find balanced information about the digital revolution from their news outlets.

In addition, individual journalists tend to be "cheerleaders" of new technologies because these gadgets and apps are so important to their daily job tasks of gathering "newsworthy" information of short-term interest. On the whole, journalists are the early adopters, and touting each new social media such as Twitter and Facebook is directly in the interests of the individual journalists. Given the avalanche of reporting about every detail in developing and launching each new generation of digital gadgets (including worldwide reporting of the overnight lineups by fanatic consumers for the latest Apple products), it is little wonder that the citizenry is in awe about these technologies, and willing to suspend judgments about the wisdom of their uses and misuses. Parents are especially caught up in this vortex, as the marketing directed at their children complements the attempt of parents to "stay informed." Thus, regardless of any corporate directives to individual journalists about what is "newsworthy" vs. "off-limits," individual journalists fuel to the techno-frenzy among the mainstream citizenry as part of their daily diet of pre-digested information.

But, what are discussed less often are the *macro* implications of all of these developments in digital technologies, hard and soft, and the high-tech juggernaut sweeping the developed world. For instance, the digital revolution has been a godsend for corporate capitalism. The new sources of profits range from the instantaneous transfer of money globally, through exorbitant fees and interest rates for financial services to consumers, to the sale to the citizenry (young and old) of the various "digital pursuits," noted above. Not only has the digital revolution opened vast new profitable business enterprises, it has also vastly expanded the opportunities for the consumer surveillance and new forms of marketing based on that surveillance (Morozov, 2013).

And, as we have seen in this chapter, now access is being granted corporations to mass educational systems, which were previously considered off-limits to profit taking in most countries. Since the 1980s, neoliberal government policies have starved educational institutions for operating funds. In turn, the very corporations that pressure governments to adopt neoliberal policies come to the rescue with cost-saving technologies that require educators to relinquish control of these educational systems.

In the end, at the macro level, who are the real beneficiaries of the digital revolution? In terms of material conditions, since the digital revolution began income inequality has actually grown in most Western countries (e.g., Lanier, 2013), in part because the salaries of the average *older* worker have not increased, and those of the average *younger* worker have declined (Wilkinson & Pickett, 2010). Conversely, the upper income groups have made substantial gains in wealth acquisition over this period, with an exponential growth in billionaires, as we saw in Chapter 5.

In macro terms, then, digital technologies are of most benefit to affluent people and affluent nations. As noted, massive digital divides exist within Western countries and globally between so-called developed and developing nations. Moreover, digital technologies have introduced serious instabilities in Western economies, including the dot-com bubble of the late 1990s leading to the stock market crash in 2000, and the current use of computers to control stock trading based on algorithms that take profits based on extremely short-term stock price fluctuations at the expense of long-term investors like those saving for their pensions (CBS, 2010). The most savvy among the wealthy have the knowledge and means to benefit from these market instabilities, while the less wealthy usually have neither the wherewithal nor the capital to do so, and are more likely instead to lose their investments.

Why are these big-picture issues not openly discussed? A manufacture of consent appears to have taken place where otherwise reflective people suspend their judgment and commonsense when it comes to the use and impact of technologies, forgetting the human equation in favor of the technological utopianism sold to the masses by the media (Morozov, 2013).

Conclusion: Questioning technological utopianism

Looking forward, it is apparent that the youth segment will be even further repositioned in the political economy of many countries by the digital revolution, at the same time as new cohorts are psychologically prepared from a young age to fully embrace whatever comes from these technological changes. The current socialization practices concerning the new "technological ethos" of the digital age are leading new cohorts to embrace enthusiastically and unquestioningly each new technology manufactured by corporations. Clearly, these developments should be a matter of concern among more humanistically oriented citizens; however, there is a sense of inevitably of an unpredictable future that will be governed by the digital ethos, or what Morozov (2013) calls "Internet solutionism," in part because of a "narrative collapse" of opposition from other value systems (Rushkoff, 2013).

As Morozov (2013) notes, this is not our first go-around with technological utopianism. Previous generations registered their objections, especially in the post-World War II period (e.g., Ellul, 1964). Erikson (e.g., 1968, 1975) was the first to link this Western cultural conflict with youth socialization, contrasting conformity-inducing technological socialization with humanistic values (see Côté & Levine, 1987, 1989, 1992, 2002). In 1967, he stated:

> We in the West pretend that we want to uphold only a "way of life," while in fact we too are creating and exporting technological and scientific ideologies, which have their own ways of enforcing conformity. The majority of our young adults gladly accept this as a basis for an identity of "what works is good." A minority of youth senses that what only "works" may be destructive unless restrained by a new sense of responsibility toward mankind as a species. These are two great sources of contemporary identity and identity confusion: faith in technology and a reassertion of a kind of humanism. Both are apt to be dated in their utopianism and inadequate for the gigantic struggle for man's mastery of his own powers.
>
> (Erikson, in Evans, 1969, pp. 34–5)

This Erikson quote about previous generations' resistance of technological utopianism anticipates the chapters to follow on identity. Another quote anticipates the final chapter on politics. In the following passage, a political scientist summarizes the literature to date on the impact of the "revolution in information technology" on the political sensibilities of the generation of young people now coming of age:

> The Internet has transformed the world of information and communication, but we must still ask, will the emerging generation be able to participate politically as informed citizens? Those lacking the skills to make sense of what is happening in the political world cannot be counted on to partake meaningfully. New technologies provide new ways of paying attention and participating, but they require not only access to networks, but also the skill to use them effectively.
>
> (Milner, 2010, p. 75)

Recommended readings

Sue Bennett, Karl Maton, & Lisa Kervin (2008). The "digital natives" debate: A critical review of the evidence. *British Journal of Educational Technology, 39,* 775–86.
    This paper is a critical analysis of the claim that young people are uniformly proficient with new technology. Finding they are not thus, the authors offer explanations for the "oversell" of new technologies in educational settings.

Chris Durrance, John Maggio, & Martin Smith (Producers) (2010). College Inc., *Frontline* PBS Retrieved from http://www.pbs.org/wgbh/pages/frontline/collegeinc/
    This American documentary explores how for-profit education has developed in the United States, becoming driven by corporations seeking profit-maximization. These corporations engage in "hostile takeovers" of colleges in financial difficulties

and lure students into online universities that they cannot afford and from which they are unlikely to graduate. This PBS documentary is also available for free viewing online.

Gregor T. Kennedy, J. B. Dalgarno, & J. Waycott (2010). Beyond natives and immigrants: Exploring types of net generation students. *Journal of Computer Assisted Learning* 26, 332–43.

This article empirically examines Prensky's claim that two types of people exist with respect to new technology use.

Paul A. Kirschner & Aryn C. Karpinski (2010). Facebook and academic performance. *Computers in Human Behavior,* 26, 1237–45.

This empirical article examines an example of the displacement effects of new technology use: the popular social medium, Facebook.

Mark Prensky (2001). Digital natives, digital immigrants. *On the Horizon,* 9.5, 1–6.

This is the original article proposing that people can be divided into "digital natives" and "digital immigrants."

Douglas Rushkoff (Producer) (2010). Digital_nation: Life on the virtual frontier. *Frontline*, PBS. Retrieved from pbs.org/frontline/wgbh/pages/digitalnation/view/

This 90-minute documentary is available for free viewing on the PBS website. Rushkoff examines recent trends in digital technology use and where these trends might be taking us.

Part III

The Changing Experiences of the Youth Period

Whereas the second part of this book examined the antecedent and emergent factors that have produced and continue to transform the youth period in Western countries, this third part explores the emerging outcomes of these casual factors. In this context, we explore the social and psychological forms that the youth period is taking within the current historical period of the West. As with the chapters in Part II, the chapters in Part III focus on key debates that have arisen in interpreting the causes and consequences of the youth period and experiences thereof. We begin with a look at the topic of youth culture in Chapter 8, a topic that has occupied youth researchers since the early days of this field and is central to many sociological approaches, often offered as an alternative to the "transitions" approach (e.g., Furlong, Woodman, & Wyn, 2011; MacDonald, 2011). We then shift to a consideration of the issues associated with the study of identity formation and social identity during the youth period, in Chapters 9 and 10, respectively. Part III ends with a chapter examining the position of youth people within the polity of several Western nations in terms of their potentials as political agents within this historical period.

Youth Culture: In Whose Interests?

8

From a historical perspective, the institutionalization of the period of adolescence over the past couple of centuries and the more recent lengthening of it to the "youth" period in the past few decades has been accompanied by a gradual separation of the daily lives of Western "young people" from those of "adults." In pre-industrial Western societies, young and old alike from the "masses" shared work roles and a common culture, including a popular culture of musical entertainment for leisure, celebrations, and festivals. However, during the transition from agrarian to industrial society, those in their teens were gradually segregated from older people as work roles changed. In the transition to so-called post industrial society, those in their twenties also came to experience a similar workplace segregation as a result of the decline of the industrial labor markets that previously accommodated them.

This loss of productive roles required a number of adjustments by the young people affected, as well as by the adults directing the economic and social changes of the times. The emergence of mass educational systems (secondary systems for adolescents and tertiary ones for youth, as we saw in Chapter 4) was an obvious response on the part of adult society to fill this void, but successive youth cohorts also responded to this hiatus by developing their own meaningful activities, ranging from small peer groups to more widespread, informal youth cultures, subcultures, and countercultures.

In addition to a loss of work roles, there are a variety of other possible reasons for this age-segregation that are not always discussed by those studying youth culture. At the same time, the very concept of "culture" is a contentious one, but is often taken for granted. Moreover, the reasons for, and consequences of, the age-based segregation constitute a major disagreement representing a fracture in the field of youth studies. To try to sort out the basis of this disagreement, this chapter focuses on the extent to which youth cultures are spontaneous creations of the young and the degree to which they are "manufactured" for them by adult interests. Before exploring this disagreement, though, it is useful to understand why the concept of "culture" is a contentious one.

What is culture?

The term "culture" has such a variety of possible uses in the social sciences and humanities that many believe it has lost a meaning that can be widely taken for granted. For instance, Swidler (1986) argued some time ago that a "debate has raged for several academic generations" among sociologists and anthropologists over how to define "culture." Generally speaking, its application has been too broad and its usage often carries connotations about human behavior that are difficult to defend, undermining the meaningful use of the term. In effect, broad definitions can make "culture" a constant, rather than a variable, rendering it less useful from a social-scientific point of view. Such definitions also have deterministic connotations, implying that everyone is equally affected by certain cultural values, leaving little room for human agency. Related to this problem is the difference between seeing culture as an organic cause of behavior (as in generally conservative views) as opposed to being the result of economic forces that produce behavior for which "culture" becomes a symbolic justification (as in political-economy views where the relationship between culture and behavior is often seen as spurious, due instead to economic factors).

By the same token, Swidler (1986) noted that older all-encompassing and deterministic views of culture were supplanted by characterizations in which people are seen to agentically use symbols as part of their cultural "tool kit" to solve various problems through "strategies of action" (p. 273; cf. Geertz, 1973). Based on this position, Swidler argued, "culture consists of such symbolic vehicles of meaning, including beliefs, ritual practices, art forms, and ceremonies, as well as informal cultural practices such as language, gossip, stories, and rituals of daily life" (*ibid.*).

These various uses of the concept of culture can be found in the youth-studies field. Some researchers tend to use the idea of youth culture as the product of economic forces inducing mass conformity among the young, while others have used the notion of youth culture in terms of the "tool kit" it can provide young people in fashioning identities and negotiating their daily activities with peers. Still, the end result for the field is not always clear-cut, for there is evidence for both the agentic use of cultural tools *and* mass conformity. Accordingly, to argue that one position should hold sway would commit the error of homogenization: logically, like other age groups, young people would be neither entirely agentic in all matters nor entirely conformist. Furthermore, to complicate matters further, certain conceptions of agency do not preclude mass conformity, as in the case of "individuality" and "cool" where there are massive social pressures on people to conform to the dictates of being "individuals" in their own right or to always being "cool," with the only alternative being a "loser" if that status is not attained (e.g., Niedzviecki, 2004). In these cases, agentic capacities appear to have been redirected or appropriated by other self-interested human agents (e.g., marketers working for corporations), as discussed below.

To muddy the waters further, the notion of "subculture" has become very popular, especially in cultural-studies approaches. In this case, a subculture is seen to provide a toolkit for constructing collective identities with co-members of the subculture as well as negotiating oppositional relationships with non-members (especially older people). Subcultural research has produced some useful ethnographies (e.g., Cohen, 1972; Hall & Jefferson, 1976; Willis, 1977, 1978), but in some analyses it is not clear whether youth culture in general is the object of study (i.e., a culture shared by all youth in a particular age range), or whether youth itself is seen as a "subculture" (e.g., Brake, 1985). This appears to be the case especially for some contemporary cultural-studies postmodernists who tend to see the study of youth culture as the study of youth itself (e.g., Cieslik & Pollock, 2002; cf. Blackman, 2005). At the same time, as we see below, some postmodernists reject the subcultural approach, arguing that the concept itself no longer has an agreed-upon meaning (e.g., Bennett, 2011).

The focus of the next section is on the dispute about whether current youth cultures are the culmination of the agentic efforts of young people or are the creation of (some) adults who seek to control young people culturally in order to profit from identity-based consumption patterns. For general reviews of youth culture theories, see Brake (1980, 1985), Cieslik and Pollock (2002), and Fornäs and Bolin (1995).

Youth culture: Spontaneous or manufactured?

Spontaneous-culture arguments

Two influential approaches have taken the view that youth culture, in its various forms, is the spontaneous creation of young people. As noted in Chapter 2, youth-subcultural analysis began in the United States early in the twentieth century in the Chicago School under the direction of Park. These efforts were focused on studying specific subgroups of young people who were particularly marginalized, but there was no intention to generalize these findings to the entire youth population. Subcultural analysis then spread to the United Kingdom, and grew roots in the Center for Contemporary Cultural Studies (CCCS) in response to the emergence of class-based youth subcultures (e.g., the Mods and Rockers) that created widespread concerns among adult society, in what Cohen (1973) labeled moral panics. In analyzing these trends, the CCCS was distinguished by its development of Gramsci's (1971) Marxist-based notion of cultural hegemony (Bennett & Kahn-Harris, 2004; Jones, 2009).

Studies produced by the CCCS were based on the assumption that working class youth in Britain developed, largely on their own, various forms of resistance to the oppressions and cultural contradictions they experienced. Working-class youth did so by forming subcultures marked by distinctive appearance and dress styles, as well as through specific attitudinal and behavioral patterns. This distinctively British approach to youth culture morphed into a more recent approach, which is still current, premised on the argument that young people do not form class-based subcultures so much as belong to "neo-tribes," or as adopt lifestyles, representing creative consumption patterns and hedonistic behaviors (these are referred to as "post-subcultures"). Both the subcultural and post-subcultural approaches have tended to focus on "spectacular youth" who engage in the more flamboyant music-based activities and lifestyles, a methodological flaw according to MacDonald (2013) because they have ignored "ordinary youth."

Subcultural analyses are not as common in other countries, even where the adolescence/youth has been prolonged, presumably because the vast majority of the young conform either to the dictates of mainstream society or to the local mass-marketed variation of popular youth culture "imported" from the United States or United Kingdom (e.g., Brake, 1985). For obvious reasons, youth cultures and subcultures are absent in countries where adolescence/youth have not been developed as age periods or become very prolonged. In addition, this sub-field of youth cultural studies tends to be Anglocentric (or increasingly "UK-Aussie-centric"), with most of the research carried out where music-based youth-driven popular cultures have emerged (cf. MacDonald, 2011, 2013). Studies elsewhere that could be considered "subcultural" tend to be examinations of how the large amounts of leisure time available to "ordinary" contemporary youth are spent (e.g., Greenberg, 2007). For example, Brake argued that in Canada youth cultures "lack the dramatic, socially visible forms that they take in Britain or the United States. They tend to be derivative, and insufficiently large to form any sense of moral outrage" (1985, p. 152).

Beginning in the 1990s, the post-subculture approach grew in the United Kingdom largely as a reaction to the CCCS, with a number of British postmodernists (or poststructuralists) concerned about what they saw as the limitations of the neo-Marxist approach taken by the CCCS. This postmodernist influence produced a shift from realist to nominalist assumptions regarding youth culture at the CCCS. Interestingly, a similar ontological shift took place for Marx, but in the other direction with his "epistemological break" from nominalism early in his career to realism later in his career (Burrell & Morgan, 1979, p. 22).

Bennett and Kahn-Harris (2004) list these critiques as follows:

- failing to take into account the involvement of young female's involvements, with subcultures conceptualized as "masculinist";
- contending that consumption is a form of resistance, without presenting empirical evidence for the claim;
- subcultures as serious class struggles rather than hedonistic outlets;
- the forms of resistance studied did nothing to alter the supposed class basis of youth oppression, except in imaginary ways;
- an over-generalization of their findings about local subcultures, claiming a universal relevance to all localities;

- an over-reliance on white, male, working class, British youth in the post-World War II era, with little applicability to other subgroups of youth in the United Kingdom, and especially in other countries;
- an excessive focus on structural concerns of class, ignoring race, culture, locality, and nation;
- a neglect of the role of the media and various cultural industries, both as causes of youth cultures and as resources used by youth in constructing identities; and
- focusing too much on the age category of 16 to 21, rather than seeing "youth" as a state of mind.

The efforts of post-subcultural theorists and researchers to overcome these problems have been based on the premise that youth cultures are fragmented, giving rise to a variety of styles that are mixed individually and collectively, depending on the locality (Bennett & Kahn-Harris, 2004). Under these conditions, post-subcultures are argued to involve "neo-tribes" that fluidly form and disperse as occasions arise, and are predicated on the free-floating identities of their members. The preferred focus of investigation of these post-subcultures is on subjectivities and consumption patterns associated with these neo-tribes. The value-priority stance is one of youth advocacy–liberation along with a celebration of the purported creativity and agency of young people thus involved. For many post-subculturalists, the term "lifestyle" is preferred over subculture, as is the term "scene" in the case of music. According to Bennett and Kahn-Harris (2004), post-subculturalists have "taken seriously contemporary critiques of 'essentialism' and the concomitant emphasis on fragmented contradictory practices and identities" (p. 14).

A lively dispute developed recently between Blackman (2005) and Bennett (2011), with Blackman critiquing the claims of post-subculturalists and Bennett defending them. Blackman sees some value in postmodern subcultural analysis in pointing out creative aspects of youth culture, but argues, "the new conceptual developments of 'post-subcultures', tribe and 'lifestyle' lack theoretical coherence and explanatory power at the level of the social" (Blackman, 2005, p. 17).

Blackman characterizes the post-subculture approach as follows:

> For postmodernists, subcultures react imaginatively through consumption and identity to construct creative meanings that can be liberating from subordination. Postmodern subcultural theory seeks to move away from models of social constraint and places greater emphasis on agency in the search for individual meaning in subcultural practice. The postmodern milieu of spatiality and cultural pessimism valourizes locality and the power of individuals in subcultures to imaginatively reappropriate global commodities for emancipation.
>
> (*ibid.*, p. 8)

He identifies in these postmodernist formulations of youth culture the famil-iar boilerplate assumptions of postmodernist conceptions of identity (as we see in the next chapter): fluid, multiple, and not centered on any stable structures. In effect, then, youth identities are argued by postmodernists to be individualistic, inauthentic performances rather than stable character traits, derived from picking and choosing among "consumer goods, which allows them to feel unique" (Blackman, 2005, p. 14, quoting Miles, 2000, p. 22). Thus, Blackman argues, "postmodern subcultural theory reduces 'real' subcul-ture to surface signifiers without authenticity where identity is determined by choice" (2005, p. 15).

In Blackman's view, these postmodernists have unfairly and prematurely rejected the CCCS. He sympathizes with the structuralist roots of the CCCS in Marxism, and its investigation of class-based subcultures as forms of cre-ative resistance to the various forms of oppression associated with capitalism in class-based British society. The goal of the CCCS, according to Blackman, was to challenge the "bourgeois order and celebrate creative resistance to order" (2005, p. 16). Research produced by the CCCS placed identities within structures, especially social class structures, which limit some young people's consumption choices; financial constraints are consequently a major impediment to free-choice and identity construction.

We see here that the tension between nominalism and realism might explain some of the disagreement between these approaches: youth-culture postmodernists appear to have negative reactions to anything structural (dis-missing them as "essentialist" in lockstep with their "anti-realist" belief system), a position apparently derived from the postmodernist boilerplate (see Chapter 2). Blackman says as much in the following passage, pointing out the ideological nature of postmodernists' views of youth subculture:

> Postmodern subcultural theorists employ Maffesoli concept of the tribe to suggest the existence of a "postmodern age and postmodern sensibilities". Here the concept of tribe acts as a carrier for postmodern theory or ide-ology. The postmodern subcultural theory of neo-tribe is closely linked to theories of consumption and lifestyle that posit the centrality of choice and individualism as key factors in identity formation. The idea is that neo-tribes confirm our sense of identity and individuals take pleasure in the hybridity of consumerism. The centrality of choice in postmodern theories of subcul-ture argues that social categories such as social class, sexuality and ethnicity are too reductive and universalistic.
>
> (Blackman, 2005, p. 12)

He goes on to point out how this rejection of realism carries the risk of missing the sources of oppression experienced by some youth:

> The reluctance to consider the way in which choice is also imposed on young people by capital, structures and institutions fails to give voice to different

young people's experiences of marginality . . . . On this basis postmodern theories of subculture do not address or critique the relations of dominance and subordination exercised through social and cultural structures of society.

(*ibid.*, p. 12)

In contrast, Blackman is much more convinced by a structural analysis, taking what is essentially a political-economy position, as follows:

> Consumption is not [equally] available to all and thus is a marker of inequality. Young people can be resistant and attempt to challenge dominant values, but young people's encounters with social exclusion and zero tolerance policies show that consumption is a chimera of choice in constructing subcultural identities (Blackman 1997; Williamson 1997). Young people desire subcultural expressions and commodities that are themselves defined by the power of the market. Bennett's priority on individual consumption at the expense of production misrecognizes youth marginality under postmodernism. Youth consumers may have developed into a specialized subcultural market niche but capital actively denies youth economic stability that prevents them from participating in cultural consumption.
>
> (Blackman, 2005, p. 14)

Finally, reminiscent of Heath and Potter's (2004) critique of "rebel identities" (discussed below), Blackman believes that the postmodernist critique of structuralism and its celebration of consumption naïvely feed into the capitalist mode of production. Far from being a radical critique, it resembles a form of conservative functionalism that justifies neoliberal policies (Blackman, 2005, p. 15) supportive of the promotion of free choice in free markets as a laudable goal. Moreover, in doing so it is fraught with contradictions, including asserting relativism as an "absolute." Blackman summarizes this lethally mix of inconsistent assumptions as follows:

> Postmodern subcultural theory wishes to retain the notion of emancipation, but through denouncing universals as oppressive it ignores the power of capital, thus without a means of understanding collective forms of oppression postmodern emancipation remains a "speculative exercise."
>
> (Blackman, 2005, p. 16)

In a ten-year retrospective, Bennett (2011) responded to this critique in a remarkably conciliatory fashion that is exemplary of what is needed to bridge the epistemological divide. He notes the following criticisms of the work produced by the "post-subcultural turn:"

- it does not provide a consistent, alternative theory of youth culture;
- its celebratory stance overlooks the role of corporative interests in shaping youth identities and lifestyles;

- structural inequalities continue to influence the life chances and cultural memberships of youth, even if class-based youth identities are less important now;
- youth culture is depoliticized with the emphasis on reflexive individualism; and
- the fluidity of youth cultural styles is over-emphasized.

After reviewing these criticisms, Bennett offers a number of recommendations about how the field of youth cultural studies might move forward in a unified manner:

> Ultimately then, there would seem to be increasing mileage in the development of a refined strand of youth cultural studies in which elements of post-subcultural and subcultural theory are combined to forge a more effective mapping of a contemporary youth cultural terrain in which youth identities forge an increasingly complex mix of global and local cultural influences. Thus far, little progress has been made in this direction with subcultural and post-cultural studies continuing to be represented, by and large, as discrete areas of youth cultural research.
>
> (Bennett, 2011, p. 502)

Although the subcultural approach continues to generate research based on structural assumptions that are "essentially quite negative toward theoretical and methodological interventions of post-subcultural theory," Bennett admits that research based on the postmodernist perspective is "compromised through reliance on small, qualitative data-sets." After recognizing the limited empirical base of post-subcultural theory, he continues by arguing, "in order to determine more fully the nature and extent of the interplay between local experience and global flows of consumption, leisure and lifestyle among young people, *large-scale qualitative and quantitative data-sets are required*" (Bennett, 2011, p. 502, emphasis added).

In other words, Bennett is tacitly admitting that the nominalism-based methodologies favored by postmodernists need to be combined with more realism-based ones. As encouraging as this insight is, this recommendation is in part a "back to the future" recommendation, because (as noted in Chapter 1) this combination of qualitative/quantitative, idiographic/nomothetic methodologies informed some of the biggest research programs in the social sciences from the beginning, before the move to disciplinary specialization in the latter part of the twentieth century (e.g., Hollingshead, 1949; Sherif, 1958), including the rise of postmodernism. The difference now is that, with excessive specialization, there are antagonisms among various approaches so that rather than a "live and let live" attitude, there are dogmatic specializations, as in the "anti-realist nominalist" strand of postmodernism. In this light, Bennett's call for compromise will likely be considered heretical by some postmodernists.

Regardless of the rankles Bennett might raise among those in the post-subcultural subfield, his insights are extremely useful in highlighting that the postmodernist boilerplate needs to be addressed if we are to bridge the epistemological divide. Most significant in this regard is his admission that the core assumptions of the postmodernist ideology have never been tested and that doing so might help to bridge the divide between structuralism and poststructuralism, as follows:

> A project combining subcultural and post-subcultural perspectives would also *ideally address three critical "givens" as these arise in the discourse of the post-subcultural turn—"fluidity", "multiplicity" and "temporality". In post-subcultural discourse, it is largely taken for granted that young people's tastes, interests and cultural affiliations are fluid and inter-changeable.* However, beyond the small handful of published studies discussed above, *there is very little in the way of reliable data to assert such claims* at a wider sociocultural level. Nor is there any clear understanding of how such identified post-subcultural shifts in the youth cultural landscape are in themselves patterned by forms of local experience. Similarly, further and more rigorous testing is required to ascertain the extent to which young people's identities are "multiple", in the sense of being divided between a number of simultaneous interests and affiliations.
>
> (Bennett, 2011, p. 503, emphasis added)

In calling for "a rigorous empirical assessment of the key tenets of post-subcultural theory" with large samples that are still sensitive to localized expressions of youth culture, Bennett essentially calls for an exposure of the boilerplate of post-subcultural theory, namely, "the tendency to begin with the assumption that [class, ethnicity and gender] do structure youth identities to a significant extent and work back from this position" (Bennett, 2011, p. 503). This collaborative research would include analyses of these structural influences, but also of other influences of interest to poststructuralists, like "nuanced and locally [variable]...patterns of consumption, leisure and lifestyle" (p. 503). Remarkably, this is an implicit admission of the limited critical thinking by postmodernists in this area of research because their assumptions determine the conclusions of their investigations; that is, without any methodology adopted for reducing the confirmation bias, they violate a first-order principle of critical analysis (see Chapter 1).

Manufactured-culture arguments

There is not an organized group of youth researchers who argue that popular youth culture is "manufactured," especially in comparison with those who argue that post-subcultures are "spontaneous." Instead, evidence and arguments come from a number of quarters, loosely connected by affinity with the assumptions of a political-economy perspective.

Those taking a manufactured view of youth culture tend to take a macro view and place the youth segment implicitly or explicitly in a political-economy context: politically without a voice and economically exploited because of the progressive disenfranchisement over the past several decades (e.g., Côté & Allahar, 1996, 2006). In this context, youth culture is seen as principally an identity-based consumer culture orchestrated by consent-manufacturing processes.

These contentions about the deliberate manipulation of youth culture currently find empirical support in research into the practice of "branding" commonly employed by corporations (e.g., Klein, 2000; Quart, 2002). These branded products all have in common an identity-conferring quality. The message in the branding campaigns is that to be "someone" one has to be "cool," and to be cool, one has to have, wear, or consume the properly branded items and publicly display the appropriate corporate labels and logos. Under these conditions, young consumers are perfect targets for such manipulation so long as they are kept "identity hungry" (Côté & Allahar, 1996).

When the sense of personal identity is fragile and partly formed (or perhaps fluid and de-centered, in postmodernist terms) among a sufficient proportion of consumers, corporations can change their products year after year, confident that these conformist consumers will follow the trends they arbitrarily set and announce through the various carefully crafted marketing techniques discussed in the preceding chapter. From the political-economy perspective, the entire consumer–corporate system works in unison and is the perfect arrangement for capitalist enterprises that have as their primary objective profit maximization: in the case of youth, they have been made into both a source of cheap labor and a massive consumer segment (with many young people in more affluent societies now financially subsidized by their parents well into their twenties and even thirties).

Thus, when we update the political-economy perspective from its early tenets in the mid-twentieth century to look at how young people in more recent generations have fared, we find evidence that the manufacture of consent has been ever more perfected in producing a youth culture complementary to the interests of Capital, especially through advertising and marketing. Moreover, as argued in the previous chapter on mediated technologies, corporate marketers now have much more effective technological mechanisms for penetrating people's lives (and consciousness) on a 24/7 basis that were unimaginable a generation ago, except in science fiction genres. The multimedia penetrations into consumers' lives are now far deeper than were simple advertisements. Added to this influence are social media. For example, Facebook tailors ads to the profiles of each user, and the search engine Google does the same. As noted, these penetrations also involve viral marketing in which specifically targeted young people who are "alphas" among their peers (and hence, cool) are hired to encourage their friends (or strangers, depending on the venue in which the marketing takes place) to try or buy a product. A steady stream of studies and books has been documenting the perfecting of these marketing strategies for some time (e.g., Klein, 2000; Quart, 2002; Schor, 2004).

Among those examining the relationships between youth culture and corporations from the political-economy perspective, the consensus is that youth culture (which is now indistinguishable from popular culture in countries such as the United States) has been hijacked by this predatorial corporate marketing. As young people turn to youth culture because of their marginalization from the labor force and adult roles in society, the various anti-adult attitudes and activities of this manufactured youth culture can push adulthood further beyond their emotional grasp if they are taken seriously by young people. A number of books on this issue have also been published over the last few years (e.g., Calcutt, 1998; Danesi, 2003; Heath & Potter, 2005).

As noted above, the separation of young people from mainstream society has taken place slowly over time, beginning over a century ago. It began with a series of laws concerning employment practices and compulsory education that set the basis of new customs and institutional practices that rigidly separated adolescence and adulthood. From this de jure exclusion from mainstream society, and in conjunction with a series of economic and political arrangements that developed over the twentieth century, corporations learned through careful research and marketing experiments that they could sell "identity packages" to mainstream youth (e.g., "cool" coordinated fashion accessories) and "packaged identities" to those who aspire to some sort of subculture membership (e.g., Goth). In these respects, a smorgasbord of commodities has been marketed for young people to use depending on their identity needs. Young people can make statements of "individuality" (by mixing and matching), group solidarity (by adopting a "uniform," or by simply wearing certain jeans or running shoes), or "rebellion" (through body piercing or other forms of dress and behavior objectionable to adults; cf. Niedzviecki, 2004). Corporations have also included music, movies, and various technological gadgets into the mix, providing a sense of unlimited freedom and individuality for many unsuspecting young people. As we saw in the last section, these are the types of behaviors that post-subculturalists have celebrated as evidence of youth creativity. The political-economy perspective casts doubt on the authenticity and originality of this creativity, even if a small segment of trendsetters are being truly creative (only to be studied by marketers so that the outcomes of their creativity can be packaged and sold back to the conformist masses; Rushkoff, 2001).

Regardless of whether one accepts the spontaneous or manufactured view of youth culture, it is difficult to deny that corporations have become a new and massive structural force in the lives of the young in many countries over the past half century. On the other hand, there has been evidence of individual resistance to consumerism among some young people ("culture jamming," "subvertizing," and so forth; Quart, 2002), and many young people do not buy into the corporate–consumer model of identity formation, preferring instead to establish their own life styles (cf. Raby, 2005). In addition, there has been periodic collective resistance (e.g., Juris & Pleyers, 2009; Farthing, 2010), but the latter may be more appropriately considered political movements than youth cultures or subcultures (e.g., see Chapter 11).

Nevertheless, from a political-economy perspective, it is not necessary to argue that all people mindlessly buy into the mass-cultural messages that are bombarding them. People in general are able to resist these messages if they are so motivated. However, there is compelling evidence that marketers have learned how to feed off some of this resistance, especially from young people, in the various youth-oriented industries that emerged in the latter half of the twentieth century. Now, many symbols of youth resistance to mainstream society and market forces are commodified and sold to younger cohorts so they too can feel "hip" or "cool" as an integral part of their sense of identity.

In sum, from a political-economy perspective, when a population is controlled educationally and economically, it is then possible to initiate efforts to control them emotionally—to try to define their sense of self and to manipulate their identities. Indeed, much of "mainstream" youth culture appears to constitute a special type of consumer culture: an informal organization of individuals eager to have their emotions, identity, and tastes defined and redefined for them by the youth-oriented "leisure industries" that market fashion, music, art, new digital technologies and gadgets, and other consumer items. It is further argued that even the rebels of this system can be caught up in this consumption vortex as a function of their own identity needs (the need to be defined as a cool trend-setters, nonconformists, avant-garde, etc.) or because of their own competitive consumption habits by which they distinguish themselves from what they see as "lesser beings" among the "non-cool," commonly referred to as "losers" (Milner, 2004).

The strengths and weaknesses of each perspective

Readers are reminded here of the discussion in Chapter 3 of the focus and range of convenience of theories: most theories are very useful in focusing on a limited set of phenomena, but beyond a certain range, their explanatory power diminishes. There is also a tendency for theorists to try to over-extend their own theories, especially in the current era of academic specialization. It remains then for other theorists to employ a critical-thinking methodology to determine the extent to which a particular theory is the most useful approach in analyzing specific phenomena or whether that theory has been employed in ways that overreach the mark.

Overreaching is basically what the poststructuralists accused structuralists of doing in the debate regarding post-subculture vs. subculture theories. But, in claiming its superiority, the poststructuralists seem to have done the same. As Blackman (2005) points out, in their attempt to refute all other approaches and claim the supremacy of their own, the poststructuralists seem to have introduced contradictions into their claims especially around grand or totalizing theories (having created their own), the "absoluteness" of relativity, and the universality of fluidity, multiplicity, and fragmentation.

In retrospect, subculturalists appear to have stretched their findings from specific subcultures to all manifestations of youth culture, but post-subculturalists have similarly overreached in claiming that all youth behaviors are evidence of fluid culture and multiple, unstable identities. Both approaches are impeded by their respective boilerplates, whereby their assumptions influence the conclusions drawn by their empirical research, thus violating a primary rule of critical thinking.

Both approaches are more defensible and valid when they do not over-extend themselves from their focus of convenience. The postmodernist approach, with its nominalist assumptions is best suited to micro-level behaviors and idio-graphic, ethnographies; this is an honorable tradition that dates back to the early days of the social sciences, as noted above. Unfortunately, it appears that the dogmatism of the anti-realist wing of this faction unduly restricts its research potential, putting researchers into a never-ending task of setting up research questions to prove boilerplate assumptions regarding fragmentation, multiplicity, and fluidity (as implied by Bennett, 2011).

As Bennett (2011) argues, the way forward is to collaborate, not reject each other's efforts offhand, and to put assumptions to empirical tests that can determine their validity and applicability; in other words, to test their focus of convenience (or scope conditions). This would require sincere attempts to bridge the epistemological divide, which will not be spanned so long as post-structuralism is predicated on bashing structuralism rather than testing the applicability and validity of its own claims.

Conclusion: Towards a shared frame of reference

In view of the above considerations about the conceptual problems in defining "youth cultures," "subcultures," and the like, as well as the problems in over-extending the scope of theories, the following assumptions and research questions are offered as a starting point for collaborative research.

Assumptions:

- the majority of youth belong to the dominant culture for most of their day-to-day activities, but they participate in various popular cultures for leisure and fun; these activities constitute only part of their overall identity (especially in the case of "weekend warrior" activities, such as raves);
- a small minority belongs to youth subcultures, and these are subcultures of youth culture, not adult culture; there is a need to distinguish on a case-by-case basis any that might be subcultures of the dominant "adult" culture;
- young people have a variety of roles and involvements by merit of their youth status in a society, but these would only qualify as subcultures if they spent

most of their time in them and they were separate from mainstream society (accordingly, peer group and school-clique activities are not subcultures, or "post-subcultures");

- what many cultural studies theorists have been calling youth cultures of the present era may more closely resemble *generational popular cultures* not tied to age because each generation takes its popular culture with it as it gets older (in actuality, for example, the elderly who are still listening to Elvis Presley are not trying to be "young" or are refusing to "grow up"; rather, that popular culture became part of their formative identity and consciousness, along with their tastes and preferences);
- population-level trends in popular youth cultures are best approached with realist assumptions that can detect macro-level trends; the experiences of "youth cultures" personally and locally are best approached with nominalist assumptions to see how people manage their impressions with the resources provided by that culture;
- post-subcultural theorists tend to use a lens of cultural "separation" where distinct cultures do not exist—much of popular culture involves mass-entertainment events, often staged by adults for profit.

Research questions to be investigated derived from the political-economy perspective:

- To what extent do mainstream youth cultures derive directly from the dominant consumer culture and therefore support it economically and ideologically?
- Is there a symbiotic relationship between many corporations and young people, especially the major mass media and new technology producers? Does a "giant feedback loop" characterize this relationship (cf. Rushkoff, 2001)?
- To what extent is the agency most young people exercise in their youth-culture activities a form of a "multiple choice agency," with the choices set for them? Even if this the case, in what ways might young people benefit from this situation in terms of their identity formation; and in contrast, what are the potential pitfalls to consumption-based identity formation, especially when it is the result of predatorial marketing strategies?

Finally, older subcultural studies utilized nominalist as well as realist assumptions, so they were not anti-realist. Current researchers need to be more respectful of others' assumptions, with critiques based on the recognition of their respective focus and range of convenience. Researchers also need to be mindful of the value-priority basis of their involvements in the field (Chapter 1). No one of these four stances is the only or best stance to take; in fact, too strong of an adherence to any one blinds researchers to the sincere commitments of other researchers, creating ideologies based on dualistic us/them thinking.

Recommended readings

Richard Griffiths (2010). The gothic folk devils strike back! Theorizing folk devil reaction in the post-Columbine era. *Journal of Youth Studies*, 13, 403–22.

This article is an examination on the Goth subculture and media reactions to it following the Columbine massacre in an American high school.

Joseph Heath & Andrew Potter (2002). The rebel sell: If we all hate consumerism, how come we can't stop shopping? Retrieved from http://www.thismagazine.ca/issues/2002/11/rebelsell.php

These Canadian professors take current countercultural rebels to task for actually contributing to the "conquest of cool" by providing marketers with ever-new symbols of youth dissent that corporations can use to define their products as cool. According to them, capitalism feeds on change, not conformity, so youth culture has identified the wrong "enemy" in resisting symbols of conformity.

Douglas Rushkoff (Producer) (2001). The merchants of cool. *Frontline*, PBS. Retrieved from pbs.org/wgbh/ pages/frontline/ cool/

This is a landmark film documenting the marketing techniques used in the manufacture of American youth culture, based on the theory of the "conquest of cool." This 90-minute documentary is available for free viewing on the PBS website, which provides additional analysis of, and content from, the video.

From the ancillary interview material provided on this website, see the transcripts of the interview with Malcolm Gladwell. Retrieved from pbs.org/wgbh/ pages/frontline/ cool/interviews/gladwell.html. Gladwell wrote an essay for *The New Yorker* in 1997 called "The Coolhunt." www.gladwell.com/1997/1997_03_17_a_cool.htm

Youth-Identity Formation: Agentic Potentials or Inevitable Confusion?

9

As the youth period has been extended in Western societies, identity formation has taken on different forms, attributed by many observers to changing societal conditions that have made the consolidation of a coherent sense of identity more problematic (Côté & Levine, 2002). However, the reasons for these problems and how extensive they are among the youth and adult populations have been disputed in youth studies along the epistemological divide.

In examining the basic assumptions on both sides of the divide, this chapter thus focuses on competing claims concerning the extent to which young people, on the one hand, can establish a coherent sense of identity or, on the other hand, will inevitably experience a constant sense of identity fragmentation. This is an extremely important question that has implications for the entire life course: if younger people cannot establish some sort of stable, coherent sense of identity, then older people must not be capable of it either, so the life course for all people in current Western societies would be one of continual identity-based struggles.

In order to attempt to answer this question of potential coherency vs. inevitable fragmentation, the focus of this chapter is on the "agency side" of the structure–agency debate as it is relevant to identity. In the chapter to follow, the focus shifts to the "structure side" of that debate. One reason for separating the discussion of "identity" into two discrete chapters is to show how academics are often talking past each other across the epistemological divide in the sense that they are often actually referring to different types of phenomena, in this case "identity" as it is manifested at different levels of analysis.

The Ivory Tower of Babel: The need for a taxonomy of identity concepts

The types of identity most relevant to the "agency side" pertain to the more personal aspects of identity—those that people have more experience with and control over in their daily lives. These personal aspects include the subjective aspects of identity and its formation—what psychologists often refer to as *ego identity* and sociologists refer to as *self-identity*. These subjective aspects of identity are distinct in many ways from the more objective or societal forms of identity—what are generally referred to as *social identities*.

Sociologists and macro-oriented social psychologists often study social identities in terms of the societal meanings attributed to group-based attributes such as ethnicity, gender, and class; this approach thus overlaps with the field of *intergroup relations* (e.g., Seeman, 1981) and has a firm basis in sociological social psychology (e.g., Rosenberg, 1981). In youth studies, it has generally involved the types of social identities associated with youth cultures.

At the same time, psychologists and micro-oriented social psychologists tend to study the subjective side of these social identities, especially in terms of the developmental processes people experience, and stages through which they pass, in forming a sense of themselves in relation to their ethnic, gender, and class identities. These identities are complex because they are also strongly influenced by societal definitions of ethnicity, gender, and class (and other socially defined locations, inclusive of sexual orientation and minority status). Consequently, psychologists and social psychologists focus on the individual differences in what these social identities mean to the person and how salient they are as a part of an overall sense of identity consolidation. Importantly, though, these researchers are also mindful of societal and cultural differences in how these social identities are defined and what these differences mean for experiences of discrimination and other forms of differential treatment.

As we see, by sorting out the confusions among these different types of identity and levels of analysis, a way of bridging the epistemological divide becomes possible. Côté & Levine (2002) called for the identity-studies community to develop a taxonomy of identity-related terms to help clear up misunderstandings and obfuscating duplications of research efforts, so the field might progress more effectively. Without a common language, numerous misunderstandings are inevitable among those ostensibly studying the same phenomena. In generic terms, the problem seems to be captured by the idiom "comparing apples and oranges."

The roots of the youth-identity studies field

The study of identity formation in adolescence and young adulthood dates back to the mid-twentieth century, stimulated by the early work of Erikson (1950). Although Erikson was not a psychologist per se (e.g., see Roazen, 1976, for an intellectual biography of Erikson), his work has strongly influenced the developmental-psychology approaches to identity formation, spawning a variety of empirical models (e.g., Marcia et al., 1993).

Erikson's work also influenced sociological approaches to identity, especially symbolic interactionism. Noting this influence, Weigert, Teitge, and Teitge (1986, p. 29) argued that Erikson's concept of identity became a "reasonably value-neutral and interdisciplinary term" with which to describe the effects of social change on social status, group allegiances, value acquisition, and the process by which people develop a sense of meaning and purpose in life.

Erikson's model of the *formation* (or development) of identity as an approach to understanding youth identities was only seriously contested in the 1990s, largely by the postmodernists examined below. Feminists and others critiqued Erikson's original writings over the years, but these critiques focused on his general model of the life cycle rather than youth itself (Côté & Levine, 1987; Sorrell & Montgomery, 2001).

The postmodern challenge: Identity confusion vs. coherence

Rattansi and Phoenix (2005) launched a vigorous challenge to the Eriksonian model of youth-identity formation. This challenge is particularly useful because it was republished so that it could be answered on a point-by-point basis by leading neo-Eriksonians in ways that bring out many issues that are often not openly discussed (Côté, 2005). In addition, Phoenix and Rattansi (2005) provided a rejoinder defending their positions.

Rattansi and Phoenix self-identify as postmodernists, explicitly challenging what they call Erikson's "modernist" position as well as the more purely psychological empirical derivatives that can be classified as neo-Eriksonian approaches, focusing on Marcia's (1993; Marcia et al., 1993) identity status paradigm. They argue that the Eriksonian approach in general, and the dominant neo-Eriksonian empirical paradigm in particular, decontextualizes and ignores the "subjectivities" of young people's identities. They propose an alternate framework to what they perceive as the errors of Erikson's modernist approach, based on six theoretical axioms organized under the "twin-headings of the 'de-centering' and the 'de-essentialisation' of identities" (Rattansi & Phoenix, 2005, p. 103), which can be summarized as follows:

(1) Identities are "relational" in character, hinging their definition in relation to other identities, so they are not "centered" in the "subject."

(2) Identities are not "essential" and are not formed in "stages." Instead, identity relations are inherently unstable and oppositional, but social institutions function to normalize this opposition to disguise power relationships.

(3) People occupy multiple and contradictory positions and therefore have a range of identities, with different identities having salience in different contexts. Accordingly, young people blend identity elements from their multiple positions.

(4) Identities are always in process, and identity is never complete. Any apparent identity closures are "provisional and conditional," as dictated by the various contexts in which the person must function.

(5) The self is de-centered not only by social contexts, but also by unconscious mental processes that are often conflictual.

(6) Identities are uncertain and fragmented in ways that reflect dysfunctional and disjointed institutional and social contexts.

These proposed axioms illustrate the stakes inherent in this dispute: namely, if these are true, the period of youth is the beginning of *inevitable* lifelong identity confusion and crises, where young people *and adults* are all destined to a lifetime of de-centered existence with no stable, core sense of themselves. In contrast, as we see below, the neo-Eriksonians who responded to this critique argue that a full reading of the Eriksonian model that Rattansi and Phoenix are contesting actually proposes that adolescence/youth *can be* a period of growth of agentic strengths that *can* culminate in a coherent sense of identity (consolidating various self-concepts and identities) in spite of societal conditions that might alienate, manipulate, or confuse young people. As we also see below, *late-modernist* sociologists such as Giddens hold positions that are compatible with the Eriksonian model while acknowledging the disorienting influence of fragmented social contexts.

Sorting out the validity of these opposing stances takes us to the heart of the human condition, and therefore merits close attention. Accordingly, it is important to examine these postmodernist claims in terms of (1) how accurately they depict the Eriksonian approach and (2) how well they are supported by empirical evidence, either produced by postmodernists themselves or by neo-Eriksonians. In the next two sections, the above-listed axioms are examined in terms of the two boilerplate assumptions professed by postmodernists and reiterated by Rattansi and Phoenix, namely, that identities are fragmented (fluid and temporally-spatially contradictory) and not "essentialist" (un-fixed, de-centered, and multiple).

Fragmented identities

Rattansi and Phoenix contend that Erikson's

> form of theorisation produces a strong individual/society dichotomy, which obscures understanding of the complex ways in which identities are formed and operate dynamically in different social contexts. It also runs counter to attempts to understand identities as more fluid and fragmented, as in cultural studies and some sociology.
>
> (2005, p. 101)

Is this contention really true? This criticism appears to have some merit with respect to the identity status paradigm, but this criticism is not new. As a matter of fact, the identity status paradigm has been the subject of an internal debate for some time (e.g., Berzonsky & Adams, 1999; Côté & Levine, 1987, 1988a,

1988b; Schwartz, 2001; van Hoof, 1999; Waterman, 1988), and attempts have been made to correct its limitations (e.g., Yoder, 2000). But the thrust of this internal critique of Marcia's empirical model is that it does not do justice to the complexities and nuances of Erikson's writings, especially his specification of the importance of cultural, societal, and historical contexts for ego identity formation, as well as the content of social identities.

As it turns out, not only does Erikson's original work explore societal contexts in detail, he was a pioneer in the study of how identities are made precarious by experiences in certain social contexts. Understanding the history of identity studies helps us to understand the roots of these "postmodernist" claims and Erikson's role in pointing out how "identities are formed and operate dynamically in different social contexts" (to reiterate this portion of the above quotation from Rattansi & Phoenix, 2005, p. 101).

In actuality, the rise of identity studies follows the intensification of "identity anxieties" in the twentieth century in relation to a number of socio-historical developments (Côté, 2006a). Using the proliferation of publications on the topic as an indicator of the growing attention to these anxieties in the academic literature, by mid-century there was a palpable increase in anxiety among social scientists about the rise of "mass society," with its decline in community, the ascendance of anonymous bureaucratic control—along with the technological transformation of human activities—and a consequent rise in problems of personal definition. A volume documenting this anxiety, appropriately titled *Identity and anxiety: Survival of the person in mass society*, was published in 1960 with Erikson's essay "The problem of ego identity" as the lead, and organizing, chapter (Stein, Vidich, & White, 1960). Selections in this landmark book were drawn from the various social sciences to represent the diverse explanations of the growing problems of social integration and personal meaning.

Over the decades following the 1950s, these concerns about identity problems rooted in mass society morphed into other approaches. In sociology, the concept of mass society has been generally replaced by the concepts of postmodernity and late-modernity, yet many of the same problematic societal conditions remain as likely sources of identity problems (Côté, 2000, 2006a). In this sense, some postmodern claims about the "state of society" are in many ways "old wine in new bottles."

Erikson was in these ways a pioneer in this area, with his early work first popularizing the idea that human identity had become problematic (e.g., 1950). His later work went into depth with respect to the cross-cultural and historical variations in identity problems (e.g., 1958, 1968). At the same time, Erikson influenced the study of identity in adolescent psychology with his proposition that the key psychosocial task of adolescence—the identity stage—involves developing a viable sense of identity that links childhood with adulthood by consolidating identifications rooted in childhood and roles learned in adolescence into a coherent identity that would provide for a functional adulthood. Consequently, the psychosocial task of identity formation was identified as a "normative" event of adolescence within and between cultures (Erikson, 1950, 1968). It is important to note that he used the term "normative" in the descriptive sense of being the *norm for the majority of the population*, and not in the prescriptive senses involving sanctions against minorities or moral obligations to abide by certain rules.

In addition to his normative descriptions, Erikson also pointed out ways in which significant deviations from contemporaneous cultural models of adult identity could take place for certain people in particular cultural and historical contexts, especially with individual prolongations of the stage. His psycho-historical analysis of Martin Luther's identity struggles stands as an exemplar of Erikson's (1958) thinking on this matter. At the height of his writings some 50 years ago, these extensions of the identity stage were thought to be exceptions, found only in some cultures and then mainly among the affluent and others who could "afford" a prolonged identity stage, as in the case of university attendance. With the recent prolongation of the youth period, though, the extension of the identity stage beyond the late teens now appears to be a normative event in Western societies.

Erikson also viewed identity formation as a lifelong process that can be deeply affected by a variety of socio-cultural factors (e.g., 1950, 1975) and symbolic community processes (e.g., Erikson & Erikson, 1957). In fact, he wrote that identity "is always changing and developing: at its best it is a process of increasing differentiation, and it becomes ever more inclusive as the individual grows aware of a widening circle of others significant to [him/her], from the maternal person to [humankind]" (1968, p. 23). Erikson provided numerous illustrations of the lifelong aspects of identity formation through his favored qualitative method of writing life histories of key historical figures such as Mahatma Gandhi (Erikson, 1969). A common theme in these studies was the interrelationships between identity and ideology, and how the personal identity conflicts tackled and resolved by key historical figures led to massive ideological changes at the societal level.

Thus, for Erikson, the fragmenting influences on identity, and its formation, are individually variable, not constant, as the postmodernist assumption would seem to have it (i.e., postmodernists make blanket claims that the fragmentation is universal and apparently equally experienced by everyone, a logically tenuous assumption; e.g., Kroger, 2005). Erikson also wrote of the cultural variability in tendencies for individuals to experience fragmentation. For instance, tacitly anticipating the late-modernist perspective, Erikson proposed that "the more highly structured a culture is, the less likely there will be an overt conflict of identity, while the less structure there is...the greater will be the conflict" (Erikson, in Evans, 1969, pp. 37–8). On the issue of historical change, he wrote:

> In some young people, in some classes, at some periods of history, the...identity crisis will be noiseless and contained within rituals of passage marking a second birth; while in other people, classes, and periods, the

crisis will be clearly marked off as a critical period intensified by collective strife and epidemic tension.

(Erikson, 1975, p. 21)

For Erikson, then, fragmentation is a matter of degree: some societal contexts will be more fragmented than others, and historical variations will be apparent over time. Erikson was keenly aware of these variations.

In sum, when Erikson's many works are consulted and given a full reading, contrary to Rattansi and Phoenix's contentions, his model does not appear to decontextualize identity formation or ignore the influences that fragment identity and its formation. To the contrary, Erikson was pointing out as early as the 1940s what later came to be diagnosed as problems like "the malaise of modernity" (e.g., Taylor, 1991). Moreover, in many ways Erikson anticipated the late-modern model of identity represented by Giddens (1991) and Beck (1992), which shares postmodernism's concern with context-fragmentation but stresses the importance of agency in dealing with fragmented and thus unsupportive social contexts.

Rattansi and Phoenix are correct in their criticism that Erikson did not consider the multiple problems associated with ethnicity, gender, and class, along with their intersections, with the level of sophistication that can currently be found. Nevertheless, many of these current formulations are not incompatible with his early work, and the existence of this recent work does not justify jettisoning the entire Eriksonian approach to identity formation. Phoenix and Rattansi would prefer that these forms of identity were approached from a "discursive" or "narrative" perspective (p. 216), but as noted in Chapter 3 there is no reason why a mature field cannot study identity problems from multiple perspectives with multiple methodologies (cf. Syed & Azmitia, 2008, 2010).

Non-essentialist identities

For Rattansi and Phoenix, an *essentialist* position would deny " 'human nature' is itself a historical product, [but rather is] . . . simply the unfolding of an essence inherent in human beings regardless of specific institutions and cultures" (2005, p. 104). Rattansi and Phoenix argue that identities are "non-essentialist" because they are fluid, and not fixed to any one marker (social or biological); they are also multiple, with people pulled in often contradictory directions. According to them, postmodernist positions on identity

are particularly inimical to the idea of a "core self" that is established relatively early and remains as an essential organiser of the subject's relations with the social world. Instead, the emphasis is on the ways in which individuals occupy multiple positions and therefore have a range of identities, with different ones acquiring salience in different contexts. The differing positions are seen to derive from particular social positions—class, gender, ethnicity—and also from the insertion of subjects into discursive formations and ideologies, such as racism.

(Rattansi & Phoenix, 2005, p. 104)

Paradoxically, if these positions are the hallmark of postmodernist views on the "essential nature" of identity, then Erikson could be viewed as an early postmodernist. Actually, he wrote about a tendency of fluidity in identities as part of the problem people face in mass societies. For example, in postulating the rise of "Protean man," attributing it in part to the rise of relativism, Erikson thought "the notion that everything is relative has undoubtedly contributed to the character of contemporary identity formation in many subtle as well as blatant ways." For instance, he noted the increasing tendency for people to enact "a number of seemingly contradictory characters [i.e., social roles] in one lifetime" (Erikson, 1974, pp. 106–7).

However, whereas some postmodernists like Rattansi and Phoenix apparently celebrate this fluidity and relativity, Erikson pointed out the limitations and pitfalls in taking identities too far in this direction. To illustrate, in his reference to "Protean man," Erikson also observed that Proteus (a god in Greek mythology who could change shape) in the end was compelled to show his "core identity" when he was unable to "escape into different beings [and] was...forced to be himself and tell what he knew." Accordingly, Erikson was skeptical that people can function effectively as entirely superficial role-players without any stable, interior substance. He expressed this skepticism as follows:

But what if role-playing became an aim in itself, is rewarded with success and status, and seduces the person to repress what core-identity is potential in him? Even an actor is convincing in many roles only if and when there is in him an actor's core-identity—and craftsmanship. Comparably, there may well be some character types who thrive on Protean possibilities, even as there is, by definition, a developmental period (namely, youth) when the experimentation with a range of roles and alternating states of mind can be a way of personal growth. What is described as a Protean personality today may, in fact, be an attempt on the part of adolescent personalities— and America has always cultivated them—to adjust to overwhelming change by a stance of deliberate changeability, of maintaining the initiative by playing at change so as to stay ahead of the game.... Those who are gifted in this game and, therefore, truly playful in it, may with luck make it an essential part of their identity formation and find a new sense of centrality and originality in the flux of our time.

(1974, pp. 106–7)

Erikson's position was thus that there are *real* constraints on the elasticity of the *processes* of *ego identity* formation and maintenance undergirding a sense of temporal-spatial continuity. When the concept of ego identity is separated from the concept of social identity, the definitional confusion in Rattansi and Phoenix's critique becomes clearer. Indeed, it cannot be stressed enough that much of the postmodernist literature confuses *identity construction* with *identity formation*. That is, the "contents" and "processes" of identity formation, respectively, are conflated with each other, leading to the types of misunderstandings underlying Rattansi and Phoenix's critique of Erikson (Berzonsky, 2005; Kroger, 2005; Levine, 2005; Phinney, 2005a).[1]

Further, to assert that subject multiplicity transcends cultural context is to confuse level of analysis: in order to cope with and adapt to fragmented contexts, people require a multifaceted self. But this self logically needs to have some "core" in the form of underlying functional mental capacities to manage the various selves. Without some core functional capacities, we would all develop multiple personalities or wake up each morning with little recall of our past selves. As it happens, it was from Erikson's experiences as a clinician treating what were called "shell-shock" victims from World War II that he developed his first insights into the importance of ego processes in maintaining a unity of personality functioning—core mental operations sustaining a sense of temporal-spatial continuity—in the face of extreme stress (Erikson, 1968). The traumas these victims experienced created severe symptoms of identity confusion, amnesia, and the like, which we now call post-traumatic stress disorder (PTSD). Again, Erikson was a pioneer in investigating these sorts of identity disorders.

Later, Erikson noticed the trend toward more problematic identity functioning among the general population of Americans, writing extensively about the "identity crisis" that he saw as a rising epidemic in modern societies, especially among "severely conflicted young people whose sense of confusion is due to a war within themselves" (Erikson, 1968, p. 17). From these insights, Erikson went on to think broadly about the identity problems of adolescence and adulthood that he saw to be "normal" responses to the vicissitudes of mass societies. Importantly, he did not believe that everyone experienced these things to the same degree, nor did he argue that a severe identity crisis was "normal" (normative) or necessary for further identity development. To the contrary, he was interested in how some people can survive these severe stresses while others have a difficult time doing so. His conclusion was that basic differences in *ego strengths* are key to the various ways people handle stress, and he developed his theory of *ego development* to try to explain this.

To return to Rattansi and Phoenix's position, they are adamant about their postmodernist boilerplate assumptions in emphasizing "the multiplicity, fluidity and context-dependent operation of youth identities" (2005, p. 98). To understand this position, as discussed in Chapters 1 and 2, the moniker "postmodernist" can sometimes more productively be read as "nominalist," because it often involves a reiteration of nominalist assumptions. It is important to note these assumptions, because had Rattansi and Phoenix simply stated their position as a form of nominalism (that favors discursive and narrative approaches) without the postmodernist boilerplate, they might have been more sensitive to the distinction between *processes* of identity and identity *contents*, that is, between ego identity and social identity. The conflation of these two levels of identity is apparent in the following passage from Rattansi and Phoenix:

> Following the work of the psychoanalyst Erik Erikson, for example, it is often asserted that adolescence is a "critical" phase or period in the life course when identity has to be established in order for young people to become ready to assume adult sexuality and other adult responsibilities. Erikson's ego identity approach consisted of a series of age related stages, with identity being the main task of adolescence. He theorised identity as having integrity and continuity and as important in keeping the internal and external worlds aligned to each other. *Following Erikson, many psychologists construct identity as an inner-core which is the self and which requires continuity if it is not to experience threat.*
>
> (2005, p. 101, emphasis added)

The highlighted sentence shows where Rattansi and Phoenix's reasoning does not distinguish between process and content. Eriksonians discuss ego identity as the process by which the ego maintains a sense of temporal-spatial continuity when acting as a kind of "central processing unit" of the mind. But, Rattansi and Phoenix appear to be referring to identity contents, which as noted above can take any form.

An analogy with entirely neutral terminology can perhaps clear up this confusion. Following a computer analogy, imagine the ego as the CPU—the central processing unit, the indispensable hardware that makes a computer what it is and enables it to function as such. At the same time, imagine various social identities as software programs or apps.[2] Confusing the CPU with apps is a "rookie error" if one is trying to understand how computers work; it is likewise a folly to confuse mental processes with learned contents when trying to understand how the mind works. As Rattansi and Phoenix continue, we can see how this confusion compounds their misunderstanding of the nature and role of ego identity, as well as how they return to the nominalist starting point of their critique:

> Inevitably, this form of theorisation produces a strong individual/society dichotomy, which obscures understanding of the complex ways in which identities are formed and operate dynamically in different social contexts. It also runs counter to attempts to understand identities as more fluid and fragmented, as in cultural studies and some sociology ... and as not being crucially organized around age-stages and critical periods.... *The notion of coherent, stable identities is, however, increasingly coming into question* within the burgeoning field of identity ...
>
> (2005, p. 101, emphasis added)

The claim that humans are not capable of forming coherent and stable points of reference in organizing information about the world and regulating their behavior makes about as much sense as the claim that computers do not have (relatively) stable hardware with which to process software. So, when we recognize Rattansi and Phoenix's critique as a nominalist rejection of realism (colored by an underlying anti-psychology bias, implicitly dismissing psychology as "essentialist"), it is easier to understand their rejection of the Eriksonian position on ego identity as a rejection of any processes that are independent of social constructions. And, when we place these nominalist assumptions within the postmodernist boilerplate, we can see how they are actually seeking to reinforce the epistemological divide rather than bridge it. As a matter of fact, in their rejoinder to the Eriksonians, Phoenix and Rattansi argue "there are important differences of emphasis on structure, process, and content in identity construction that mean that approaches cannot simply be reconciled or synthesized" (2005, p. 216). More recently, Phoenix (2010, p. 300) repeated this misconception in her justification for rejecting stage theories of ethnic identity formation.

Occam's razor: The late-modernist approach to identity processes

Based on the above discussion of Erikson's corpus of works, it would appear that Rattansi and Phoenix's critique is replete with errors and exaggerations. These misrepresentations of Erikson's work appear to be largely the result of a loyalty Rattansi and Phoenix feel with postmodernism, and their consequent application of the postmodernist boilerplate. Unfortunately, these types of criticisms of Erikson have been repeated so often that many youth researchers, who have no particular allegiance to postmodernism yet little firm knowledge of the corpus of Erikson's work, are spreading them without knowing they are baseless (e.g., Jones, 2009).

So, what happens when a similar sociological framework is used to update the Eriksonian model and place it in a more sociological perspective, but without the postmodernist fanfare of cultural studies? The late-modernist framework provides a useful comparison because it is less burdened by the postmodernist boilerplate, and on the whole takes a more straightforward approach. In comparison, it applies "the rule of Occam's razor," namely, that the simplest explanation is probably the most useful one.

For instance, like other identity theorists, Giddens also argues that sustaining a sense of identity has become more difficult, but he attributes the difficulties to conditions associated with advanced capitalism that have "heightened" modernity (Giddens, 1991). These conditions have "undercut traditional habits and customs," radically altering "the nature of day-to-day social life" and affecting "the most personal aspects of our experience" (Giddens, 1991, p. 1). Yet, in contrast to some postmodernists, he ascribes agentic capacities to the person (the subject) to resist and adapt to this destructuring. At the same time, this need to adapt puts demands on people's intentional qualities that they cannot always meet, so those with lower capacities for agency do not cope as well in late-modern contexts, especially in terms of identity formation and maintenance (cf. Côté, 2002).

Thus, for Giddens, it is important in late-modernity for the individual to develop agentic capacities with which to construct reality and act in the world. He describes the agentic person as an "intelligent strategist" (1994, p. 7) who learns how to deal with the abstract dimensions of "place" and "space" in the late-modern world. For the late-modern citizen (subject), "the self becomes a [lifelong] reflexive project" (Giddens, 1991, pp. 32–3), because of continual institutional destructuring and restructuring. Consequently, the life course in late-modernity now follows a larger number of trajectories than in the past, determined in part by individual preferences and agentic capacities (the process of *individualization*), and in part by the uncertainty and risks of living in, and attempting to cope with less predictable concrete, day-to-day structures.

Giddens's perspective is entirely compatible with the Eriksonian one, but is not encumbered by the boilerplate assumptions of postmodernism requiring that all things are to be seen as fragmented, de-centered, and non-essential, and that only nominalism-based evidence is acceptable.

Empirical evidence: How fragmented? How coherent?

As argued above, Rattansi and Phoenix's postmodernist approach to identity depicts the period of youth as the beginning of *inevitable* lifelong identity problems, with everyone destined to a lifetime of fragmented and conflictual experiences without "core" organizing mental processes with which to agentically manage their lives. However, when we examine the empirical evidence they present for these (boilerplate) claims, we find two chief problems in the relevance of their evidence as a refutation of the Eriksonian perspective.

First, their real-life examples of "identity" are more about youth cultures, sociological manifestations of how youth organize themselves in some contemporary Western societies (principally the United Kingdom, which is the bellwether nation for youth culture as collective expressions of dissent). As we see in this section, this is an entirely different set of phenomena than those studied by Eriksonians, who are focused on *individual identity formation* rather than *collective identity displays*. The topic of youth culture looms large in youth studies, as we saw in the previous chapter, but is peripheral to the concerns of the Eriksonian approach.

Second, the perspective taken by Rattansi and Phoenix as a basis for selecting evidence is strongly influenced by cultural studies, with its heavy reliance of nominalism-based qualitative methods and a value priority of advocacy. This combination of perspectives begins with conclusions based on boilerplate assumptions, so there is little new to be discovered by empirical inquiries; instead, evidence is sought that confirms preconceptions. As noted in Chapter 8 with respect to the same drawback in postmodernists' approach to youth culture, this is problematic from the point of view of critical thinking.

How well do their claims hold up when we expand the radius of empirical research to include other disciplinary concerns, ontologies, and methodologies that focus on individual differences in agency-based identity formation? It is important to examine this research because Rattansi and Phoenix (1997) mischaracterize the Eriksonian and neo-Eriksonian approaches as holding a homogeneous conception of identity formation—that all young people supposedly experience the same form or trajectory of identity development (cf. Kroger, 2005). In fact, Eriksonians view identity formation as far more complex, nonlinear, and varied than Rattansi and Phoenix's account suggests, and individual differences in the capacity for personal agency are in reality the key dimensions differentiating these identity-formation trajectories.

The most consistent finding of the neo-Eriksonian literature is that adolescents/youth in late-modern societies differ in terms of how actively they engage themselves in their identity formation toward formulating and consolidating an identity with which to eventually integrate into the adult sphere of their society. Instead of using the specialized language of this literature, the terms "proactive" and "inactive" will be used here to describe the most contrasting ways in which the tasks of identity formation can be approached.[3] *Proactive* approaches involve a willingness to think ahead in one's life in a planning and purposive manner, thereby exploring and experimenting with possible goals, commitments, values, and roles, upon which to base adult identities. In contrast, *inactive* approaches characterize a reticence to think ahead, experiment and explore, or to commit.

Those who take more *proactive* approaches to their identity formation, in comparison with inactive ones, empirically exhibit

- higher levels of personal agency (Côté, 1997; Côté & Schwartz, 2002);
- higher achievement motivation; lower neuroticism and use of defense mechanisms; more robust cognitive processes (functioning better under stress, exercising more balanced thinking, being more planful, and demonstrating higher levels of moral reasoning and ego development) (Boyes & Chandler, 1992);
- better interpersonal skills and mature interpersonal relationships (higher intimacy, self-disclosure, and more secure attachments) (e.g., Dyk & Adams, 1990; Kroger, 2003; Orlofsky, Marcia, & Lesser, 1973);
- stronger relationships with family and friends (but are better able to resist peer pressure), greater self-efficacy, and more self-reflexivity and self-confidence (e.g., Jakubowski & Dembo, 2004; Marcia et al., 1993); and
- a sense of self-esteem that is more stable and less prone to contextual influences because of their greater capacity for internal self-regulation (e.g., Marcia, 1993).

Inactivity in identity formation shows a contrasting litany of characteristics associated with lower levels of functioning. Those who are inactive

- are more prone to drug abuse, risky sexual behavior, eating disorders, and susceptibility to peer influence and academic failure (Jones, 1992, 1994; Jones & Hartmann, 1988; White, 2000);
- tend to be less adaptable, experiencing difficulties adapting to new environments (including university settings);
- have lower levels of self-esteem and are more self-focused;
- tend to have more disorganized thinking, an external locus of control, and a tendency toward procrastination and defensive avoidance of issues in their lives; and
- score lowest on measures of moral reasoning and ego development (Kroger, 2003).

In light of these findings, an important conclusion can be drawn from this extensive neo-Eriksonian empirical literature that helps address the coherence vs. fragmentation question in contemporary Western societies: most people seem to be able to arrive at a reasonably coherent and stable resolution of the identity stage and become functioning adults in their communities—in effect, to have a sense of ego identity that is flexible enough to adjust to multiple and changing social contexts (Côté, 2009a).

This literature suggests a developmental sequence beginning with the transformation of self-concepts (and identifications) formed during childhood into more coherent identities in adolescence/youth, which can carry on into adulthood. Although one might think that young people begin their teen years without any prior identity-formation activity, this does not appear to be the case, nor did Erikson claim it to be the case (e.g., 1959). Most young teens appear to have been active to some extent in childhood, at least in terms of building self-concepts into more coherent identities. The empirical literature indicates that only about 30 per cent of young teens would be classified as inactive, and this proportion drops to about 20 to 25 per cent in the late teens and early twenties, and to about 15 per cent thereafter. If identity-formation inactivity persists beyond these years, it can become a permanent stance (Kroger, Martinussen, & Marcia, 2010). Thus, by its very nature, inactivity can become a permanent approach to identity maintenance, although some people can pass through it as a temporary respite when they are not ready for a particular developmental challenge or are confronted with an obstacle that precludes them from forming certain commitments (Côté, 2009a).

In contrast, the majority of young people in Western societies appear to manage some form of identity synthesis into coherent adult identities, based either on a functional (active) identification with their parents (about 20%) or on their own proactive experimentation with values, beliefs, roles, and commitments (about 20% of those in their late teens, 30% in their twenties, and 50% in their thirties). When these latter two types of commitment-based identity synthesis are considered together, the neo-Eriksonian literature thus provides an estimate that about 50 per cent of the young adults, and 70 per cent of the adult-aged population, in contemporary Western societies have consolidated a coherent identity that provides a stable basis for adult roles (Côté, 2009a; Kroger, Martinussen, & Marcia, 2010).

Conclusion: Bridging the epistemological divide

When a wide-reaching approach is taken that examines a range of issues, the postmodernist debate of the Eriksonian approach to identity formation turns out to be somewhat of a "tempest in a teapot" based on a caricature constructed by Rattansi and Phoenix (and others). Postmodernists are basically referring to different manifestations of identity—social identities, with a focus on youth culture—while Eriksonians focus on the ego identity and the formation of various types of personal and social identities during the adolescence/youth period.

Rattansi and Phoenix's insistence that only nominalist assumptions can be adopted in studying "identity" is shortsighted—limiting the scope of inquiry and potential for this field to advance. The discursive and narrative approaches recommended by Rattansi and Phoenix are useful, but constitute only two approaches that shed light on only certain manifestations of identity (Côté, 2009b).

What these nominalist approaches do not illuminate are the mental processes underlying the ability to communicate the stories we tell each other and ourselves about our identities. That is, these approaches do not tell us "what" is responsible for the human ability to engage in discourse and narration in the first place, and this question is precisely what Eriksonians are interested in, dating back to Erikson's epiphany that shell-shock war victims experiencing amnesia had lost the ability to engage in identity discourse and narrative. Those suffering these symptoms do not have a sense of ego identity that is sufficiently functional to provide the sense of temporal-spatial continuity necessary to tell others who they "were," "are," or "will be."

For Eriksonians, the empirical puzzle to solve is how people develop the abilities—and differences in the development of these abilities—to maintain continuity in their lives, especially in the face of stresses, contradictions, fragmentations, de-centering influences from competing identities, their own unconscious conflicts, and so forth. In this sense, the incompatibilities in perspectives identified by Rattansi and Phoenix are illusory—mainly a product of Rattansi and Phoenix's own social constructions that are heavily biased by postmodernist boilerplate assumptions and an insistence that only nominalist assumptions and methods can be productively used in the field of identity studies. The rejection of anything that smacks of "essentialism" eliminates from consideration the basis for the human mental capacity for self-reflection as well as for the communication of those self-reflections to others.

The hiatus in youth-identity studies supports the warning, offered in Chapter 1, that unless researchers are willing to consider the range of ontologies, and to suspend their boilerplate assumptions long enough to understand the point of view of other youth researchers, the field of youth studies will remain stalemated by the epistemological divide. Recommended readings for this chapter include Syed and Azmitia (2008) for an example of how this divide can be bridged empirically, and McAdams (2011) for a theoretical discussion that bridges this divide (see also Chandler, 2001, and Syed & Azmitia, 2010). The next chapter picks up on content-process dimension as it applies to the objective and subjective experiences of identity during the youth period.

Recommended readings

James M. Glass (1993). Multiplicity, identity and the horrors of selfhood: Failures in the postmodern position. *Political Psychology*, 14, 255–78.

    This article provides a critique of the glorification by some postmodernists of "subject multiplicity." After discussing the Dissociative Identity Disorder in general and a particular case of it, this psychiatrist concludes that "postmodernism's dalliance with disconnection and chaos" is "dangerously irresponsible" and that "this kind of 'freedom' is not liberation, but enslavement" by "emotional fragmentation and psychological dislocation" (p. 276).

Charles Levine (2005). What happened to agency? Some observations concerning the postmodern perspective on identity. *Identity: An International Journal of Theory and Research*, 5, 175–85.

    In this rejoinder to Rattansi and Phoenix's critique of the Eriksonian approach to identity formation, Levine takes them to task for misunderstandings of that approach and the inability of their own postmodernist approach to account in a theoretically consistent manner for the role of human agency in identity formation.

Dan McAdams (2011). Narrative identity. In S. J. Schwartz, V. L. Vignoles, & L. Koen (eds.), *Handbook of Identity Theory and Research* (pp. 99–115). New York: Springer.

    This handbook chapter reviews the field of research on identity using a narrative approach, recognizing that both nominalist and realist approaches are useful.

Moin Syed & Margarita Azmitia (2008). A narrative approach to ethnic identity in emerging adulthood: Bringing life to the identity status model. *Developmental Psychology*, 44, 1012–27.

    This article presents the findings from a study that used both the conventional quantitative approach to ethnic identity formation and a narrative approach, providing evidence for convergence between two approaches by linking ethnicity-related narratives to the ethnic identity status model.

Youth Social Identities: Structurally Determined or Agentically Mediated? 10

This chapter picks up on content-process dimensions of "identity" that are central to a major fracture among youth researchers interested in how young people define their "spaces and places" in the world. As noted above, this disagreement is relevant to a number of seminal debates, including the structure–agency debate, which in this case calls for distinguishing between the objective and subjective aspects of the youth period. As we see in this chapter, when social identities are viewed as having two principal facets, a more complete picture of the youth period emerges. These two facets involve external features—identities viewed from "the outside in"—as well as internal features—identities viewed from "the inside out." "Outside in" features comprise objective, structural aspects and social influences, while "inside out" aspects encompass subjective, agentic characteristics and psychological influences. As such, they are "two sides of the same coin."

Social identities from the outside in

This chapter broadens the coverage of disputes from the preceding chapter to include considerations that return us the "youth question," and thus the fundamental nature of the youth period itself. Based on the material covered in a number of above chapters, we are now in position to delve deeper into the youth question in terms of the objective conditions of the youth period as it is constituted in contemporary Western societies. For instance, some theorists have argued that other social identities are more salient than age/youth in setting people apart in various societies. Jones (2009) follows this debate, as manifested between functionalists and the CCCS, quoting Stuart Hall as claiming that there is "no sociology of youth, since differences of class, race and sex mean that young people experience very different types of youth.... Youth as a concept is unthinkable. Even youth as a social category does not make empirical sense" (Hall et al., 1976, quoted in Jones, 2009, p. 21).

Other theorists have argued that gender is more important than age/youth, such that young women experience an entirely different youth period (e.g.,

McRobbie, 1980). Yet others have argued that ethnicity is more important. More generally, a common criticism is that the youth period has been conceptualized as "normative" in terms of the majority group in a society or in terms of the typical male, heterosexual experience (e.g., Aapola, Gonick, & Harris, 2005; Tyyskä, 2009).

We saw in Chapter 1 that broad cultural and historical distinctions are important in locating "youth" as a period of the life course, because in some cultures (and throughout most of human history) there were no age-periods that correspond to adolescence or youth as constituted in contemporary Western societies. With these distinctions in mind, there are two ways to approach the issue of the importance of youth as an objective social identity: (1) in a given society comparing all youth fractions with all "adult" segments—that is, contrasting youth identities with adult identities—and (2) making comparisons within the youth segment—that is, examining social identity differences among youth identities. In both cases, empirical evidence is needed that allows comparisons of the different structural categorizations of both youth and adults in terms of important criteria such as the material circumstances of their daily lives.

Youth identities vs. adult identities

As noted above, Jones (2009) recorded the earlier debate among youth researchers as to whether youth makes empirical sense as a social category. Developments since the 1970s may have changed matters in many countries, though, solidifying youth as a social-structural category in its own right. Two developments in particular are noteworthy: (1) the collapse of the youth labor market sparked by the ascendance of neoliberalism, along with the dramatic rise in educational requirements for entry into the labor force, and (2) the targeting of young people by corporations as consumers of identity-conferring products, as discussed in the youth culture chapter.

As we saw in Chapter 5, not only is the youth period associated with increasing material disadvantage in relation to adult status, but this period of economic disadvantage is also lengthening. Certainly, other forms of status advantage–disadvantage based on class, ethnicity, gender, sexuality, ability, and so forth are experienced by people of all ages. However, it becomes an empirical question regarding how much the youth status cuts through each of these other statuses, potentially placing younger members of each status at an economic disadvantage in relation to older members in each of those statuses. If this is the case, aside from these other sources of status disadvantage, young people will have a greater chance of being disadvantaged than adults with whom they share other social statuses like ethnicity.

At the same time, the sources of disadvantages may multiply, producing double and even triple jeopardies. For example, age can combine with race and gender in many countries, creating compounded economic disadvantages in relation to adults of different races and gender (what postmodernists refer to as intersectionality). While these experiences are real and serious in their consequences, and should be vigorously studied, if the field of youth studies were only concerned with documenting every combination and permutation of disadvantage that compounds with youth status, it would lose its "identity" as a discrete field, and would become a cataloguing of compounded disadvantage rather than an analysis of the youth period, both as an identity/culture and as a transition to adulthood.[1] The fact that the youth period of the life course is consistently overlooked—even dismissed—as a source of structural disadvantage (e.g., as demographers are wont to do; Beaujot & Kerr, 2007) makes it even more crucial that this field maintains its unique focus.

In pursuing the issue of within- vs. between-age differences, a useful heuristic is to ask whether young people in a given society considered as a group have more in common on key indices (e.g., work roles and earning power) with each other or with those who are older but who share another characteristic, for example, gender as in the following illustration.

A historical analysis undertaken by Jordan (1978) provides such an example. In reference to early American history (which can be used as an exemplar of a traditional society), Jordan argued that gender roles overrode age roles. In this traditional Western society, "manhood" and "womanhood" were widely believed to be distinct and superordinate but complementary social statuses. Consequently, it was more important normatively for people in that traditional society to distinguish men from women than to distinguish young people from older people. Thus, males and females had more in common with those of the same gender regardless of age. Over time, Jordan argued, these statuses reversed in importance, with age-related roles becoming more important than gender roles in a number of important material respects. Currently, on key economic criteria, adult men and women have more in common materially with each other than with younger people of the same gender, and males and females in the youth period have more in common with each other than with younger or older people of the same gender.

To bring this American example up to date, as we saw in Chapter 5, when current salaries are compared in the United States, because of a severe drop in youth wages, young men and women (aged 16 to 24) now have only a 5 per cent difference in median weekly earnings, a significant convergence from just 40 years ago. Remarkably, the difference in earning power between younger and older workers (aged 25 and older) is now 50 per cent for males and 40 per cent for females, a dramatic difference from 40 years ago when the difference was only 26 and 6 per cent, respectively (Sum & McLaughlin, 2011).

Variations among youth identities

As argued in the preceding section, simply cataloguing various disadvantages when investigating potential "multiple youths" within the youth segment would distract from the task of identifying what is unique about historically specific forms of youth in contemporary Western societies. To argue that there are different "youths" in a society because advantages vary among them would be similar to arguing that there are different "childhoods" or "adulthoods" in the life course, but it is clear that there are substantive differences between these life phases that warrant their independent study.

In these respects, the postmodernist approach may have more utility when identity is viewed from the perspective of structural effects on aspects of *social identity*. At the same time, structures are double-edged, providing opportunities for some people and constituting obstacles for others. On the one hand, these opportunities/obstacles are related to the social identities of the person (e.g., gender, ethnicity, and class). On the other hand, the agentic capacities of people appear to be relevant in terms of both taking advantage of opportunities and overcoming these obstacles. With the structure–agency debate in mind, the key problem in analyzing youth as a social identity is to clearly identify the distinctive features of the youth period as constituted in contemporary societies without homogenizing young people in terms of structural obstacles/opportunities or agentic potentials.

To complicate matters, current emphases on "diversity" risk potentially diverting attention away from the increasing polarization of wealth, and the growing poverty and social exclusion in some countries (Michaels, 2006). The general case about the importance of "class" appears to be especially relevant to the youth field, as the disadvantages associated with the youth period itself increase. Sociologists, as a rule, have an acute concern with social-class differences, and this can be clearly seen in UK youth studies (Furlong, 2013; MacDonald, 2011). While this is valid concern, as argued above, there is the jeopardy in youth studies of missing the point that young people collectively now confront structural obstacles, as well as new opportunities, by merit of their age status. As also argued above, the attempt to document all possible variations in these obstacles and opportunities based on structural differences begs the question of the existence of a young period in the first place. That is, it assumes the very thing in question, in this case the factors that create the conditions that set young people apart from older people in a given society.

The youth-studies community seems to have fumbled the ball on these issues in a number of respects. As we have seen, adolescent psychologists tend to view adolescence/youth ontogenetically, so have not addressed the question of the deteriorating material basis of the youth period itself. Functionalists view this age period as the result of evolving cultural expectations, but have avoided the issue of the origin of those expectations in power structures. Functionalists describe youth as an age-status, a useful but potentially incomplete depiction in many societies, especially neoliberal ones. Political economists have been the only ones to take the question on more directly, positing "youth as class" (Côté, 2014b; Côté & Allahar, 1996, 2006; Rowntree & Rowntree, 1968).[2] For political economists, the youth period has become a new filter for the social reproduction of class inequalities.

A useful way forward on the issue of within-youth differences is to estimate the structural resources (e.g., economic advantages/disadvantages) different young people have access to, in conjunction with the agentic resources they are capable of mobilizing (e.g., level of interpersonal functioning). An algorithm for calculating "structure by agency" resources is provided in Côté (2013b). This method allows us to detect variations at the individual and collective levels without homogenizing young people, as in the case of concepts such as "emerging adulthood" or "vanguard generation." Importantly, this method avoids the tendency of "recommending" an extended youth period as advantageous to all young people (e.g., Arnett, 2004; Wyn, 2008), as discussed in Chapter 5. Serious resource differences do exist among the youth segment, but not all of these differences are material. Some differences relate to agency-based identity formation potentials, as we see in the second part of this chapter and as we saw in the preceding chapter.

Approaches to youth social identities that emphasize structure without taking into account agency tend to be deterministic and ignore the massive social transformations that have taken place in the transitions from traditional to post-traditional societies. In traditional societies, social identities are often strictly ascribed at birth and there is little or no latitude for the person to change these social identities during life-course transitions because of strict social norms, mores and folkways (e.g., peasant females had narrowly defined roles and opportunities in feudal societies that would not change as a result of moving through any phases of the life course). As societies move from traditional to "post-traditional" (or modern) social organizations, these forms of ascription tend to weaken, allowing certain forms of achievement over ascription (e.g., McClelland, 1961).

Nonetheless, as Durkheim (1893/1964b) originally noted, and as late-modernists have taken up, the gap between "ascription" and "achievement" is often left as a normative void in post-traditional societies. These gaps create "fragmentations" in social organization, as traditions are shed that loosen up ascriptive processes. In this context, postmodernist approaches to identity, while noting these societal fragmentations, tend to confuse levels of analysis and thereby mis-define different types of identity—mistaking psychological and interpersonal levels of analysis with social levels, conflating ego and personal identities with social identities (e.g., Wetherell, 2009; Wetherell & Mohanty, 2010). This category error (Berzonsky, 2005) is compounded by a reticence to deal with individual differences, a tendency endemic to those nominalist approaches that reject "variable analysis" (Blumer, 1969). Consequently, identities are often approached as constants, rather than in terms of multiple manifestations at different levels of analysis. These misunderstandings seem to be related to the persistent, but misguided, charge that realist approaches to identity are "essentialist" and therefore must be wrong (e.g., Phoenix, 2010; Rattansi & Phoenix, 2005; Wetherell, 2009).

In light of these considerations, when "identity" is viewed in terms of the effects on the person of structures, including the social class, ethnic, and gender stratification systems in a given society, an appropriate level of analysis involves "objective" social identities, namely, the location(s) of the person in the society as manifested in the social roles enacted and the relative status of these roles. By the same token, to avoid over-generalizations, or a "one-size-fits-all" error that Kroger (2005) identified with Rattansi and Phoenix's approach, it is necessary to recognize that modern Western societies rarely have completely rigid, impermeable stratification systems: although these systems still influence life outcomes at a population level, many people are able to penetrate and cross certain structural barriers. Because all people are not ascribed social identities at birth that absolutely dictate their fates, as was/is the case in many traditional societies, when assessed in terms of life-course outcomes such as sharing national affluence and wealth, social categories can be more permeable objectively and fluid subjectively (as both late-modernists and postmodernists argue). As we saw in Chapter 3, this position is currently a postulated resolution of the structure–agency debate in youth studies (e.g., Evans, 2002).

Additionally, in many Western countries, as people of different backgrounds have shared more in national economies, schools, and workplaces, their social-identity differences have become more salient interactionally, with many people sharing multiple positions (creating hybrid ethnic identities; e.g., Brunsma, 2006) or multiple contradictory positions (e.g., Costigan et al., 2010). This is likely to produce the types of subjective "de-centering" and "multiplicity" referred to by postmodernists, and has sparked interest in the idea of *intersectionality* (Phoenix, 2010; especially in terms of compounded disadvantages) and "hybridity" (e.g., bi-racial identities; see e.g., Brunsma, 2006). The postmodernist perspectives on identity likely have their greatest strengths in investigating nominalist aspects of these phenomena (i.e., subjective experiences of structural fragmentations as multiple identities are negotiated and maintained). However, as noted, those perspectives can fall short in terms of adequately acknowledging or theorizing the agency that people can have to cope with those identity issues (e.g., Côté, 2006a; Costigan, Su, & Hua, 2009; Phinney, Jacoby, & Silva, 2007; Rotheram-Borus & Wyche, 1994; Sundar, 2008).

This contrast between traditional and post-traditional societies provides another way to understand structure and agency in societies where identities can be constructed and negotiated. This complexity requires a multidimensional approach. This multidimensional approach identifies factors at three levels of analysis: (macro) social structure, (micro) social context, and (subjective) agency of the self/ego. At each level of analysis there are variations that help to take into account the different experiences and outcomes of individual efforts to exercise agency, as follows:

- social structures can differ in terms of "permeability," ranging from closed through open;
- social contexts can vary in terms of "goodness of fit" for different people, which can range from poor to optimal; and

- agency differs with respect to "proactivity," with some people being inactive, others more active, and yet others proactive (i.e., reflexively anticipating future possibilities).

Thus, to understand the complexity of structure–agency interactions, it is useful to know (1) how inactive or proactive a person is in approaching social contexts, (2) the extent to which specific contexts provide a good fit for them that opens up possibilities of social-structural permeability, and (3) how open specific social structures are to being "penetrated." In post-traditional societies, the resources people have in terms of actualizing certain identities can be key to their ability to exercise agency and thus have more control over their experiences with social structures, as in the case of attempts to be upwardly mobile through an educational system (Côté, 2013b).

In the above respects, the youth period in contemporary Western societies has become both a potential obstacle and opportunity: a social location that can deny the person certain material gain and social status, but can also provide the opportunity for forms of personal growth and life satisfaction. In post-traditional societies where ascriptive processes have diminished, whether the youth period is an obstacle or opportunity to social-identity formation can depend on the person's other social locations and identities and whether these are a net advantage or liability in terms of life chances (Côté, 1996). Additionally, the structural fragmentation in post-traditional societies can be a liability for young people regardless of their other social locations, but it can also provide potential advantages to the extent that old social norms have lost their salience as ways of positioning people in terms of their social statuses (e.g., norms concerning sexuality, as discussed in Chapter 2). In these cases where social ascription has lessened and structural fragmentation has occurred, individual agency potentially becomes more variable and important.

Social identities from the inside out

Having examined the more objective and material aspects of youth social identity, we can now review the empirical literature on the subjective experiences associated with forming various social identities, focusing on ethnicity, gender, class, and various minority statuses. This literature, which is based primarily in contemporary Western societies, illustrates how agency-based identity formation is related to various social identities. This literature tends to be more psychological, exploring the mental processes associated with how social-identity formation takes on various meanings.

As we see, there appears to be some validity for Rattansi and Phoenix's assertion (discussed in the preceding chapter) that the empirical derivative of the Eriksonian approach ignores ethnicity, gender, and class, especially class. Still, the problem remains with respect to Rattansi and Phoenix's confusion between identity processes and identity contents. As we see, while identity contents do differ, identity *processes* have been found empirically to be "universal" in the Western societies studied in that people of all categories of social identity share the same mental operations (or ego/self mechanisms) for processing identity-relevant information and constructing the individual *contents* of their various social identities. At the same time, Rattansi and Phoenix (2005) might dismiss this empirical distinction because the research verifying it does not accord with their anti-realist, nominalist ontology. They express this general disapproval as follows:

> A clear research implication here is that studies of youth identities cannot rely on methodologies such as survey research which only take account of "attitudes" while ignoring the ethnographic necessity of close or "thick" description of the myriad ways in which actual identities are constructed and reworked in different social contexts. (p. 107)

Readers can judge this claim for themselves, but they are reminded that the Eriksonian approaches are concerned with the mental processes that make it possible for humans to construct identities in different social contexts (i.e., addressing the question of "what" or "who" is doing the identity construction). The following literature pertains mainly to research exploring how these under-lying mental processes operate in response to the need to construct various types of social identities.

Ethnicity

Initial attempts to study ethnic identity formation attempted to operationalize it solely in terms of respondents' specification of their ethnic group member-ship. But, treating ethnic identity solely in terms of "group membership" makes several errors. First, and most obviously, ethnic groups are often difficult to define and are most certainly not homogenous in sharing all of life's circum-stances. Second, people of a particular ethnic group do not uniformly define (construct) themselves in relation to their "own" group. And third, people of a particular ethnic group do not uniformly define themselves in relation to other ethnic groups. Thus, simply using a categorical approach to ethnic identity fails to distinguish ethnic group membership from the subjective identification with that group. It also fails to assess a sense of difference from other eth-nic groups. The categorical approach that uses self-designated "membership" thus conflates the social and psychological dimensions of identity, and ignores individual differences in the extent to which people relate to their ethnicity (cf. Phinney, 1989).

The problem in using ethnic group membership as an indicator of ethnic identity is highlighted in a Canadian study investigating self-perceived ethnicity among Aboriginal youth (Hallett et al., 2008). This study found that only half of the sample consistently self-identified as Aboriginal on a longitudinal survey.

This anomaly is also found in the United States among Hispanic adolescents (Eschbach & Gómez, 1998) and among the U.S. American Indian population in general (Eschbach, 1993). Research of this nature underscores the fact that ethnic self-identification is more complex than it appears at first blush and that there are different reasons for people to identify with their ethnic origins and thus how salient ethnicity might be in their overall sense of identity consolidation. Ethnicity tends to be more salient among minority groups—often as a function of the amount of discrimination they have experienced—and therefore is more likely to be a prominent aspect of how they consciously see themselves.

The most common quantitative approach to agency-based identity formation examines three dimensions of the salience of ethnic-group origin: (1) self-identification of a sense of belongingness to a particular group, (2) ethnic affirmation and belonging, and (3) ethnic-identity resolution (Phinney, 1989, 2006). This approach defines ethnic identity as a self-constructed internalization of the meaning and implications of a person's group membership based on that person's attitudes and feelings toward his or her cultural background, ethnic heritage, and racial phenotype.

In this model, ethnic-identity formation involves people resolving positive and negative understandings and feelings about their own group in relation to other groups that impinge upon their life. This is seen to involve a three-stage process (Phinney & Rosenthal, 1992). In the first stage, ethnicity remains unexamined, having been internalized from significant others in the family/community. The unexamined stage is more common in early adolescence. It usually takes a significant experience of prejudice or discrimination to make a person's particular ethnicity salient in identity formation, by triggering the second stage—a period of exploration leading the person to question what it means to have that ethnicity in his or her society. A person who becomes proactive in this way will explore cultural differences between his or her ethnic group and the other groups in the society. In this model, this proactive period is optimally followed by a third stage wherein people develop a "commitment to a particular way of being a member of their group" (Phinney & Rosenthal, 1992, pp. 150–1).

Research based on this model has been carried out largely in the United States, finding that there is significant movement through these three stages between ages 16 and 19. This empirical research supports the conclusion that those "who have made a commitment to their group and have a secure understanding of their group membership show more positive psychological profiles than those who are unclear about the meaning of their ethnicity or dissatisfied with their group membership" (Phinney, 2005b, p. 190).

American research based on this model finds that the meaning and strength of ethnic identity differs among ethnic groups, with African Americans having the strongest ethnic identities, presumably in response to the stronger negative stereotypes and discrimination they can face daily. Asians and Latinos also have strong ethnic identities, but are less likely than African Americans to move developmentally through the three stages. European Americans have the least salience and overt commitment, even those living in diverse communities and attending mixed schools (Phinney, 2005a).

This approach to studying ethnic identity is widely accepted in adolescent psychology, largely ignored in sociological approaches, and rejected by postmodernists in ways examined in the preceding chapter (Rattansi & Phoenix, 2005). Phinney responded to the postmodernist critique by emphasizing that Rattansi and Phoenix conflate sociological and psychological aspects of ethnic identity:

> Ethnicity, although fluid and changing, is meaningful and useful as a psychological construct.... The existence of identifiable ethnic patterns at the group level is not inconsistent with the reality of individual differences within groups in the ways adolescents understand and experience their ethnicity.
>
> (Phinney, 2005b, p. 189)

Phinney also argues that

> Rattansi and Phoenix overstated the difficulty of maintaining an ethnic identity over time and place. The *evidence* indicates that an ethnic identity, although dynamic and influenced by the historical and social contexts, can provide for ethnic group members, to varying degrees, a stable "core" sense of belonging that is a central aspect of the self.
>
> (Phinney, 2005b, p. 193, emphasis added)

In responding to Phinney's defense of her approach, Rattansi and Phoenix dismiss these empirical findings as "somewhat essentialist" (Phoenix & Rattansi, 2005, p. 220). In doing so, and by failing to examine the specific merits of the empirical research, they exhibit a fixation on an anti-realist, nominalist approach.

Unfortunately, this rare exchange across the epistemological divide does not appear to have accomplished much rapprochement between developmentalists and postmodernists with respect to how to understand and study ethnic identity (or other forms of identity). For instance, Phoenix (2010) has since gone on to reiterate the same critique, asserting that Phinney's conclusion (concerning the empirical findings that proactive ethnic-identity formation is associated with a more positive psychological profile) is "somewhat essentialist in imposing notions of what ought to be the case on identities that demonstrably have been in flux over the last 50 years" (Phoenix, 2010, p. 300). Again, we find the same conflation of identity processes and contents, or in other words, psychological and social levels of identity, and the insistence that identity politics must underlay the study of identity.

Phinney's rebuttal of Rattansi and Phoenix (2005) is suggested as a further reading at the end of this chapter to allow readers to gain a firmer grasp of the issues dividing identity researchers—issues preventing the type of rapprochement that might advance this area of study.

Gender

Considerable research attention has been given to identity formation among young women, looking for contrasts with the experiences of young men. Although there was a certain amount of confusion in the 1970s in terms of how to characterize gender differences in agency-based identity formation (Marcia, 1993; Marcia et al., 1993), the general consensus is now that there are no significant differences among contemporary Western females and males in terms of psychological processes (ego identity formation) or timing of these processes (e.g., Sorell & Montgomery, 2001). This may be due to significant improvements in the opportunities available to women in Western countries over the past few decades, or it may be that the initial research was inadequate to the task of assessing gender differences.

In addition, differences have been identified in terms of several specific "domains" or *content* areas of identity issues. Archer (1993) concluded that females experience more proactive identity formation in resolving identity issues pertaining to family/career plans (cf. Archer, 1989), sexual experiences (cf. Waterman & Nevid, 1977), and personal friendships (cf. Thorbecke & Grotevant, 1982). However, the body of empirical research shows no reliable differences in other domains such as occupational and religious identities. In other words, more females appear to be exploring issues related to certain interpersonal concerns, thereby increasing the scope of their identity explorations. Conversely, females and males do not differ in the ways in which these identity explorations are processed psychologically at the level of ego identity (cf. Waterman, 1992).

Social class

In contrast to ethnicity and gender, the agency-based identity literature has been starkly inattentive to social class, a common limitation of the Eriksonian literature, which is principally rooted in psychology. Psychology-based models for conceptualizing the effects of economic disadvantage on identity formation appear to be limited by several discipline-based factors. For example, much of this research is based on convenience samples of secondary and post-secondary students, biasing the samples toward more affluent youth, and effectively eliminating socially excluded and poor youth from study. Research in general psychology tends to be based on large-scale samples of young people in schools (mainly because of the ease of access), governed by the assumption that psychological processes are generally universal, varying only by degree in different social contexts and among different segments of the population. Disadvantages among youth tend to be viewed in terms of the psychological disadvantages some have, especially in terms of emotional (e.g., depression and anxiety) and health (e.g., eating disorders, risk-taking) issues.

In contrast, sociological research has a long history of targeting social-class differences in material resources and social-status benefits (e.g., Hollingshead's,

1949, seminal study *Elmtown's Youth: The Impact of Social Class on Adolescents*), and this "face" of youth studies has a long-standing interest in "the transmission of advantage and disadvantage across generations" (Furlong, 2013, p. 8). This concern has prompted the focus of sociologists on socially excluded (marginalized) and working-class youth more so than youth from other class segments (MacDonald, 2011; Roberts, 2011).

Although there has been recognition of this lacuna in adolescent psychology research (e.g., Lerner & Steinberg, 2009), there is yet to be a systematic examination of the effects of social class on identity formation, perhaps because much of this research comes from the United States, where there are widespread beliefs in a "classless society." In one of the few statements touching on this assumption, it was concluded that "empirical support for...lowered expectations for identity achievement among minority group members has been mixed" (Rotheram-Borus & Wyche, 1994, p. 67).

Several psychology-based models have been proposed to rectify this gap in the literature. For instance, Phillips and Pittman (2003) proposed a model that identifies the types of "identity work" that economically disadvantaged adolescents might undertake in coping with disparaging self-relevant information, limited opportunities, and chronic exposure to high levels of stress and negative life events. This model predicts that those who are unsuccessful in overcoming these problems may avoid or prematurely end agency-based identity explorations, thereby increasing their risk for future failures and underachievement.

Similarly, Yoder (2000) developed a model with which to understand how structural barriers to identity formation could be conceptualized. Like Rattansi and Phoenix (2005), she argued that most models of identity formation adopt a static view of the environments in which identity exploration might take place. She further argued that these models tend to assume that social structure is clearly defined for all adolescents, that there are few physical or economic limitations confronting them, and that all adolescents understand the work and life options ostensibly available to them. Yoder proposed a model in which the barriers to agency-based identity explorations and commitments are absent, present, or have been overcome. Unfortunately, no empirical research has been reported based on this model.

Perhaps because there are few studies to confirm assumptions that social-class disadvantages produce different identity-formation processes, the "default" assumption among identity researchers is that identity formation among the disadvantaged is hampered by forms of discrimination and underprivilege that create difficulties in the transition to adulthood (e.g., in the United States and Canada it is assumed by default that everyone who is not middle class or above will encounter special and/or more severe problems).

Aries and Seider (2007) put some of these assumptions to an empirical test in a mixed-methods study of American college students, comparing lower-income students with affluent students. They found that the affluent students were more conscious of the structural advantages they had for their (higher) future prospects, while lower-income students developed ways of ratio-nalizing and minimizing threats to their sense of self-worth associated with their economic disadvantages. Additionally, using the identity status approach, lower-income students attending an élite college were found to have engaged in more proactive identity explorations than both lower-income students attend-ing a State college and affluent students attending the same élite school. Their explanation for this finding was that these lower-income students' sense of contrast with affluent students was more salient because they faced it on a daily basis. This study is included as a recommended reading at the end of this chapter (among other things, note how the authors overcame the difficulties in quantifying "social class").

At the same time, there is some evidence that young adults from less affluent backgrounds "grow up" faster in terms of subjectively feeling like an adult as well as being treated like one, and integrating into an adult community. The key factor appears to be the extent to which parents are willing to finance a pro-longed transition for their children (cf. Hamilton, 2013). When young adults (especially males) must pay their own way through higher education, they appear to resolve identity issues in the transition to adulthood more quickly (Côté, 2002, 2006b).

When we turn to the more general empirical literature on specific facets of self-identity formation, we find a more extensive literature that suggests lower socio-economic status (SES, typically based on father's education and income) has a negative relationship with attributes such as self-esteem that strengthens from adolescence into adulthood. Self-esteem is thought to suffer because the implications of socio-economic disadvantages become more apparent to peo-ple as they experience the realities of adulthood. Studies find even stronger effects when they look more closely at how the daily experiences of lower SES affect young people's self-esteem (e.g., whether they are on welfare, have an unemployed father, the condition of the neighborhood; Wiltfang & Scarbecz, 1990).

More general sociological studies have reported that social class can have "hidden injuries" (Sennett & Cobb, 1972) because unlike other stigmatized groups, the blame is more often placed on the individual than the group (e.g., an ethnic group), so lower-social-class members have fewer avenues for establishing mutual solace with other group members in a way that peo-ple from stigmatized ethnic groups can. For example, as Phinney's research shows, ethnic group membership can be protective when it is construed as a source of pride, so the sense of self can be associated with the group's positive aspects.

Lower-social-class membership apparently does not have this self-protective feature in societies where citizens predominately believe they are "classless," as is the case in many Western societies. Indeed, studies find that poor adolescents tend to internalize blame for their economic circumstances more so than others blame them (McLoyd et al., 2009). Young people from lower-social-class back-grounds have also been found to be highly cynical of their future opportunities and meritocratic aspects of the opportunity structures of their society, and have lower educational and occupational aspirations as a result, believing that effort and ability will not be duly rewarded (McLoyd et al., 2009). This should not be surprising because, as we saw in Chapters 4 and 6, lower-income parents also tend to be less encouraging of academic and occupational achievement in their offspring (Lareau, 2011; Schunk & Meece, 2006).

Minority-status youth

Social identities are also affected by a number of ontogenetic factors that inter-act with social contexts, such as disabilities, "other abilities" (e.g., deafness), and "other sexualities" (e.g., LGBT). Unfortunately, the vast majority of the agency-based identity literature has been directed at "normative" samples, especially from regular school systems, as noted above. The default hypoth-esis would be that young people with special needs (e.g., physical, mental, or learning disabilities), and family-origin issues (e.g., adoption), or stigmatized sexualities, would face challenges with respect to proactive types of identity formation, but that the underlying psychological (ego/self) processes would be effectively the same. Given that so many young people in normative sam-ples experience difficulties with less severe challenges and obstacles, those with special needs and circumstances would understandably be less active in their identity formation, possibly internalizing the stereotypes about themselves. Unfortunately, systematic studies of this assumption have yet to be published.

Again, though, as with other social identity categories, there are so many types of minority youth, and so much possible variation of needs within each type, that generalizations about the effects of "minority status" are difficult to make (e.g., Most, Wiesel, & Blitzer, 2007). This is perhaps one reason why there has been little published concerning the agency-based identity formation of youth with special needs or special minority statuses, including Deaf youth (Small, Cripps, & Côté, 2012).

The empirical literature is in fact sparse, even among specific types of special needs and circumstances, but the relationships are not always consistent or as one would expect. For instance, a major longitudinal study of adopted ado-lescents found no differences in identity formation (or self-concept formation) in relation to a comparison sample of non-adoptees (Stein & Hoopes, 1985). Similarly, some researchers suggest that all minority youths can develop posi-tive identities similar to those postulated by Phinney's ethnic identity formation model. In some cases, what is normatively defined as a disability can be con-structed differently to see it as a positive resource for developmental benefits (Hauser-Cram, Wyngaarden Krauss, & Kersh, 2009; Most, Wiesel, & Blitzer, 2007; Small, Cripps, & Côté, 2012).[3] The same logic applies to young people who experience a stigma because of a social identity ascribed to, or chosen by, them, including LGBT (or LGBT2Q) youth. After reviewing various models of sexual identity formation, Savin-Williams (2011) drew a similar conclusion regarding the same underlying mental processes in conjunction with different constructed contents, as follows:

> any presumption that teens have more in common with others of their sexual orientation than with their peers in general simply because of that orientation is questionable and perhaps implausible.... [T]o understand the development of sexual identity among same-sex-oriented teenagers, scientists must first understand the development of personal identity in general. A critical aspect of this understanding is the recognition that sexual diversity is becoming normalized among current cohorts of youth. Same-sex-oriented adolescents have the same developmental concerns, assets, and liabilities as do other-sex-oriented adolescents. (p. 686)

Conclusion: Youth and adulthood as roles and identities

This chapter examined the (often implicit) structural aspects of the youth period, that are independent or, or additive to, other structural factors associated with social class, gender, ethnicity, and minority statuses. The operant proposition in this examination is that the destructuring in post-traditional societies can make the youth period itself a structural obstacle because of the ambiguities associated with the individualization process. At the same time, this destructuring can open the way for forms of agency-based identity formation that can mitigate these other structural barriers. Within each structural category, we looked at evidence of a convergence of young people's life experiences with different social identities, especially in terms of their social-identity formation during the youth period.

In many ways, youth has become an identity in itself as the period of transition to adulthood has expanded in Western societies, coincident with youth becoming a prolonged period of identity formation for the myriad roles and statuses that people can assume. The convergence of experiences associated with youth as an identity was illustrated in objective terms in the case of the paralleling decline in earning power of young American men and women, supporting the political economy position that youth has taken on class-like characteristics.

In more subjective terms, young people can experience ethnic-, gender-, class-, and minority-identity formation as psychosocial tasks, with a variety of outcomes depending on the degree and types of agency exercised by the person. The individual differences in these forms of social-identity development were examined in terms of the methodologies that investigate conditions that make those identities more salient and therefore the object of more reflection and exploration (agency). These types of identity formation have been the object of study in adolescent psychology for decades but have been almost entirely ignored in the other youth-studies approaches, which tend to downplay individual differences in the subjective experiences of different types of social identity and therefore miss these within- and between-age variations of the youth period.

Recommended readings

Michael Apted (Director) (1964–2013) *The Up Series (DVDs)*, Retrieved from http://en.wikipedia.org/wiki/Up_Series
   This British documentary series follows a group of working-class children along with a roughly matched group of upper-class children from age seven in 1964, re-filming every seven years since, with the most recent release in 2013 when the participants were in their fifties. Although not pretending to be scientifically systematic, there are myriad insights to be gained from viewing any of the eight episodes, including instances where social-class destinations do not turn out the way one would predict when personal agency is included in the equation.
Elizabeth Aries & Maynard Seider (2007). The role of social class in the formation of identity: A study of public and elite private college students. *The Journal of Social Psychology*, 147, 137–57.
   This article reports a mixed-method study of differences in identity formation at two American universities, one of which is highly selective and one of which is a mass institution with lower admission standards. Affluent students in the more selective school were the most "class conscious" while lower-income students in the more selective school undertook the most identity explorations. In both schools, lower-income students developed rationalizations for accepting differences in class origins in face of their higher-educational opportunities.
James Côté (1996). Sociological perspectives on identity formation: The culture-identity link and identity capital. *Journal of Adolescence*, 19, 417–28.
   This article places identity formation in a broad socio-cultural context, tracing changes from pre- to late-modernity, and sets out a number of propositions concerning identity formation in late-modern societies.
Jean Phinney (2005). Ethnic identity in late modern times: A response to Rattansi and Phoenix. *Identity: An International Journal of Theory and Research*, 5, 187–94.
   This article presents Phinney's response to the postmodernist critique of the Eriksonian model of ethnic identity formation.

Youth Politics: Engaged/Alternative or Disengaged/Resistant

11

A great deal of attention has been devoted to various issues concerning young people's active political engagements as well as reactive behavior patterns. Active political engagements refer to conscious, direct, formal involvements in the country's political structures (e.g., voting, actively promoting causes) and/or intentions to contribute to social change in some way, even if outside mainstream structures (e.g., protests). In contrast, reactive behavior patterns represent disengagement from, or resistance to, the "system" in some way. These patterns are not necessarily consciously intended (cf. Raby, 2005).

Varying positions in youth studies with respect to these two sets of behaviors have been slowly congealing. However, in contrast to many other areas, it is difficult to identify specific camps that are sharply in contrast to other factions. Instead, publications in the field tend to represent individual efforts to make sense of the situation in the absence of sufficient evidence or in terms of offering "better" interpretations of evidence (cf. Kimberlee, 2002). Other efforts have emerged out of the conservative nominalist paradigm identified in Chapter 1, which examine micro-level behaviors and subjectivities but often do not put those phenomena in wider theoretical or macro contexts, limiting their contributions to the field.

With respect to political engagements, the debate can be discussed in terms of the contrast between a new "techno-politics" and an old formal politics:

- On the one hand, there are numerous claims that the young have found new types of informal political expression through the Internet and the new information and communication technologies (ICTs), and many of these involvements are individualized (i.e., take a "cafeteria" approach of picking and choosing various single issues on the basis of personal preference).
- On the other hand, concerns have been expressed that in many countries the majority of the young are emotionally and cognitively disengaged from older, formal politics. It is argued that this is to their detriment because politicians will not attend to their interests as long as they do not constitute a voting bloc; and it is to the detriment of democracies because power is given up to the élites to the extent that the youth voting bloc is not mobilized (e.g., Milner, 2010).

In reference to reactive patterns, the debate seems to have been taken up between those advocating "youth resistance" and those cautioning about mass conformity among young people that passes for resistance. As noted above, it is common for youth-studies researchers to valorize "youth resistance," but critics point out that some resistance may simply be mass conformity in most cases or "bad behavior" in other cases. As we saw in the youth culture chapter, the mass conformity arguments take the position that some individualized forms of lifestyle "rebellion" are not a threat to the capitalist system, but instead are integral parts of it, providing marketers with ideas about what "cool" products to market to disaffected and identity-seeking young people. At the same time, some observers caution that "bad behavior" is mainly a nuisance to the young person and those in his or her immediate social environment, and not even a remote threat to the economic system as a whole.

Perhaps because of the embryonic nature of the evidence in this field, unlike other disagreements and debates examined in this book, a major dividing line in the area of "youth politics" tends to be drawn between value-priority stances, and not on ontological grounds. As we see, those who take an advocacy approach set their claims against other value-priority stances, especially against those who take a critical emancipation approach, but also against the two social control approaches.

White, Wyn, and Albanese (2011) explicitly draw out this value-priority divide, reiterating their earlier work (e.g., White, 2007), critiquing all of those who apparently take a position that young people might not "know their own minds" (p. 138). Although this critique is ostensibly directed at the media and policy-makers, there is a tone in their critique that it also applies to youth researchers who take positions that do not correspond to the "youth can do no wrong" advocacy position (identified in Table 1.2).

Although the advocacy position may be a noble one to take, and useful if it is supported by evidence and logic, in this case it sets an impossible standard that no one can meet, regardless of a person's age. Logically, no one can be fully aware of all political issues all of the time; we are all influenced to some degree by the larger forces that shape our consciousness regarding what is important; and, none of us is always right in everything we think or say. We have already seen, and revisit below, the strong case that is made that young people's tastes and values are targeted and manipulated by special interests—as are people of all age groups—so that it is very difficult for them, or anyone, to always "to know their minds."

Techno-politics vs. formal politics: Political participation

The "problem" under contention can be stated as follows:

- Researchers in countries such as the United States, the United Kingdom, and Canada have documented a progressive disengagement of the youth population from the formal political process in terms of both low levels of rudimentary knowledge of the political systems in their own countries and little involvement in basic political activities especially voting (e.g., Brooks & Hodkinson, 2008; Gidengil et al., 2003; Kimberlee, 2002; OECD, 2011). Two concerns can be identified about this political disengagement, which are related to the value-priority assumptions of the youth observer:

o Those who adopt a facilitation-guidance perspective worry that the lack of representation of youth issues in the political agenda is exacerbated by young people's lack of involvement. This would include the OECD, which notes in its 2011 report: "The higher participation of elderly people in national elections, as well as the growing share of older people as population ageing takes place, may also influence the political process, increasing the risk of electoral sanctions for governments introducing cuts to social programs that disproportionately benefit the elderly" (p. 96).

o In contrast, those who take a critical-emancipation perspective are concerned that young people have been manipulated to distance themselves from mainstream politics, leaving élites to pursue agendas that are harmful to the young and others (e.g., Côté & Allahar, 2006; Milner, 2010). This manipulation is seen as part of a larger manufacture of consent of disenfranchised groups in societies; however, if mobilized, these disenfranchised groups could use existing democratic measures to neutralize some of the excesses of the élites and support more socially just political reforms that correct for the worst practices of neoliberal capitalism (e.g., Heath & Potter, 2004).

• Other researchers point to the new technologies that can enable informal political involvements, especially more personal, local, and single-issue ones (e.g., Brooks & Hodkinson, 2008). This technologically mediated, alternative engagement appears to follow the principles of the more general individualization of the life course, by which people pick and choose from a variety of options in determining their values and commitments according to issues that are relevant to their own "life politics" (cf. Furlong & Cartmel, 2007).

o Many of those who explore these alternative involvements adopt an advocacy position, often being very defensive about the activities of the young and rather hostile toward those who believe that more young people need to be more formally engaged in mainstream politics for the reasons cited above (e.g., Vromen, 2003). An older variant of this position is that informal politics activities include lifestyles choices involving the green movement and dietary habits (e.g., organic food, vegan or vegetarian diets) and that these "personal statements" suffice as political actions (cf. Milner, 2010).

Unfortunately, as noted, investigations of this "problem" can take on an adversarial stance based on value-priority differences even before researchers go into the field, thereby reducing the critical quality of some research. Consequently, many research findings are determined by starting assumptions, which is a violation of the first rule of critical thinking. The present chapter concludes by suggesting a way of correcting this deficiency in the literature.

In the next section, we first consider the evidence and arguments in favor of the benefits of alternative political involvements, and in the following section turn to critiques of these positions based on concerns that these alternative involvements, in the absence of formal participation, can paradoxically place young people at an increased disadvantage in their societies.

Technologies, lifestyles, and the individualization of youth participation

As noted, this is a rather undeveloped area of study, with arguments varying widely, and few uniting framework emerging, other than an academic "silo" based on advocacy assumptions. There have been several attempts to bring researchers together with special issues in the *Journal of Youth Studies* in 2003 and 2008 (Brooks & Hodkinson, 2008), and several collections of essays (e.g., Buckingham & Willett, 2006; Dahlgren, 2007; Loader, 2007). The publications in this area provide useful examples of how informal politics are enabled by various technologies (e.g., Farthing, 2010; Juris & Pleyers, 2009; Vromen, 2003), showing there is little question that there are strong merits to the many positions put forth by the advocates of this side of the debate. By the same token, as with all areas of study, it is prudent not to over-extend arguments beyond their focus of convenience (see Chapter 1), and the enthusiasm for the perspectives adopted by many advocates can lead them to overestimate the validity of their own research or research confirming their views. For instance, Milner (2010) is critical of "Internet idealists" whose enthusiasm for the utility of the Internet appears premature, especially given the evidence that it is mainly those who are already interested in politics who will use the Internet for political engagement or will take advantage of the various initiatives that are undertaken by politicians and others to reach young people through the Internet.

Brooks and Hodkinson (2008) and Livingstone (2008) wrote "bookend" articles in the 2008 special issue of the *Journal of Youth Studies*, providing useful contexts within which to understand this literature. For example, Brooks and Hodkinson note that some of the enthusiasm during the 1990s for the revolutionary potential of "new media" has been muted as the complexities of the situation have become more apparent, particularly the appropriation of these media by dominant interests for a variety of purposes, which ranges from monetization to surveillance. Facebook is an excellent example of both monetization and surveillance, including providing people with opportunities for "click-on activism" and forming various political action groups (cf. Lanier, 2010).

In a similar vein, the content of the Internet is now so vast that many people, younger and older alike, tend to "cocoon" themselves as a defense against information-overload and to maintain close in-group ties (cf. Bauerlein, 2008; cf. Lanier's, 2010, concept of the "hive mind"). A consequence of this can be a narrowing, rather than a broadening, influence of the Internet.

And, it is more entertaining to simply get political news filtered by the various old and new media that spoof politics (e.g., *The Onion*; http://www.theonion.com) or the TV shows of American political satirists (currently the comedians Jon Stewart and Stephen Colbert are very popular). Unfortunately, as informative as these sources may be, they tend to reinforce the idea that formal politics are "uncool" and these sources therefore tend to feed a sense of "righteous disengagement." Although there is much to be cynical about in terms of how the present political process is constituted in many parts of the world, this disengagement can push the young to move further from the centers of political and economic power; as we see below, political disengagement may be exactly what the élites want.

From their appraisal of these types of influences, Brooks and Hodkinson (2008) conclude the following:

> For these and other reasons, the somewhat idealistic predictions of the 1990s have largely been replaced by more cautious and less deterministic approaches to the role of new media in relation to young people's political engagement. Nevertheless, there remains extensive interest among academics, policy makers and other practitioners both in the general implications of different forms of new communication technologies for young people's levels of political engagement and in the kinds of interventions which might be made in order to maximise any possible opportunities to garner such engagement. (p. 476)

Indeed, with respect to Brooks and Hodkinson's last point, some politicians have been looking for ways of using the new technologies to engage young people in formal politics in the United States and the United Kingdom, although these experiments have not been as successful as politicians would like (Livingstone, 2008). Conversely, politicians in other, non-democratic countries have been trying to find ways to nullify the potential of these technologies to foment dissent and rebellion, but often do so with limited success (Hammelman & Messard, 2011). Political consumerism via these technologies can also include outcomes that many academic advocates would not endorse. These outcomes include supporting neoliberal, or even extreme Right-wing and racist causes, rather than progressive reforms (Livingstone, 2008).

Commenting on the role of social media in the "Arab Spring" in Egypt, especially in January 2011, Hammelman and Messard (2011) document the role played by these new technologies, but also note that it is important to recognize the role of more traditional forms of political organizing, along with the importance of the interplay between these two forms of engagement. In addition, they "caution against overemphasizing the effect of social media tools" and note "the tendency of some journalists and others to overlook months and years of labor, campus and political organizing in favor of an overly simple 'Facebook' explanation for Egypt's profound social movement" (p. 21). One issue that is played down by techno-advocates is that only a minority of people in many countries, including Egypt, has access to computers and the Internet, or mobile phones, especially "smart phones." It is thus important not to underestimate the role of "old technologies" such as television, including the role played by news outlets such as Al Jazeera is providing real-time coverage of events to the entire population (it is telling that the Egyptian government closed the local Al Jazeera office for a period and arrested some of its journalists).

Finally, Brooks and Hodkinson (2008) note that many academics are investigating ways in which new forms of political expression may be emerging in Western countries through the use of some new technologies. These emergent movements tend to be decentralized and non-hierarchical, mixing lifestyles, personal beliefs, and cultural values and affiliations (cf. Juris & Pleyers, 2009). The claim is that applications of the technologies are potentially limitless, ranging "from regularly reading the website of an environmental pressure group, to campaigning on discussion groups to keep a local music venue open, to joining a Facebook group campaigning on eating disorders, to the ideologically motivated sharing of one's music and video files on peer-to-peer sites" (Brooks & Hodkinson, 2008, p. 477).

Unfortunately, as Livingstone (2008) notes, because many of these studies are qualitative, there is no way to know how extensive the new forms of political consciousness are among the youth population (in terms of depth and breadth). The line also becomes blurred with respect to whether the activity involves informal politics or is a manifestation of youth culture that has more to do with personal lifestyles than political engagements. Although some researchers would argue that these are now often the same thing (e.g., Farthing, 2010), as Juris and Pleyers (2009) argue, certain informal actions are politically "imaginary" when they have no effect on "underlying structural contradictions" (p. 59).

Distractions, manipulations, and the political economy of youth participation

Whatever transformations may be underway in how people informally express their political engagement, with respect to formal participation, the extent of disengagement is greater in some countries than others. Brooks and Hodkinson (2008) note in their review of the literature that "concern about youth disengagement is driving public debate in countries as far apart as Canada, Germany and Australia" (p. 473). In this context, the OECD (2011) monitors voting patterns of the electorate in its member countries, producing very helpful statistical information that puts this debate in context, including the fact that there is not a youth–adult difference of formal participation in some countries:

- overall voter turnout (i.e., all age groups) varies greatly, ranging from less than 50 per cent (Korea) to over 90 per cent (Australia), with an OECD average of 70 per cent;
- overall voter turnout has declined generally in most countries since the 1980s, with an OECD average decline of 11 per cent;
- those with more education are more likely to vote, with an average difference of eight percentage points between those with a university education and those without a secondary education; and
- older people (55 and older) are more likely to vote than younger people (16 to 35) by 12 per cent, with wide fluctuations by country (e.g., a 38% difference in the United Kingdom vs. near equity in Australia).

If we take Canada as a representative country where there is a youth–adult discrepancy in voter turnout, we can gain an idea of what might be behind those cases where there is a decreased involvement of the youth segment in the "old" polity.

Elections Canada (2012a) reported a decline in overall Canadian voter turnout since 1980, dropping from an average of about 75 per cent dating back to the 1940s to about 60 per cent in 2011. This decline appears to be due mainly to the lower participation of young Canadians aged 18–24 (Elections Canada, 2012b), with only about 40 per cent voting in the four federal elections held between 2004 and 2011 (compared to over 70% of those 55 and older).

Based on data that decomposes turnout by age, Adsett (2003) also found that this pattern of lower youth voter turnout began in the 1980s, which she observed coincides with "the emergence of neoliberalism and globalization, which have narrowed the political conversation" (pp. 248–9). She noted that historically, before 1984, "there were few clear and consistent age-specific patterns in the turnout rates and the spread between the rates by age group was relatively small (i.e., life cycle effects were relatively weak)" (p. 251).

Adsett argues that since the 1980s a life cycle effect has set in, with indications that younger cohorts of Canadians will be less likely to vote even as they get older (see also, Human Resources Development Canada, 2003). To explain this, she identified a period effect—neoliberalism—that has altered young Canadian's relationship with the State:

With the emergence of neo-liberalism, the Canadian state has reduced if not retracted its support to Canadian youth in their transition to adulthood (e.g., post-secondary education, unemployment insurance and housing) in its dismantling of the welfare state. In addition, it has given a low priority to the types of programs and initiatives that have traditionally concerned Western youth (e.g., equality, and individual and human rights).

(Adsett, 2003, pp. 261–2)

Canadian research is consistent with the OECD (2011) data that age and education are the strongest predictors of voting, and that those with university educations are more likely to vote regardless of age (Gidengil et al., 2003). This research also finds that while many young people are disaffected with party politics, this cynicism is equally spread across age groups. Instead, the primary reasons for lower voter turnout include low levels of political interest and knowledge; thus, the research suggests that younger Canadians are more likely to be "tuned out" of formal politics, rather than "turned off." This research also seems to apply to "old-school" alternative and activist political behaviors. Young Canadians are not more likely to be involved in activist initiatives, such as environmentalism: the middle-aged are more likely to be activists, and young Canadian activists are more likely to be engaged in conventional party politics (Elections Canada, 2012b; Gidengil et al., 2003). Specific (marginalized) subgroups of youth have also been identified as less likely to vote, which include "Aboriginal youth, ethnocultural youth, youth in rural areas, youth with disabilities and unemployed youth not in school" (Elections Canada, 2012b, p. 1).

Although this examination of within-country variation in formal political engagement seems clear, at least in the case of Canada, explanations for between-country variations are not so clear. The OECD (2011) estimates for the lowest age-group differences in voting behaviors tend to be in countries that have social-democratic political systems (vs. liberal democratic ones[1]). For instance, in Sweden, the OECD estimates only a 2.6 per cent difference between those aged 16 to 35 and those 55 years and older, with about 80 per cent of both age groups voting, a 9 per cent decline for all groups since 1980.

Compared to Canada and other similar liberal-democratic countries, Sweden has a more progressive system of political socialization, including political socialization in schools (e.g., Côté & Allahar, 1996, 2006). Milner (2010) describes the various program initiatives in Swedish, which include "Time for Democracy," a program that targets young people and ethnic minorities who might be disaffected with the formal political system. Sweden's efforts to maintain a high level of literacy and engagement appear to have been highly effective. For example, 70 per cent of 16–24-year-old Swedes regularly discuss politics, compared to only about 40 per cent of young Canadians who follow any politics at all (O'Neill, 2003). Formal politics thus seems to be more a part of the daily lives of most young Swedes: surveys show that 70–80 per cent would wear a badge to express a political opinion; 60 per cent are or would be a member of a political party; and 80 per cent have or would contact a politician over an issue (Swedish Institute, 1993; Swedish National Board for Youth Affairs, 1999a). The Swedish educational system also appears to nurture greater political knowledge. One international survey of world knowledge found that young Swedes (18–24 years old) scored highest of the nine nations included in the study, answering three quarters of the questions correctly whereas young Canadians (and Americans) could not correctly answer even half of the questions (National Geographic Education Foundation, 2002). We return to the political situation in Sweden in the concluding section of this chapter.

Another contrast sheds some useful light on this debate. Although many observers focus on the age differences in voter turnout, even for lower-turnout countries such as Canada, consider the following internal contrast: 40 per cent of younger people *do* exercise their voting franchise, but also 40 per cent of older people *do not* exercise it. Accordingly, it is important not to exaggerate the situation as an either–or situation in comparing younger and older voters. Instead, the first question to ask should be why a citizen *of any age* would not vote, and then a follow-up question would be why age is now a factor. This approach leads to an analysis of the reasons for political disengagement (alienation) in general and specifically in terms of age differences. In other words, why would so many people in specific modern democracies, which took centuries of class-, race-, and gender-struggles to develop, be so *tuned out* (as above) of formal politics—ignoring political events and not developing a rudimentary knowledge of the political system governing them. The political-economy perspective offers some possible answers to these questions.

As noted in Chapter 2, political economists argue that the roots, characteristics, and maintenance of social structures lie in objective conditions produced by the distribution of power, particularly economic and political power. It is further argued that in contemporary neoliberal societies, young people have increasingly become a disenfranchised "class" without significant economic, political, or social power. Political economists look to ways in which young people are induced into a state of false consciousness to mask this as part of a manufacture of consent so that they accept practices and beliefs that work directly against their own interests (Herman & Chomsky, 1988).

A primary assumption of the political-economy view is that in the more laissez-faire capitalist societies the consent manufacturing efforts are directed at creating a widespread state of *false consciousness*. The intention of these efforts is to persuade the citizenry (of all ages) to accept and support arrangements that work directly against their own interests, but in the favor of certain élites. This citizenry constitutes the non-wealthy wage earners and salaried employees, as well as their families. In particular, these consent-manufacturing processes engender in workers an alienation from themselves as agentic, creative individuals, and an acceptance of that state of alienation as normal and inevitable. It is argued by political economists that these processes begin in childhood, with children, adolescents, and youths taught to believe that

- their society in general is benign;
- the capitalist economy functions in their interests and is the best of all possible economic systems;
- the educational system is based on merit and it will lead to a rewarding job if they behave themselves and work hard in school;

- they will be duly rewarded if they work hard and conform to the dictates of workplace; and
- they will be happy if they adopt a conventional, consumption-based life style, especially with an "individualistic flair."

If all of these things are believed, people will also accept the assumption that if something bad happens to them or to one of their peers, the fault lies with the person, not the economic system. If this form of consent is successfully manufactured by the current capitalist élites, the citizenry will give a resounding endorsement to individualism within the context of laissez-faire capitalism, where structural explanations for individual successes and failures are dismissed and people are given individual praise or blame for what happens to them (cf. Furlong & Cartmel's, 2007, epistemological fallacy).

In this context, the lower levels of involvement of the general population in countries such as Canada are of general concern because those who do not exercise their franchise tend to come from groups that have been disenfranchised economically (Milner, 2010). Consequently, they rightly feel the political system does not work in their interests, and thus do not believe there is much point in voting. The OECD recognizes this issue with the following statement: "While low voter turnout might reflect satisfaction in the country's management, it also implies that the political system reflects the will of a limited number of citizens" (OECD, 2011, p. 96).

Yet, while the economically disadvantaged are correct that the dominant interests in society will generally not act in their interests, because they do not vote, the dominant interests are not held accountable for the policies that undermine the material conditions of the disadvantaged. Moreover, were the various disadvantaged groups to mobilize their vote, they could collectively have a dramatic effect on policies in countries that have (hard-fought-for) formal democratic political apparatuses. They could do so directly through their own representatives and indirectly by making individual political candidates answerable to them as a constituency. The struggles for political freedoms in the so-called Arab Spring attest to the importance placed on the political freedoms for those who do not have them, and their willingness to die for those freedoms, as did previous generations in Western countries (cf. Hammelman & Messard, 2011).

Young people constitute one such disadvantaged group, but given their proportion of the voting-age population (some 20% of prospective voters are between ages 18 and 30 in many countries; e.g., Lee, 2010), should they collectively mobilize their vote, would constitute a potentially formidable segment of the population, as in the 2008 U.S. election of President Obama. It is for this very reason that dominant interests would want to create and maintain a situation where the majority of young people are politically disinterested ("tuned out," as above) and thus do not exercise their voting franchise or mobilize in any concerted manner.

The low level of political engagement of the electorate in general in many countries is thus particularly concerning from a political-economy perspective.

Regardless of how effective the individualized, single-issue political activities of people of any age might be, on the issue of withdrawal from formal participation, there is a special concern about the present and future health of democratic societies from a social justice point of view (Milner, 2010). In fact, individualized political orientations can be in the interests of political and economic élites to the extent that they keep the focus off capitalist exploitation and the control of capitalists of the political economy. In the current era of neoliberalism, which began in the 1980s—the point at which many young voters began to tune out—it is especially important for élites to maintain their control of the political agenda because neoliberal principles strip away the social welfare entitlements that were put into place in many countries after the Second World War to prevent the types of mass destitution that characterized the Great Depression of the 1930s.

Indeed, Steger and Roy (2010) argue that neoliberalism entered its "first phase" in the 1980s as a reaction against the "egalitarian liberalism" that represented "the golden age of controlled capitalism" of the post-World War II period, the longest economic boom in the history of capitalism (Hayes, 2002, p. 148; Steger & Roy, 2010, p. 7). This economic boom was based in part on government regulation of business and industry, and a high level of taxation of wealthy individuals and corporations, along with a redistribution of that wealth to provide widespread welfare entitlements. This period was a reaction to the excesses of unregulated capitalism that led to the Great Depression. This redistributed wealth helped create the large "middle class" for which the twentieth century is noted. It also provided widespread economic benefits for workers and helped build the transportation and communication as well as educational and health-care infrastructures that benefited everyone. At the time of writing, in the aftermath of the Great Recession, the lessons from the Great Depression seem clear, but are falling on many deaf ears (cf. Wilkinson & Pickett, 2010).

However, this redistribution of wealth in the post-World War II period threatened the control of the economic élites, both in terms of accumulation of capital and the use of that capital to maintain positions of extreme power. After several decades of fighting egalitarian liberalism, gains were finally made in the 1980s in taking back control of the political agenda, especially in the United States and the United Kingdom through the regimes of Reagan and Thatcher, respectively. In so doing, the shift began where governments became less concerned with "pursuing the public good ... by enhancing civil society and social justice" and more concerned with business principles (Steger & Roy, 2010, p. 12). Among other things, these principles include redefining "citizens as 'customers' or 'clients'" at the same time that public institutions, including universities, were forced to become entrepreneurial by cutting "waste," ostensibly to become more efficient, effective, and accountable.

Many of these cutbacks have severely affected the current living conditions of young people, as well as their future prospects, on matters ranging from minimum wage levels to post-secondary tuition fees. For this reason, it is very much in the interests of economic élites both to "cover their tracks" concerning how they brought about these cutbacks and to normalize the situation so young people accept their diminished circumstances as justified and inevitable. A variety of means are at the disposal of the élites, especially consent-manufacturing influences like the media and education systems. Other influences merely have to be complementary to their interests, like the pleasurable distractions that put the focus of people's consciousness away from the machinations of the élites (cf. Lanier's, 2010, warnings of the "hive mind" of the Internet).

In the case of the "pleasurable distractions" of ICTs, although these technologies have numerous benefits, including political ones, these technologies can constitute distractions for some people that are complementary to the interests of those in power, as in the cocooning effect noted above. At the same time, while the fervent pursuit of single-issue politics—whether technologically mediated or not—may address issues that are important in themselves, if not accompanied by knowledge of the "big picture," these forms of political pursuits can misidentify "the enemy," distracting people away from the real source of their problems. When people are distracted through misdirection about important political issues, not only will they not address the exploitive aspects of capital accumulation in neoliberal countries, but they might also identify the wrong cause and in doing so engage in fighting with people who would otherwise be fighting for the same cause.

When this misdirection is successful, dominant interests benefit from the age-old "divide-and-conquer" strategy, even if they did not orchestrate it. And as we saw in Chapter 5, for the political economist, the major "story" with regard to youth transitions has been covered up or re-interpreted in various ways. Consequently, addressing the age-based redistribution of wealth associated with current forms of capital accumulation is not part of the public agenda in many countries, except to the extent that it reached more affluent youth as a result of the Great Recession interfering with their university-to-career plans. But, as we saw above, this age-based redistribution of wealth began in the 1980s, affecting less affluent youth from the beginning. Its cover-up has been accomplished in part by a manufacture of consent that has "normalized" the disadvantages of the youth segment in many countries, especially liberal-democratic ones that have been given over to neoliberal principles: low wages for young workers, a lower than minimum wage in some youth-dominated jobs, fewer social and health benefits, and the introduction of, or increase in, post-secondary tuition fees.

Resistance vs. mass conformity

As noted in several chapters, youth "resistance" to the status quo has been heralded from an advocacy position by a number of sociologists dating back to early days of the CCCS and more recently by postmodernists (e.g., Raby, 2005). Unfortunately, it is often difficult to define "resistance" and distinguish it from "bad behavior" and various forms of deviance, in part because of incomplete definitions of the "status quo" and a misidentification of "the enemy" as in the case of some alternative, individualized political protest, as described in the previous section.

Because the general concept of "resistance" was examined and critiqued in the youth culture chapter, in this section, we will briefly examine the more specific concept of political resistance, defining it literally as one would identify a political resistance or underground movement in wartime (e.g., the French Resistance of World War II). Placed in this real-world context of clashing material and ideological interests, there does not appear to be a political revolution on the horizon in the West that would eradicate the problems facing contemporary youth that stem from their exploitation under neoliberal conditions. The situation in some places has been explosive, though, but it is still not clear what long-term changes have resulted from youth street-protests. In the recent past, youth political resistance has been evident in various parts of the world, gaining considerable media attention, with young people taking to the streets in often violent conflicts with authorities, notably in northern Africa with the so-called Arab Spring (Hammelman & Messard, 2011), in Europe (among immigrant youth in England and France), and in Québec among university students protesting against tuition increases (Weinstock, 2012).

On the one hand, neoliberal economies provide many people with abundant material rewards, including cheap consumer items and technological gadgets, making it unlikely that they would support a revolutionary movement that threatens those rewards. On the other hand, many of those who are not rewarded in these economies have been so mystified by consent-manufacturing enterprises that they would not know what to fight for or whom to fight against. These mystification enterprises help explain why the signs of political dissent we are now witnessing among many young people seem to be simply individualist forms of conformity to an anti-mainstream youth culture (Niedzviecki, 2004) or stylistic, self-enhancing statements of rebellion (Heath & Potter, 2004). There appears to be little sense in many countries, even among the young, regarding how youth disenfranchisement is an issue of social justice and certainly there are few political platforms upon which to proceed. As such, as noted in the youth culture chapter, this dissent appears to actually feed the system exploiting young people (Heath & Potter, 2004) and is therefore unlikely to culminate in a political movement beyond "imaginary" resistance (cf. Juris & Pleyers, 2009).

From a political-economy perspective, in addition to being marginalized producers in the economy, the young are targeted by massive marketing campaigns that seek to promote a high level of consumerism that is essential for contemporary corporations. This is a potentially unstable situation because of the obvious contradictions between wage exploitation and the need for compliant consumers. One solution to this contradiction seems to have been found by corporations in appropriating the symbols of political resistance in terms of lifestyle identities that require the support of various aspects of the capitalist machine of popular-culture production (and, as noted, parents often compensate for the wage exploitation by providing room and board, as well as various income supplements; cf. Schoeni & Ross, 2005).

As also noted in the media and youth culture chapters, over the late-twentieth century, corporate marketers learned that displays of "individuality" could be defined as symbols of political dissent, even as they represent forms of mass conformity (i.e., Frank's "conquest of cool" and Heath & Potter's "rebel sell"). Thus, the fashion industry now feeds consumers various self-presentation accouterments that can be supplemented with badges of "rebellion" (e.g., styles associated with hair styles, body piercing, tattoos). Young people can then combine these identity-ingredients in individualistic ways that provide the illusion of dissent. However, from the point of view of "outsiders," individual young people do not stand out as "individuals" so much as different fractions of people who look virtually identical. In this way, mass conformity has been disguised as individuality.

While mainstream urban youth apparently have been easy targets of these marketing efforts, even the trendsetters involved in various anti-capitalist movements seem to get caught up in the "resistance-as-display-and-consumption" marketing archetype. As it happens, imaginary "rebel identities" (Heath & Potter, 2004) have become part of the stock and trade of many forms of contemporary youth fashion and lifestyle: not only is this no threat to corporate capitalism or neoliberalism, but it also feeds it (Rushkoff, 2001). This transformation of protest into consumption is especially concerning with the increasing emphasis placed on a "feel-good" existence, with young people encouraged to escape into technological "trivial pursuits" that entertain them while leaving the power structure intact.

In point of fact, marketers have continued to work on new ways to appropriate potential youth resistance by nurturing hedonistic consumption patterns. For instance, in the late 1990s, marketers began targeting children with this formula, now defined by marketers as "tweens" and "pre-tweens," a demographic previously off-limits to predatorial marketing (Nader & Coco, 1999). This branding of today's children will affect the political consciousness of tomorrow's youth, potentially creating generations that feel perfectly happy living in neoliberal societies, with their extreme polarizations of wealth, of which age is becoming an increasingly important axis. For impassioned critiques of these practices—which have also been questioned by the American Psychological Association and the American Academy of Pediatrics—see Schor (2004) and Linn (2004). For a more general treatment of this problem, see Bakan (2004).

The Swedish example: Understanding all forms of political engagement

Are the two forms of political engagement really so different, especially in the eyes of young people everywhere today? Is it inevitable that dominant economic interests can manufacture a consensus in favor of neoliberalism and instill false consciousness among the citizenry, old and young alike? Is it impossible for a progressive polity to resist these threats to democracy?

A report from the Swedish National Board of Youth Affairs (SNBYA) about the ongoing situation in Sweden provides a very useful framework within which to answer these questions. The SNBYA (2011) reports that although the electoral participation of young Swedes has declined slightly (recall from above that it is already high and only slightly lower than that of older Swedes), surveys show that the level of interest of young Swedes in politics is actually on the rise (as it is for Swedes of all ages). Moreover, these surveys show that young Swedes born since 1965 actually "are interested in politics to a greater extent than previous generations were at the same point in their lives" (p. 52). The SNBYA interprets this to mean that the future of political engagement is bright in Sweden, especially as young Swedes find new ways to express their political interest as they age.

This SNBYA (2011) report also takes a prudent position concerning the potentials of new forms of political involvement. Their data show that young Swedes are more likely than older Swedes to use innovative methods, but it is not always clear whether the involvement is entirely new or replaces older forms, as in online petitions replacing older hardcopy petitions. This report also warns against romanticizing the new technologies, including the Internet:

> Our analyses have shown that the internet and social media have a great potential as arenas for dialogue, organisation, mobilisation and political involvement for young people, but also that there are a large number of limitations and democratic challenges that remain to be resolved.
>
> (SNBYA, 2011, p. 43)

As research in other countries shows (Milner, 2010), the use of the Internet requires individual initiative and motivation. Even if many people are communicating with each other on political issues, it is difficult to say with certainty "how effective these new forms of political participation are when it comes to conveying the political messages of young people and to their views producing the desired effect" (Milner, 2010, p. 43; cf. the political economists' concerns, outlined above).

Finally, the SNBYA (2011) report places the formal and informal types of political engagement within the national context of contemporary Sweden—a country with a high level of citizen participation in political affairs. The report utilizes the concept of "political consumption" which is defined as constituting an individualized form of political participation based on collective action "driven by both solidarity and the responsibilising citizenship ideal" (SNBYA, 2011, p. 42). Political consumption is "a reflection of a new view of citizenship that is linked to sustainable development (sustainable citizenship) that attempts to exert influence not only in relation to the state, but also in relation to businesses, organizations and our very lifestyle" (*ibid.*, pp. 41–2). This report continues by noting that political consumption is becoming so common, especially among young people, females, and the more affluent in general, that it should no longer be considered unconventional or a rejection of formal politics, at least in Sweden.

In view of this Swedish example, when conceptualizing forms of political/community engagement along with "lifestyle choices," it may be more useful to think of a typology of "political consumption" that would have high/low (formal) political engagement as one dimension, and high/low (informal) alternative, lifestyle engagements as the second dimension. When this is done it is likely that a minority—a small minority in some cases—of young people would be identified as low in both forms of engagement.

Table 11.1 illustrates the rough approximations that can be made of the cross-tabulation of formal and informal political involvements while contrasting youth–adult patterns. In this example, which approximates a country such as Canada, only a minority of younger and older alike would be classified as engaging in high levels of both forms of political engagements ($.4 \times .4 = .16$, or 16% for younger people; $.7 \times .4 = .28$, or 28% for older people). At the same time, a minority of both age groups has low levels of both forms of political engagements, leaving two-thirds of young people as politically engaged in some way.

If we use the Swedish example to designate a country on the leading edge of innovation in political engagement of the youth segment, in the case of the alternative engagement of "buycotting" (favoring only those businesses that practice social responsibility), we find an even more positive situation and outlook from the point of view of the potentials for active citizenship (SNBYA, 2011, p. 41). In this example, almost half of young Swedes (48%, $.60 \times .8$) engage in both forms of political activity, while a very small minority engages in neither (8%, $.2 \times .4$) (Table 11.2).

In sum, these Swedish examples show that the two forms of political engagement need not be mutually exclusive. Moreover, as we saw earlier in this chapter, political and educational institutions in countries like Sweden can engage in concerted efforts to increase the civic knowledge and engagement of their citizens, counteracting the attempts of economic interests to manufacture consent in favor of neoliberalism. With the political will, it is apparently possible for a progressive polity to preserve the democratic rights achieved by previous generations.

Table 11.1 Formal and informal political engagements: Hypothetical population estimates for younger (18–24) vs. older (55–64) citizens

		Formal (18–24) (55–64)	
		High (40%) (70%)	Low (60%) (30%)
Informal	High (40%)	+/+ (16%) (28%)	+/− (24%) (12%)
(alternate/lifestyle)	Low (60%)	−/+ (24%) (42%)	−/− (36%) (18%)

Table 11.2 Formal and informal political engagements: A Swedish example of 18–29-year-olds

		Formal—voting	
		High (80%)	Low (20%)
Alternate—	High (60%)	+/+ 48%	+/− 12%
buycotting	Low (40%)	−/+ 32%	−/− 8%

Conclusion: Beyond politics as an either–or involvement

There is no doubt that the political landscape has become very complex in many societies, especially with the advent of the Internet and its various digital platforms, including social media and ICTs. To date, strong contrasts have been drawn between "old" formal political engagement and "new" informal ones. But, is this a false dichotomy? Is the line between the two artificial?

Can a lifestyle constitute political engagement? Certainly, many Baby Boomers thought so when they "dropped out" in the sixties. As history showed, this was a temporary experiment for the vast majority of those trying it. But do some lifestyles necessarily preclude formal political engagements? Cannot someone who follows the green movement and is a vegan not also be politically informed and engaged, and thus working toward building a world that more closely resembles his or her individualized philosophy of life? The Swedish example discussed in the preceding section suggests that the two types of political engagement indeed can be complementary, and that widespread political participation and political knowledge is possible for citizens of all ages.

In some countries, there are concerns about the fragility of democracies in the face of interest groups that try to maintain control of the political economy, including a manipulation of the circumstances defining the current youth phase. Creating and maintaining youth political disengagement is clearly in the interests of certain élites in sustaining their manufacture of consent and preserving widespread false consciousness. In some more progressive countries, the stereotype of "disengaged youth" simply does not find support. It may well be that by better understanding the emerging political consciousness of people in these more progressive countries, younger and older alike, that the countries whose democracies are threatened by widespread disengagement can find useful models with which to understand how diverse political engagements of citizens can nurture democracies.

Finding new models of political engagement would continue the centuries-long social-justice struggles to develop polities where all citizens share in the wealth of their nation and have the opportunities to realize their inner potentials, struggles currently in their infancy in many parts of the non-Western world (e.g., Hammelman & Messard, 2011). The long-term goal of these struggles has been to create an economic and political "tide that will raise all boats," not just the boats of the privileged. The following well-known quotation captures the dilemma facing many Western countries that long ago overthrew dictatorships but whose citizens currently take "political freedom" for granted:

> The death of democracy is not likely to be an assassination from ambush. It will be a slow extinction from apathy, indifference, and undernourishment.
>
> (Hutchins, 1980, pp. 845–6)

Recommended readings

Colleen Hammelman & Betsy Messard (2011). Virtual public spaces: Social media and informal youth participation. In *Youth activism and public space in Egypt* (pp. 20–33). Cairo: John D. Gerhart Center for Philanthropy and Civic Engagement, the American University in Cairo and Innovations in Civic Participation. Retrieved from http://www.aucegypt.edu/research/gerhart/Documents/Youth%20Activism%20and%20Public%20Space%20in%20Egypt.pdf

This paper provides an in-depth analysis of the role of the youth segment in the Arab Spring in Egypt, including the relative importance of their use of social media.

Jeffrey Scott Juris & Geoffrey Henri Pleyers (2009). Alter-activism: Emerging cultures of participation among young global justice activists. *Journal of Youth Studies*, 12, 57–75.

This qualitative study explores various examples of youth-led political movements around the globe, looking for common features that set them apart from older political movements.

Richard Kimberlee (2002). Why don't British young people vote at general elections? *Journal of Youth Studies*, 3, 85–98.

This article reviews and critiques various attempts to explain the low youth voter turnout in the United Kingdom.

Rebecca Raby (2005). "What is Resistance?" *Journal of Youth Studies*, 8, 151–71.

Raby grapples with the concept of "resistance" and its use in the social sciences, attempting to develop a clear definition of the term.

Part IV

Conclusions: The Future of Youth Studies

In this final part of the book, I tie together the various elements of the book to draw conclusions about how youth-studies researchers have been grappling to understand the ongoing historical transformation of this culturally sensitive phase of the life course, and how the field as a whole might mature into a more comprehensive effort to understand the youth period in all of its dimensions.

As we saw in the various chapters throughout this book, youth studies is not a unified field. Different disciplines dominate different areas, and within disciplines there are disputes that appear intractable, such as the epistemological divide in the identity area. It is a fair question to ask, then, as to whether we can even speak of a distinct field of youth studies with a coherent character. I believe there is, if one defines it to include approaches that deal in some meaningful ways with the age group positioned in societies between childhood and adulthood. Adopting this definition requires broad-mindedness and a willingness to focus more on the targets of the approaches—young people—rather than on justifying the boilerplate assumptions of the approaches themselves. Too much of what is published in the field seems to be done more in the interests of the observers than the observed, based on overconfidence—even a hubris—in the abilities of specific theories to account for important aspects of the lives of the young in various societies.

The final chapter reflects on how we might move forward toward reaching the primary goals that all youth researchers ostensibly have in common, namely, to accurately understand the situations confronting the youth segment and finding ways to ameliorate problems associated with those situations.

Youth Studies' Coming of Age

Sukarieh and Tannock (2011) lay down the following challenge for youth-studies scholars to recognize their biases so that the field can become a more dynamic force of social reform and policy renewal:

> The challenge for critical analysis is not simply to replace negative stereotypes of youth with positive ones (or vice versa). It is, rather, to understand how and why particular kinds of positive and negative stereotypes of youth—or, indeed, invocations of the youth label in the first place—are mobilized by different groups in changing social and economic contexts over time. In this way, the field of youth studies and organizing can follow similar movements in women's, ethnic and race studies and organizing, to go beyond simply inverting stereotypes to critically interrogating the material and social conditions of the construction of these broad categories of identity.
>
> (pp. 688–9)

Those from different disciplines will have differing recommendations about how the field can become more socially forceful and politically relevant, but the first step would be for the youth-studies community as a whole to get beyond internally competitive disputes—especially straw arguments—and focus instead on establishing common grounds and purposes. This move toward inclusiveness would take youth researchers beyond "turf protection" to a focus on those disputes that can be discussed and debated in productive terms. The next step would be for those from each discipline and perspective to recommend their strongest evidence and arguments to others. These recommendations could then be studied from multiple viewpoints (e.g., triangulation), the results of which should produce more robust findings that have greater validity and generalizability.

For example, I have argued that the political-economy perspective has been neglected to the detriment of the field. As a macro perspective, it provides a starting point to more clearly understand the antecedents and consequences of the conditions—the root causes—that undermine the opportunities available to young people as citizens deserving of a living wage in decent jobs. At the same time, the ways in which young people are mystified by exploitative influences and ideological agents need to be brought to young people's attention. To accomplish this, youth researchers must have honest discussions with young people, as well as with each other as scholars. For the political economist, the object is critical emancipation, not simply advocacy. This political-economy position is not based on negative stereotyping; rather, it is recommending that the way to help young people is to understand the larger macro contexts that are allowing economic interests to take advantage of them while disguising their exploitation with the consent-manufacturing mechanisms, some of which use youth-studies theories, as in the case of the "positivity imperative" claimed by Sukarieh and Tannock (2011).

Of course, not all youth researchers will agree with the political-economy perspective, nor should we expect them to unless sufficient evidence for its claims can be provided. Still, skeptics must be willing to examine their preconceptions to honestly judge whether their skepticism is a matter of evidence or rather is based on a predisposition like the confirmation bias.

And, of course, other perspectives are useful in ways that the political-economy position is not. These other perspectives highlight areas that are beyond the focus and range of convenience of the political-economy perspective, at the same time that they might be able to help build the knowledge base called for by the political-economy perspective. For instance, the late-modernist perspective is a useful complement in highlighting the more micro influences of capitalism (e.g., Côté, 2014b; Côté & Allahar, 2006).

In addition, I have developed a modified Eriksonian perspective (the identity capital model) that helps place identity formation in late-modern/neoliberal capitalist contexts (e.g., Côté, 2013a, 2013b, 2014a). A guiding principle in these integrated perspectives is that not all problems are reducible to the political economy or social inequalities. Solutions to complex problems are themselves complex. To illustrate, if the wealth of a nation were magically equally distributed "tomorrow," many of the problems in people's lives would remain. This would especially be the case among those who are under-resourced agentically—regardless of social-class origin—who would still need to develop the wherewithal to use their newfound wealth on a long-term basis. The following Chinese proverb stands as an illustration of this point: "Give a man a fish and you feed him for a day. Teach a man how to fish and you feed him for a lifetime."

To understand more clearly the place of the political-economy perspective as one of many perspectives that can be applied to the youth field, it is useful to summarize the findings of the critical analysis of the field from the preceding chapters. In the next two sections, we first examine the basis of fault lines in the field and then move to the substantive areas in which the debates analyzed point to possible avenues of cooperation.

Fissures and fractures in the field

As a way of drawing attention to the pervasiveness of the fissures and fractures in the youth-studies field, Table 12.1 provides a summary of the disputes
examined in Chapter 3 and elsewhere in this book. This table alerts us to the
possibility that in all disputes, the fundamental assumptions held by researchers
that might not be specifically relevant to the task at hand can influence both
their approaches and conclusions.

Disciplinary differences emerge for both the structure–agency debate and the
stage–status dispute, with psychologists (and others sharing their paradigmatic
assumptions) tending to support both stage formulations and agency-based
views of young people, and sociologists (and others in related paradigms) tending to support age–status views of the youth period as well as structure-based
explanations of youth behavior. However, these tendencies are not absolute and
there is considerable variation (e.g., in the emerging adulthood debate Bynner
and Hendry are both psychologists disputing a fellow psychologist, Arnett; see
the disagreements among psychologists laid out in Arnett et al., 2011).

Ontological differences in nominalist–realist assumptions are associated
with both the stage–status debate and the quantitative–qualitative dispute.
Nominalists tend to view adolescence/youth as a socially constructed period
of life and prefer qualitative methods, while realists see adolescence/youth as
having their own obdurate properties and prefer quantitative methods to study
these properties.

Political agendas are related to the preference for critical or conservative views regarding social order and social change, and more generally to
Left–Right politics. In turn, general political preferences appear to be highly
predictive of social scientists' views on the relative importance of nature vs.
nurture: Left-leaning views correlate with "nurture" or environment-influenced
positions and Right-leaning opinions are associated with "nature" or genetic
explanations.

Finally, value-priority stances tend to be associated with different positions in all these debates, although it is generally those on the more liberal

Table 12.1 Fundamental assumptions driving the fissures and fractures in the chief
debates in youth studies

	Disciplinary assumptions	Ontology	Political agenda	Value-priority position
Nature vs. nurture			✔	✔
Structure vs. agency	✔			✔
Stage vs. status	✔	✔		✔
Critical vs. conservative			✔	✔
Quantitative vs. qualitative		✔		✔

advocacy–liberation side disputing those on the more conservative regulation–control side (either directly or as an imaginary audience). The more liberal views advocating youth liberation tend to emphasize "nurture" influences on the young, youth agency, age–status expectations, and qualitative methods, with the opposite tendencies more common among those taking the more conservative position of controlling youth behaviors.

Are these differences intractable? I would argue that they are not when discussed among non-dogmatic people who exercise critical thinking (Chapter 1) and consult theories of truth (Chapter 3). For the field to mature and develop adequate approaches to address all of the problems and promises of the youth period, academics need to recognize the limits of theories (focus/range of convenience; see Chapter 3) and the need for rapprochement with those who find competing approaches more convincing.

If youth researchers do engage in these détente exercises, in some cases they may realize that the basis of their disagreements can be traced to the fact that they are studying different aspects of youth behaviors, but with the same terminology. This appears to have been the problem in the area of youth identity, with postmodernists (and some others in cultural studies and sociology) focused on social identity, while psychologists are focused on ego identity, a different aspect of the phenomenon. This terminological difference appears to have been obscured by the epistemological divide, which is produced by a mix of contrasting fundamental assumptions. When it is recognized that the epistemological divide is in part a matter of "comparing apples and oranges," rather than being an entirely ontological dispute, a rapprochement may be acceptable, especially among those who can rise above their own political stances and value priorities in a collegial manner.

In other cases, youth researchers willing to find rapprochement with others may find that what appears to be an intractable ontological dispute is really a matter of their differing assumptions and methods being more suitable to different manifestations of certain phenomena. As argued in Chapter 3, qualitative methods tend to be more suited to the subjective aspects of a problem, and quantitative methods to objective aspects of the problem.

Similarly, each of the four value-priority stances can be justified in ways that all youth researchers would endorse, depending on the situation and youth segment in question. Sometimes an advocacy position would be universally seen as justified (e.g., combatting negative stereotypes about young people in the workplace), and occasionally a control position would be widely seen as warranted (e.g., dealing with incarcerated violent gang members). In some cases, an emancipatory position could be called for (e.g., helping young people become more aware of their disadvantages), and in yet other cases a facilitation-guidance position can be seen as reasonable (e.g., setting standards of conduct in learning environments and counseling students with emotional issues).

It is also recommended that youth researchers should examine their ontological assumptions, and where appropriate they should consider the merits of framing theoretical issues in terms of pragmatic constructionism (Chapter 1).

This can be done after an honest evaluation of which phenomena are best approached with nominalist vs. realist assumptions, as well as in terms of the instances where socially constructed realities act back on people. These objective social consequences are not of the same order as in the natural world studied by the sciences (e.g., the effects of electricity on the human body), but rather on a psychosocial order; for instance, with the objective consequences of rumors, gossip, ostracization, social exclusion, marginalization, and so forth, on people's physical and psychological well-being. At the very least, pragmatic constructionism avoids the problems of either extreme position: reification in the case of realism and solipsism in the case of nominalism.

Lastly, there may be instances where academics will simply have to "agree to disagree," based on a recognition that multiple interpretations can be adjudicated empirically. Differing interpretations can be put to empirical tests that satisfy those from different paradigms, and those perspectives that are found to have the strongest evidence could be duly credited in time. It would be a shame for the youth-studies field to end up like the American two-party political system where the leaders of Republican and Democratic parties have their own sets of "facts" and never the twain shall meet. Models provided by other forms of government based on consensus building, as in the Nordic countries, would be a much more desirable goal for this field.

Areas of conflict that can lead to cooperation

Broadly speaking, we could say that there are "three faces" of youth studies: adolescent psychology, sociology of youth, and cultural studies (cf. House's, 1977, similar depiction of the multifaceted field of social psychology). The sociology of youth and cultural studies appear to have found common ground ontologically, through nominalism, and methodologically, with qualitative methods; however, there are still many sociologists who prefer other ontologies and methodologies (cf. MacDonald, 2011). At the same time, adolescent psychology has become a very successful stand-only discipline with virtually no cross-fertilization with the other two "faces."

Yet, several broad areas of potential cooperation are readily apparent, so long as youth researchers are willing to step outside their comfort zones. For example, sociologists of youth have long studied social-class differences in youth, but with an obsessive attention to the lower classes and the socially excluded, as if the concerns of more affluent youth did not matter. In contrast, psychologists have been studying the concerns of those more affluent youth, primarily because of the ease of collecting data through school systems, but have very rudimentary conceptions of "class," often studying it only in terms of socio-economic status (SES, based on parental income and education). Meanwhile, psychologists acknowledge that they have been remiss in studying "the forgotten half" (i.e., those outside mainstream institutions; William T. Grant Foundation, 1988), and sociologists have recently noted that there is a "missing middle" in their studies (MacDonald, 2013; Roberts, 2011). One wonders where the youth-studies field would be today had the youth researchers from these two disciplines been more communicative over the past decades.

As a social psychologist with expertise in both sociology and psychology, I have been acutely aware of this schism throughout my career (Côté, 2013a) and have contributed to both fields, particularly with the identity capital model that links identity formation with cultural contexts (e.g., Côté, 1996, 1997, 2002, 2014a). The anti-psychology bias of the other two faces of youth studies is a problem in many ways, but particularly because the field needs models of human potential that illuminate how people can develop to their fullest. Human-potential development is viewed in various ways. For instance, we saw Bowles and Gintis's (1976/2011) conception of it in Chapter 4 with respect to what meritocratic educational systems could accomplish in terms of all people "flourishing" and sharing the benefits of affluent societies. Models of "subjectivity" coming from sociology and cultural studies are limited because they are largely "outside in," mainly in terms of how structures limit the realm of experience. Consequently, they do not help us understand what we would do if those oppressive structures were removed so that people could develop their potentials. There has been much work produced in the humanist tradition in psychology over the past century that can help the field of youth studies develop comprehensive models of human potential, including Erikson's work (and others from his generation, such as Fromm), and more recent work following the positive youth-development movement (e.g., Lerner et al., 2011).

At the same time, readers may have detected "biases" in the material I have selected for this book and my representation of that material. My defense is that this sort of "author prerogative" is inevitable. We all believe that some things are more important than others; and different authors will highlight diverse things based on their learning histories. I decided to write this book not only because I felt the fissures and fractures in youth studies need to be explicitly addressed but also because I felt that some important approaches have been underplayed, ignored, or misrepresented, especially the political-economy approach and the Eriksonian perspective. At the same time, I have deliberately offered these approaches, and those opposing them, for debate but have not insisted that they become some new orthodoxy that should dominate the field. In other words, I have elected to offer these approaches and the debates involving them to create field-wide discussions. Each chapter is intended as a teaching–learning exercise in critical thinking. Armed with critical-thinking skills, readers can decide for themselves in an informed manner how these debates might be resolved.

We can take these comparative exercises further by culling each of the topical chapters above. In the following list, I suggest several research questions and topics as a basis for researchers from different perspectives to engage in cooperative research projects that would make the youth-studies field a more dynamic force in social reform and policy renewal:

- *Education*: In recognizing the limitations of credential-driven labor markets, what models could be developed that show policy-makers how to create mass systems that have broad benefits for students from all backgrounds, namely, systems that target personal and intellectual development in ways that nurture students' critical-thinking capacities as well as critical awareness of the world around them, while still contributing to their career potentials. To accomplish this, we first need models that can produce "a tide that raises all boats," correcting the "low tide" that characterizes so many educational systems, where the "boats go nowhere."

- *Work*: Jobs available to the young are understandably at the entry level, but why do they have to be so exploitative? Following Tannock's recommendations would take youth researchers a long way in understanding youth work, in and of itself. At the same time, this understanding might encourage them to advocate ways of improving youth work so it is truly beneficial to young people, at the present and in the future. As noted in Chapter 5, for this to happen though, prominent youth theorists would need to re-examine their assumptions about the nature of youth and what is considered "natural" to that period.

- *Family*: The best practices of parenting appear to be culturally specific, but what practices are best for parents to inoculate their children so that they can cope optimally with the exploitive influences and anomic deficits of neoliberal, late-modernity—in agentic ways that help them avoid alienation and false consciousness without becoming self-entitled? The basis for this understanding might be found in an integration of the sociological and psychological approaches to parenting styles, as the relationship between authoritativeness and concerted cultivation is better understood.

- *Media and technological influence*: Understandings of the benefits of the various media and technologies are needed that are free of technological utopianism. One target for research could be to find the optimal levels for types of involvements educationally and politically so that young people can reach their potentials individually and as democratic citizens.

- *Youth culture*: The imperialist attempts of cultural studies to define the field of youth studies as "all culture" need to be better understood. The first step in better understanding youth cultures is to distinguish mainstream from spectacular youth lifestyles. With the youth period expanding, its long-term life-course effects need to be appreciated, including when youth itself is a class-like "identity," as well as the extent to which the lifestyles adopted by the young are accepted on their own terms as opposed to being the result of corporate manipulation.

- *Youth-identity formation*: A taxonomy is needed that sorts out the various types and levels of identity so that researchers can stop rejecting or ignoring each other's work because of the faulty assumption that they are studying the same things. Models can be broadened to include explorations of non-alienated identity formation that young people undertake in the face of the risks of late-modernity and neoliberal capitalist manipulation.

- *Youth social identities*: Numerous questions remain about the changing nature of the youth period, objectively and subjectively, in terms of identity formation. As the youth period has lengthened temporally and declined materially, how much has youth become a class-like "identity," how important is age-consciousness in the life course, and is the youth period itself becoming a structural obstacle for some people? Have these developments increased or decreased the experience of "multiple youths," with various subgroups differing in terms of their prospects for exercising identity-based agency in their formation of social identities? Are the differences between minority and majority youth a matter of "kind or degree" in various societies? At the same time, subjective experiences of youth-identity formation vary developmentally, and objective social identities can influence these subjective experiences. Given the assumption that all humans share the same potentials for mentally processing these experiences, just how different should we expect social-identity formation to be if/when young people are given optimal circumstances to undertake proactive development?
- *Politics*: Alternative forms of engagement, especially technologically mediated ones, need to be investigated free from technological utopianism. Although the benefits of alternative forms are being uncovered, there are few objective obstacles to engaging in both alternative and mainstream forms as full citizens. This point raises the following questions: What are the influences that alienate people away from mainstream forms, especially the young, in some countries? What is it about other countries, like Sweden, where fewer people appear to be alienated? The answers from political economists are clear, but are there other plausible explanations as well?

The youth question revisited in a cooperative field

In formulating what are arguably the most progressive youth polices in the world, the branch of the Swedish government responsible for youth policies proposed a frame that serves as a policy compass by posing a basic ontological question about the youth period (Swedish National Board for Youth Affairs, 1999b). The following alternatives were posed: Should public policy be directed to providing resources to young people that support them in their own right but might create further dependencies and prolongations of the youth phase, or should resources be provided to enable the independence characterizing adulthood as early as possible, thereby reversing the prolongation of youth? These are policy and practice questions that raise issues of whether developed societies should "support youth or end it."

This policy position recognizes that at least two different definitions of the concept of youth are relevant—one as a phase of life and the other as a social category. Policies supporting the youth phase would be aimed at "preparing young people for their entry into the adult world," while policies recognizing young people as social category (as one of several social categories in the population) would focus on the living conditions, taking into account the "relations between generations" in terms of "economic and political influence." In addition to this concern with intergenerational justice, the youth category of the population is seen to have political and economic rights, including "the right to influence policy" (Swedish National Board for Youth Affairs, 1999b, p. 10; cf. current discussions among sociologists about the "transitions" vs. "culture" approaches, e.g., Furlong, Woodman, & Wyn, 2011).

These sorts of insightful policy questions and answers highlight the youth question itself that is continually tackled by youth researchers. As noted in Chapter 1, the youth question fundamentally involves understanding the material and subjective conditions associated with the "youth period" in a given society. As we saw throughout this book, this question can be difficult to answer, not only because the societal definitions of the youth period vary widely over time and place, but also because youth researchers themselves have differing agendas based on their fundamental assumptions concerning how to approach youth research. The lessons from each chapter have reinforced the point that these differing assumptions are both useful, and limiting, to the field. They are useful to the extent that they are coherent, consistent, and correspond to empirical realities, but they can be limiting when they are over-extended or stretched beyond their optimal focus. Mapping the youth-studies field in ways that ultimately benefit the young, and the societies in which they live, requires that those working in this field recognize the strengths and limitations of their contributions and find ways to improve their relations with other youth researchers, mindful of the fact that "high fences make for bad neighbors" (cf. Archibald, 1976).

Glossary

Abstracted empiricism: A term of disparagement coined by Mills (1959) to dismiss research in which empirical observation is divorced from any theoretical grounding (contrasted with *grand theories*).

Agency: The capacity for intentional, proactive, and purposive behavior, sometimes required to overcome social-structural obstacles. Different disciplines may use other terms, such as free will, self-efficacy, and voluntarism, but each of these has specific histories and implications not necessarily relevant to youth studies. Some disciplines treat agency as a variable or individual difference, while others treat it as a constant, possessed in equal degrees by everyone.

Anomie: A condition of a society characterized by a breakdown or absence of norms and values, deriving from the Greek *anomia* meaning "lawlessness." Often used interchangeably with the psychological concept of alienation, but sociologists prefer to use it to describe a condition of society, not a property of the individual.

Boilerplate assumptions: Beliefs held by those adhering to a specific paradigm or theoretical perspective that go unquestioned by adherents, yet drive their research agenda. These implicit assumptions often lead to faulty inferences because the validity of the assumptions is not put to meaningful empirical and/or logical tests (see *theories of truth*).

Credentialism: The use of educational credentials to select and promote employees rather than with more direct criteria, some of which are determining abilities on a case-by-case basis, providing on-the-job training, or recognizing seniority as a route through career ladders. This often leads to competitions among people to outdo each other in terms of the credentials they acquire to qualify for positions, leading to credential inflation and underemployment.

Critical emancipation: A value-priority position that advocates liberating young people by helping them understand the sources of their oppression, including social practices that limit the development of their human potential, while at the same time addressing the root causes of their collective difficulties through praxis, putting theory into action.

Critical thinking: Engaging in informed observation, assessing the merits of something, both positive and negative. This requires examining the qualities of various forms of evidence and arguments, and giving reasons for conclusions about these merits based on more than emotional reactions, gut feelings, personal belief systems, or disciplinary boilerplate assumptions.

Enlightenment: A philosophical movement of seventeenth- and eighteenth-century Europe characterized by a belief in the powers of reason and observation, especially in the context of challenging religious authority and beliefs based on blind faith.

Epistemological divide: The polarized positions between those who insist that all social reality is ontologically nominal and those who insist that it is ontologically real. Generally, those positioned on either side of this divide will only accept evidence and arguments as valid knowledge if they correspond to their ontological preconceptions (the term "epistemology" is derived from the Greek for "knowledge"). The root term, *epistemology*, refers to the study of what is considered valid knowledge in different times and places.

Epistemological fallacy: The term coined by Furlong and Cartmel (2007) to character-ize beliefs that older forms of structure such as social class are no longer relevant to people's lives; instead, it is (mistakenly) believed that people's fortunes are more determined by individual factors than collective ones.

Essentialism: This term appears to have a variety of uses. It is most often used by postmodernists, as in the following example: "A position that assumes that human behaviours are rooted in some inherent, unchanging essence" (Brock, Raby, & Thomas, 2012, p. 354). For further clarifications, see the discussion of the nature–nurture debate in Chapter 3.

False consciousness: Beliefs that lead people to accept practices that work against their own interests, including internalizing the negative stereotypes about themselves and accepting economic practices that limit their life chances. Thus, people have an understanding of the world that is at odds with their true circumstances.

Grand theory: This term of disparagement was coined by Mills (1959) to ridicule functionalism that, in attempting to explain too much, become remote from real-ity. Following this sentiment, since the 1970s, there has been a general shift in many fields from studies grounded in well-developed theoretical traditions to atheoretical, topical studies, or "middle-range theories" that identify minimal intellectual heritage (contrasted with *abstracted empiricism*).

Identity terminologies

- *Ego identity*: A sense of temporal-spatial continuity that allows people to sustain a sense of themselves as agents with a past and future, a sense that is optimally meaningful and purposeful. Psychologists use this term to describe an unconscious mental quality associated with a mental strength or source of agency crucial for daily functioning, especially in societies that are fragmented or otherwise non-supportive of certain people's integration/inclusion. Suboptimal ego identity involves a lack of perceived meaning of the past and/or purpose in the future.
- *Identity politics*: Contestations of the political rights and advantage of different groups based on social identities derived from their non-normative characteristics, such as race/ethnicity, gender, sexual orientation, and so forth. Often applied to the machinations of social movements, especially civil rights and feminism.
- *Personal identity*: People's sense of themselves at the level of daily interactions with others. It includes the way they present themselves to others in normal interactions and how others perceive them as a result of those self-presentations.
- *Self-identity*: A term often used by sociologists to refer to the person's sense of self as a distinct person with a past and future, both of which are sustained by narratives the person develops to account for their unique experiences.
- *Social identity*: The meaning of this term varies but applies to people's sense of their place in society as well as how others "place" them. In this way, it has subjective and objective aspects. Social identities include occupation, nationality, race/ethnicity, gender, and so forth.

Individualization (of the life course): The general concept of individualization describes the process by which people engage in extensive choice-making concerning the direction their lives takes, the identities they assume, the communities in which they seek acceptance, and the values they adopt. This process becomes necessary as collective supports for life-course trajectories are destructured, leaving people more to their own devices in making their way in the world as adults. In youth studies, it specifically refers to a consequence of the destructuring of social markers leading to adulthood, requiring people to be more active in choosing their own paths, or series of paths, to adulthood, and then through adulthood (to be distinguished from the psychological concept of "individuation," which involves developing an emotional distance from one's parents).

Intersectionality: A term adopted by postmodernists to describe the ways in which sources of disadvantage intersect, often mutually reinforcing each other. Other perspectives refer more simply to multiple or compounded disadvantages.

Late-modernity: According to many sociologists, this is the current historical phase of Western societies. Whereas the foundation of social solidarity in premodern societies was based on primary-group relations (largely in terms of familial and intergenerational obligations), in modern societies social solidarity was based on secondary-group relations (social bonds are more voluntary and based more on rational self-interest). In late-modern societies, secondary-group relations still prevail, but have evolved to greater self-interest, especially through recent developments in neoliberal capitalism. At the same time, because of a decline in collective supports, social contexts can be fragmented and anomic, challenging people to compensate in various ways (see also *individualization*).

Manufacture of consent: The deliberate manipulation of information about the world, especially through the mass media and news sources, designed to create belief systems among the public that serve dominant interests and create social stability by heading off alternative interpretations (constructions) of reality (see also *false consciousness*).

Moral panic: Popularized in sociology by Cohen (1973) who classified moral panics among the population in terms of the singling out of certain groups and conditions as imminent threats to the social order. In this usage, moral entrepreneurs trigger these panics by identifying the source of these threats as "folk devils" and insisting they must be dealt with immediately. The term more generally is used to describe any widespread and intense feeling that the social order is threatened. In the more general usage, as well as the specific sociological understandings of forms of collective behavior, moral panics are characterized by a hiatus between evidence and reality that favors zealotry over reason.

Nominalism: The ontological position that social reality is the product human consciousness, particularly the symbols (names) humans ascribe to mental experiences and social events (from the Latin for "name"; sometimes called idealism; see *realism* for the contrary view).

Ontogenesis: The life-course development of the individual.

Ontology: The basis of fundamental assumptions regarding what is considered to be real (and by implication, "not real"). The word "ontology" is derived from the Greek word for "being"; hence, ontology involves the study of "being."

Paradigm: This term has numerous related meanings (e.g., Puuronen, 2005). Burrell and Morgan (1979) define its application to the social sciences in terms of the distinctive meta-theoretical assumptions that produce groupings of theoretical perspectives, which are often distinctive from, and in opposition to, other paradigms. Although there may be minor internal disputes within paradigms, each paradigm has boiler-plate assumptions that are taken for granted by all of those sharing them, but are disputed—or just ignored—by those in other paradigms. In contrast, Kuhn (1970) defined "paradigm" more in terms of the natural sciences and how a hegemonic paradigm defines "normal science" in a given era that is adopted by most members of the scientific community, until it is upset by a scientific revolution.

Phylogenesis: The history of the development of a species, which is often thought to influence ontogenetic development.

Plasticity: Synonymous with malleability, referring to the potential for individual change at any point in development because of interactions between nature and nurture influences.

Political agendas: The implicit or explicit assumptions underlying theories regarding "social order" and "social conflict," which in youth studies translates into disputes between positions advocating "regulation" of the status quo in societies vs. those advocating "radical change" in the basis of societies.

Postmodernity: The social conditions that are arising as "modernity" breaks down and/or is being rejected. The term "postmodernism" generally refers to those streams of thought that analyze and/or celebrate these changes. One strand of postmodernism postulates that modernist institutions based on science, logic, and reason are in decline and are being replaced by more non-rational, subjective, and relativistic social forms based on individualistic or smaller collective interests.

Pragmatic constructionism: A middle-ground position between the ontologies of nominalism and realism, which assumes that while knowledge about the social world is always formative, social constructions contribute to the objective institutionaliza-tion of that world that in turn "acts back" on individuals with objective, material consequences while also reinforcing or stimulating changes in their subjective understandings.

Pragmatism: A philosophy, dating back to William James, that people are meaning seeking, problem solving, and goal oriented. People can use these capacities to adapt to their environments in practical ways that overcome obstacles and take advantage of opportunities (Hewitt, 2003).

Premodern society: Premodern societies are often distinguished from modern soci-eties with homologies such as folk vs. urban society, agrarian vs. industrial, or *Gemeinschaft* vs. *Gesellschaft*. In most Western societies, this transformation was largely completed during the nineteenth century, but considerable variation can still be found.

Realism: The ontological position that social reality has its own properties, regardless of human consciousness and social construction (from the Latin for "thing"; see *nominalism* for the contrary view).

Reductionist constructionism: A position of extreme nominalism, which assumes that social reality is simply a product of social constructions.

Reflexive project of self: The self-conscious planning of one's self-development and life-course trajectory (see also *individualization*).

Second demographic transition: Hypothesized to follow the first demographic transi-tion of the late 1800s, which saw smaller families. During the 1960s, certain Western countries began to see even lower fertility, a greater delay of first births, and an increased diversity in familial relationships.

Social exclusion: A general term that applies differently in different contexts, some-times referring to those living in conditions of poverty and homelessness (e.g., an underclass). In other uses, refers to anyone who is stigmatized in reference to mainstream values and conventional roles, and is therefore excluded in some ways from full social participation in mainstream activities.

Structure–agency debate: The dispute as to whether human behavior is the result of intentional, proactive, and planful capacities, or is determined and constrained by normed and sometimes oppressive social structures. Although few social scientists or humanists would insist that an extreme explanation on either side is valid, in practice their analyses usually favor one side over the other, rather than using an explicitly stated model combining the two influences.

Theories of truth: Tests of the validity of a knowledge claim requires a theory or idea that (1) is agreed upon by a community of informed observers (consensus); (2) makes sense in terms of its internal logic and does not contain contradictions (consistency); and (3) has some support in a concrete reality (correspondence).

Value priority (**of youth research**): The primary obligation a researcher feels regarding the benefits of research for the young people under study, including their subjective experiences and material conditions. This can involve a fiduciary responsibility (regarding trust), a moral duty to protect the young, and an ethical obligation to help empower them. Consequently, there is a sense of how youth research ought to be carried out as well as what the ultimate goal of that research should be.

Youth question: The problem of how to conceptualize the period of youth in a given society. Its answer requires knowledge of the history of the life course in that society, as well as an understanding of the belief systems that have formed around the place of the young in that society. The question can be broken down into sub-components: who is defined as in the youth period?; what forms does the youth period take?; where do various forms of youth emerge?; when does the youth period begin and end?; and why do certain societies specify a period of the life course as "youth"?

Notes

Introduction

1. Zhikun and Xiong (2005) provide a history of government support for youth studies in China. Discussions of the evolution of Soviet and post-communist youth studies in Eastern Europe can be found in Chuprov and Zubok (2000), Helve, Leccardi, and Kovacheva (2005), and Roberts (2009).

3 Seminal Debates in Youth Studies

1. As discussed in Chapters 2 and 3, Unger et al. link personal epistemologies to positive–negative individual life experiences. My own research into this question adopted a psychoanalytic perspective, finding that professors with more intense childhood religious upbringings tend to gravitate to the humanistic disciplines, while those with more secular backgrounds go into the technological disciplines, including the natural sciences (Côté & Levine, 1992).

4 Education and the Youth Period

1. A more general manifestation of false consciousness is with anti-unionism among wage earners, an obvious area where attitudes run counter to personal financial interests. See Caldicott (1992) for a discussion of how American business interests (especially through the National Association of Manufacturers) spread anti-unionism propaganda and a fear of "communism" using public relations techniques, beginning in the 1920s just as unions were getting a foothold, while simultaneously equating "free enterprise" with "democracy" and God.

5 Work and Changing Employment Opportunities

1. It has become a common practice to "blame" the Baby Boom generation for the financial problems experienced by more recent generations. However, the data show that it was the Baby Boom generation that first experienced this economic disenfranchisement, not later cohorts, as some have claimed (e.g., Wyn & Woodman, 2006). The cohorts born in the 1930s and 1940s, which include just the earliest-born Baby Boomers, benefited most from the post-World War II affluence, not those born in the 1950s and later. The 1930s/40s cohorts entered the labor market in the 1950s and early 1960s, experiencing the so-called "'30 glorious years' (following the Second

World War) of full employment" (Roberts, 2009, p. 198). Those (Baby Boomers) born in the 1950s and 1960s found lower wages upon entering the labor force in the late 1970s and early 1980s and met recession after recession as they made their way into the labor force and through their careers (Côté & Allahar, 2006; Howe & Strauss, 1993; William T. Grant Foundation, 1988).

6 Family Life and Parental Influence

1. Strong critiques have been launched against "class analyses," for a variety of reasons, including major shifts in occupational structures and the lower salience of social class as a component of identity than in the nineteenth century when these analyses fueled social theory (e.g., Pakulski & Waters, 1996). Among the public, most people will self-identify as "middle class" even when they are low-level wage earners (e.g., Marger, 2005). At the same time, negative stereotypes about the "working class" abound, often ignoring the skilled trades that require higher levels of functioning and often pay relatively high wages.
2. Excellent-quality qualitative methods such as ethnographies are much more time-consuming than comparable quantitative studies, which is part of the appeal of quantitative approaches. Ethnographies are more easily done by academics early in a career, before facing publish-or-perish pressures, especially if they involve larger samples and more complicated topics. In fact, most ethnographies are now apparently conducted by doctoral students, before career pressures preclude the huge time investment to properly conduct them (Lareau, 2001, pp. 315–16). For an excellent ethnography of a university bar, see Spradley and Mann (1975).
3. In fairness, it is a common problem with ethnographies for those studied to vigorously object to how they are represented. Lareau's (2001) chapter on this topic is "must reading" for anyone contemplating this research method.

7 The Mediated World and Technological Influences

1. This phenomenon is not restricted to the youth segment. See Lanier's (2010) concept of "hive mind," a Borg-like Internet collective "imaginary" to which "resistance is futile" for those who allow themselves to be drawn into social media and other collectively organized digital worlds.

9 Youth-Identity Formation: Agentic Potentials or Inevitable Confusion?

1. Berger and Luckmann's (1966) social-constructionist argument that identity *constructions* are entirely "world open" is thus compatible with the Eriksonian framework. By world open, Burger and Luckmann mean that *social identities* can be given virtually any sort of *content* without necessarily affecting people's ability to engage their environments in ways that meet their basic temporal-spatial needs.

2. Of course, I am not equating humans with machines, but computers can be seen as replications of human mental processes and are therefore analogous.
3. Although the "identity status paradigm" has spawned hundreds of studies, primarily in the United States, it appears to have muddied the waters somewhat in terms of clearly mapping the developmental trajectories in the formation of coherent adult identities. However, the complexities of this debate are beyond the purview of this book (for a discussion of these complexities, see Côté, 2009a).

10 Youth Social Identities: Structurally Determined or Agentically Mediated?

1. Indeed, given that the categories of social identities can compound each other, producing complex interaction effects, their combined effects are multiplicative. For example, even if ethnicity and class were restricted to three categories each, 18 specific social identities would need to be investigated along with gender (e.g., $2 \times 3 \times 3 = 18$). No one study can realistically examine the combined effects of all possible categories; consequently, there is little research on these multiple effects.
2. Empirical investigations exploring the ramifications of "youth as class" have rarely been undertaken. However, the time is ripe for such studies at the time of writing in the midst of a global depression/recession (Côté, 2014b). These studies could include

   - a documentation of the growing income disparities in various countries between the youth and adult segments (see Chapter 5 for an analysis of this in the United States);
   - an empirical examination of the emergence of age-consciousness in terms of negative stereotypes formed by both age groups toward each other (with adult stereotypes manifesting the "ideology of youth"; and youth stereotypes toward adults showing the increase in their consciousness as a class-for-itself); and
   - an examination of the possibility that there are growing generational identities, with, for example, "being young" defined as a badge of honor set against an imaged stigmatized identity projected on "adults" as oppressors.

3. Small and Cripps (2012) make this point in comparing the situation of Deaf youth with that of ethnic-minority youth. They advocate the embracement of "Deafhood" where the emphasis is on Deaf youth positively identifying with their collective heritage in the culture of Deaf people and thus developing positive affirmations of self, while combatting "audist" attitudes that devalue Deaf culture. The Deaf community would thus constitute a minority group and be seen as a resource rather than a deficit to society.

11 Youth Politics: Engaged/Alternative or Disengaged/Resistant

1. Social democracies tend to resist neoliberalism, income inequalities, and have proportionally representative electoral systems. In contrast, liberal democracies

more closely embrace neoliberal ideals, accept income inequalities, and retain "first-past-the-post" electoral systems. An exception here is Australia, which enjoys the highest voter turnout of the OECD countries. Although it is a liberal democracy, it also has a proportional representation electoral system and all citizens are required by law to vote.

References

Aapola, S., Gonick, M., & Harris, A. (2005). *Young femininity: Girlhood, power, and social change*. London: Palgrave MacMillan.

Abar, B., Carter, K. L., & Winsler, A. (2009). The effects of maternal parenting style and religious commitment on self-regulation, academic achievement, and risk behavior among African-American parochial college students. *Journal of Adolescence, 32*, 259–73.

Adams, G. E., Côté, J. E., & Marshall, S. (2001). *Parent/adolescent relationships and identity development: A literature review and policy statement*. Ottawa: Division of Childhood and Adolescence, Health Canada.

Adsett, M. (2003). Change in political era and demographic weight as explanations of youth 'disenfranchisement' in federal elections in Canada, 1965–2000. *Journal of Youth Studies, 6*, 247–64.

Akinsola, E. F. (2011). Relationship between parenting style, family type, personality dispositions and academic achievement of young people in Nigeria. *Ife Psychologia, 19*, 246–67.

Allahar, A. L., & Côté, J. E. (1998). *Richer and poorer: The structure of social inequality in Canada*. Toronto: Lorimer.

Andres, L., & Wyn, J. (2010). *The making of a generation: The children of the 1970s in adulthood*. Toronto: University of Toronto Press.

Archer, S. L. (1989). Gender differences in identity development: Issues of process, domain and timing. *Journal of Adolescence, 12*, 117–38.

Archer, S. L. (1993). Identity in relational contexts: A methodological proposal. In J. Kroger (Ed.), *Discussions on ego identity* (pp. 75–99). Hillsdale, NJ: Lawrence Erlbaum.

Archibald, P. (1976). Psychology, sociology and social psychology: Bad fences make bad neighbours. *British Journal of Sociology, 27*, 115–29.

Aries, E., & Seider, M. (2007). The role of social class in the formation of identity: A study of public and elite private college students. *The Journal of Social Psychology, 147*, 137–57.

Arnett, J. J. (1999). Adolescent storm and stress reconsidered. *American Psychologist, 54*, 317–26.

Arnett, J. J. (2000). Emerging adulthood: A theory of development from the late teens through the twenties. *American Psychologist, 55*, 469–80.

Arnett, J. J. (2001). *Adolescence and emerging adulthood: A cultural approach*. Upper Saddle River, NJ: Prentice Hall.

Arnett, J. J. (2004). *Emerging adulthood: The winding road from the late teens through the twenties*. New York: Oxford University Press.

Arnett, J. J. (2006). Emerging adulthood in Europe: A response to Bynner. *Journal of Youth Studies, 9*, 111–23.

Arnett, J. J. (2008). The neglected 95%: Why American psychology needs to become less American. *American Psychologist, 63*, 602–14.

Arnett, J. J., Kloep, M., Hendry, L. B., & Tanner, J. L. (2011). *Debating emerging adulthood: Stage or process?* New York: Oxford University Press.

Arnett, J. J., & Schwab, J. (2012). *The Clark University poll of emerging adults: Thriving, struggling & hopeful.* Worcester, MA: Clark University. Retrieved from clarku.edu/clarkpoll

Arnett, J. J., & Tanner, J. L. (2011). Themes and variations in emerging adulthood across social classes. In J. J. Arnett, M. Kloep, L. B. Hendry, & J. L. Tanner (Eds.), *Debating emerging adulthood: Stage or process?* (pp. 31–50). New York: Oxford University Press.

Arum, R., & Roksa, J. (2011). *Academically adrift: Limited learning on college campuses.* Chicago: University of Chicago Press.

Aunola, K., Stattin, H., & Nurmi, J. (2000). Parenting styles and adolescents' achievement strategies. *Journal of Adolescence*, 23, 205–22.

Babcock, P. S., & Marks, M. (2010). *The falling time cost of college: Evidence from half a century of time use data.* Working Paper 15954, National Bureau of Economic Research, Cambridge, MA, April. Retrieved from http://www.nber.org/papers/w15954

Bakan, J. (2004). *The corporation: The pathological pursuit of profit and power.* Toronto: Penguin.

Bandura, A. (1989). Human agency in social cognitive theory. *American Psychologist*, 44, 1175–84.

Barber, B. K., Stolz, H. E., & Olsen, J. A. (2005). Parental support, psychological control, and behavioral control: Assessing relevance across time, culture, and method. *Monographs of the Society for Research in Child Development*, 70(282), 1–137.

Bauerlein, M. (2008). *The dumbest generation: How the digital age stupefies young Americans and jeopardizes our future.* New York: Penguin.

Baumrind, D. (1968). Authoritarian vs. authoritative control. *Adolescence*, 3, 255–72.

Bazuin-Yoder, A. (2011). Positive and negative childhood and adolescent identity memories stemming from one's country and culture-of-origin: A comparative narrative analysis. *Child & Youth Care Forum*, 40, 77–92.

Beaujot, R., & Kerr, D. (2007). *Emerging youth transitions patterns in Canada: Opportunities and risks.* PSC Discussion Papers Series, 21(5), Article 1. Retrieved from http://ir.lib.uwo.ca/pscpapers/vol21/iss5/1

Beck, U. (1992). *Risk society: Towards a new modernity.* London: Sage.

Beck, U. (2002). *Individualization: Individualized individualism and its social and political consequences.* Thousand Oaks, CA: Sage.

Beck, U. (2007). Beyond class and nation: Reframing social inequalities in a globalizing world. *British Journal of Sociology*, 58, 679–705.

Becker, G. (1964). *Human capital.* Chicago: University of Chicago Press.

Becker, H. (1963). *Outsiders: Studies in the sociology of deviance.* New York: Free Press of Glencoe.

Benedict, R. (1938). Continuities and discontinuities in cultural conditioning. *Psychiatry*, 1, 161–67.

Bennett, A. (2011). The post-subcultural turn: Some reflections 10 years on. *Journal of Youth Studies*, 14, 493–506.

Bennett, A., & Kahn-Harris, K. (2004). Introduction. In A. Bennett & K. Kahn-Harris (Eds.), *After subculture: Critical studies in contemporary youth culture* (pp. 1–18). London: Palgrave.

Bennett, S., & Maton, K. (2010). Beyond the 'digital natives' debate: Towards a more nuanced understanding of students' technology experiences. *Journal of Computer Assisted Learning*, 26, 321–31.

Bennett, S., Maton, K., & Kervin, L. (2008). The 'digital natives' debate: A critical review of the evidence. *British Journal of Educational Technology*, 39, 775–86.

Berg, I. (1970). *Education and jobs: The great training robbery*. New York: Praeger Publishers.

Berger, P. L., & Luckmann, T. (1966). *The social construction of reality: A treatise in the sociology of knowledge*. Garden City, NY: Doubleday.

Bernstein, B. B. (1975). *Class, codes, and control: Towards a theory of educational transmissions*. New York: Routledge.

Berzonsky, M. (2004). Identity style, parental authority, and identity commitment. *Journal of Youth and Adolescence*, 33, 213–20.

Berzonsky, M. (2005). Ego identity: A personal standpoint in a postmodern world. *Identity: An International Journal of Theory and Research*, 5, 125–36.

Berzonsky, M. D., & Adams, G. R. (1999). Reevaluating the identity status paradigm: Still useful after thirty-five years. *Developmental Review*, 19, 557–90.

Bessant, J. (2008). Hard wired for risk: Neurological science, 'the adolescent brain' and developmental theory. *Journal of Youth Studies*, 11, 347–60.

Best, S., & Kellner, D. (1997). *The postmodern turn*. New York: The Guilford Press.

Betts, J., Ferrall, C., & Finnie, R. (2000). *The transition to work for Canadian university graduates: Time to first job, 1982–1990* (Analytic studies branch research paper series No.141). Ottawa: Statistics Canada.

Blackman, S. (2005). Youth subcultural theory: A critical engagement with the concept, its origins and politics, from the Chicago School to postmodernism. *Journal of Youth Studies*, 8, 1–20.

Blackman, S. J. (1997). 'Destructing a Giro': A critical and ethnographic study of the youth 'underclass.' In R. MacDonald (Ed.), *Youth, the 'underclass' and social exclusion* (pp. 113–29). London: Routledge.

Blanchflower, D. G. (1999a). *What can be done to reduce the high levels of youth joblessness in the world?* Geneva: International Labour Office. Retrieved from http://www.dartmouth.edu/~blnchflr/papers/99–8text.pdf

Blanchflower, D. G. (1999b). Youth labor markets in twenty-three countries: A comparison using micro data. In D. Stern & D. A. Wagner (Eds.), *International perspectives on the school-to-work transitions*. Cresskill, NJ: Hampton Press Series on Literacy: Research, Policy and Practice.

Blau, P. M., & Duncan, O. D. (1967). *The American occupational structure*. New York: Wiley.

Bloom, A. D. (1987). *The closing of the American mind*. New York: Simon & Schuster.

Blumenstyk, G. (2010, August 6). Kaplan suspends enrollment at campuses where federal investigators found recruiting abuses. *Chronicle of Higher Education*. Retrieved from http://chronicle.com/article/Kaplan-Suspends-Enrollment-at/123835

Blumer, H. (1969). *Symbolic interactionism: Perspective and method*. Englewood Cliffs, NJ: Prentice Hall.

Bodovski, K. (2010). Parental practices and educational achievement: Social class, race, and habitus. *British Journal of Sociology of Education*, 31, 139–56.

Bodovski, K., & Farkas, G. (2008). 'Concerted cultivation' and unequal achievement in elementary school. *Social Science Research*, 37, 903–19.

Bourdieu, P. (1973). Cultural reproduction and social reproduction. In R. Brown (Ed.), *Knowledge, education, and social change: Papers in the sociology of education* (pp. 71–112). London: Tavistock.

Bourdieu, P. (1977). *Distinctions: A social critique of the judgment of taste* (R. Nice, Trans.). Cambridge: Harvard University Press.

Bourdieu, P., & Passerson, J. C. (1977). *Reproduction in education, society, and culture.* Beverly Hills, CA: Sage.

Bowles, S., & Gintis, H. (1976). *Schooling in capitalist America: Educational reform and the contradictions of economic life.* New York: Basic Books. (Reprinted in 2011 by Haymarket Books with a new introduction by the authors).

Bowles, S., & Gintis, H. (1988). Prologue: The correspondence principle. In M. Cole (Ed.), *Bowles and Gintis revisited: Correspondence and contradiction in educational theory* (pp. 1–4). New York: Falmer Press.

Bowles, S., & Gintis, H. (2003). Schooling in Capitalist America twenty-five years later. *Sociological Forum,* 18, 343–48.

Boyes, M. C., & Chandler, M. J. (1992). Cognitive development, epistemic doubt, and identity formation in adolescence. *Journal of Youth and Adolescence,* 21, 277–304.

Brake, M. (1980). *The sociology of youth culture and youth subcultures.* London: Routledge Kegan Paul.

Brake, M. (1985). *Comparative youth culture: The sociology of youth culture and youth subgroups in America, Britain and Canada.* London: Routledge and Kegan Paul.

Brandtstädter, J., & Lerner, R. M. (Eds.). (1999). *Action and self-development: Theory and research through the life span.* Thousand Oaks, CA: Sage.

Broad, W., & Wade, N. (1982). *Betrayers of the truth: Fraud and deceit in the halls of science.* New York: Simon & Schuster.

Brock, D., Raby, R., & Thomas, M. P. (2012). *Power and everyday practices.* Toronto: Nelson Education.

Brooks, R., & Hodkinson, P. (2008). Introduction [special issue: Young people, new technologies and political engagement]. *Journal of Youth Studies,* 11, 473–79.

Brotheridge, C. M., & Lee, R. T. (2005). Correlates and consequences of degree purchasing among Canadian university students. *Canadian Journal of Higher Education,* 35, 71–97.

Brown, C., & Czerniewicz, L. (2010). Debunking the 'digital native': Beyond digital apartheid, towards digital democracy. *Journal of Computer Assisted Learning,* 26, 357–69.

Brown, J. B., & Larson, R. W. (2002). The kaleidoscope of adolescence: Experiences of the world's youth at the beginning of the 21st century. In B. B. Brown, R. W. Larson, & T. S. Saraswathi (Eds.), *The world's youth: Adolescence in eight regions of the globe* (pp. 1–20). Cambridge: Cambridge University Press.

Brunsma, D. L. (2006). Public categories, private identities: Exploring regional differences in the biracial experience. *Social Science Research,* 35, 555–76.

Buckingham, D., & Willett, R. (Eds.) (2006). *Digital generations: Children, young people and new media.* Mahwah, NJ: Lawrence Erlbaum.

Burrell, G., & Morgan, G. (1979). *Sociological paradigms and organisational analysis.* London: Heinemann.

Bynner, J. (2001). British youth transitions in comparative perspective. *Journal of Youth Studies,* 4, 5–24.

Bynner, J. (2005). Reconstructing the youth phase of the life course: The case of emerging adulthood. *Journal of Youth Studies,* 8, 367–84.

Bynner, J., Elias, P., McKnight, A. Pan, H., & Pierre, G. (2002). *Young people's changing routes to independence*. York, UK: Joseph Rowntree Foundation.

Cahill, S., Fine, G. A., & Grant, L. (1995). Dimensions of qualitative research. In K. S. Cook, G. A. Fine, & J. S. House (Eds.), *Sociological perspectives on social psychology* (pp. 605–29). Boston: Allyn & Bacon.

Calcutt, A. (1998). *Arrested development: Pop culture and the erosion of adulthood*. London: Cassell.

Caldicott, H. (1992). *If you love this planet: A plan to heal the earth*. New York: Norton.

CBS (2010, Oct. 10). How speed traders are changing Wall Street. *60 Minutes*. Retrieved from http://www.cbsnews.com/8301-18560_162-20066899.html

Chandler, M. (1995). Is this the end of 'The age of development,' or what? or: Please wait a minute Mr. Post-man. *The Genetic Epistemologist*, 23, 1–11.

Chandler, M. (2001). The time of our lives: Self-continuity in Native and non-Native youth. In W. Reese (Ed.), *Advances in child development and behavior* (pp. 175–221). New York: Academic Press.

Cheadle, J. E. (2008). Educational investment, family context, and children's math and reading growth from Kindergarten through the third grade. *Sociology of Education*, 81, 1–31.

Cheadle, J. E. (2009). Parental educational investment and children's general knowledge development. *Social Science Research*, 38, 477–91.

Cheadle, J. E., & Amato, P. R. (2011). A quantitative assessment of Lareau's qualitative conclusions about class, race, and parenting. *Journal of Family Issues*, 32, 679–706.

Chin, T., & Phillips, M. (2004). Social reproduction and child-rearing practices: Social class, children's agency, and the summer activity gap. *Sociology of Education*, 77, 185–210.

Chuprov, V., & Zubok, J. (2000). Integration versus exclusion: Youth and the labour market in Russia. *International Social Science Journal*, LII(2), 171–82.

Cielisk, M., & Pollock, G. (2002). Introduction: Studying young people in late modernity. In M. Cielisk & G. Pollock (Eds.), *Young people in risk society: The restructuring of youth identities and transitions in late modernity* (pp. 1–21). Aldershot, UK: Ashgate.

Clark, B. R. (1961). The 'cooling-out' function in higher education. In A. H. Halsey, J. Floud, & C. A. Anderson (Eds.), *Education, economy, and society: A reader in the sociology of education* (pp. 513–23). New York: The Free Press.

Cohen, A. (1955). *Delinquent boys*. Chicago: Free Press.

Cohen, P. (1972). *Subcultural conflict and working class community*. Working Papers in Cultural Studies, CCCS, University of Birmingham.

Cohen, P., & Ainley, P. (2000). In the country of the blind?: Youth studies and cultural studies in Britain. *Journal of Youth Studies*, 3, 79–96.

Cohen, S. (1973). *Folk devils and moral panics*. St. Albans: Paladin.

Coleman, J. C. (1978). Current contradictions in adolescent theory. *Journal of Youth & Adolescence*, 7, 1–11.

Collin, P., & Burns, J. (2009). The experience of youth in the digital age. In A. Furlong (Ed.), *International handbook of youth and young adulthood* (pp. 283–90). London: Routledge International Handbook Series.

Collins, R. (1979). *The credential society: A historical sociology of education and stratification*. New York: Academic.

Condon, R. G. (1987). *Inuit youth: Growth and change in the Canadian Arctic.* New Brunswick, NJ: Rutgers University Press.

Corsaro, W. A., & Eder, D. (1995). Development and socialization of children and adolescents. In K. S. Cook, G. A. Fine, & J. S. House (Eds.), *Sociological perspectives on social psychology* (pp. 421–51). Boston: Allyn & Bacon.

Costigan, C. L., Koryzma, C. M., Hua, J. M., & Chance L. J. (2010). Ethnic identity, achievement, and psychological adjustment: Examining risk and resilience among youth from immigrant Chinese families in Canada. *Cultural Diversity and Ethnic Minority Psychology,* 16, 264–73.

Costigan, C. L., Su, T. F., & Hua, J. M. (2009). Ethnic identity among Chinese Canadian youth: A review of the Canadian literature. *Canadian Psychology,* 50, 261–72.

Côté, J. E. (1992). Was Mead wrong about coming of age in Samoa?: An analysis of the Mead/Freeman controversy for scholars of adolescence and human development. *Journal of Youth and Adolescence,* 21, 499–527.

Côté, J. E. (1994). *Adolescent storm and stress: An evaluation of the Mead/Freeman controversy.* Hillsdale, NJ: Lawrence Erlbaum.

Côté, J. E. (1996). Sociological perspectives on identity formation: The culture-identity link and identity capital. *Journal of Adolescence,* 19, 417–28.

Côté, J. E. (1997). An empirical test of the identity capital model. *Journal of Adolescence,* 20, 577–97.

Côté, J. E. (2000). *Arrested adulthood: The changing nature of maturity and identity.* New York: New York University Press.

Côté, J. E. (2002). The role of identity capital in the transition to adulthood: The individualization thesis examined. *Journal of Youth Studies,* 5, 117–34.

Côté, J. E. (Ed.) (2005). The postmodern critique of developmental perspectives [Special issue]. *Identity: An International Journal of Theory and Research,* 5(2), 95–225.

Côté, J. E. (2006a). Identity studies: How close are we to developing a social science of identity?—An appraisal of the field. *Identity: An International Journal of Theory and Research,* 6, 3–25.

Côté, J. E. (2006b). Emerging adulthood as an institutionalized moratorium: Risks and benefits to identity formation. In J. J. Arnett & J. Tanner (Eds.), *Emerging adults in America: Coming of age in the 21st century.* Washington, DC: American Psychological Association, 2006.

Côté, J. E. (2009a). Identity and self development. In R. M. Lerner & L. Steinberg (Eds.), *Handbook of Adolescent Psychology* (3rd ed.) *Volume 1: Individual bases of adolescent development* (pp. 266–304). Hoboken, NJ: Wiley.

Côté, J. E. (2009b). Youth identity studies: History, controversies, and future directions. In A. Furlong (Ed.), *International handbook of youth and young adulthood* (pp. 375–83). London: Routledge International Handbook Series.

Côté, J. E. (2010). Adolescent psychology and the sociology of youth: Toward a rapprochement. In R. Zukauskiene (Ed.), *The 12th Biennial Conferences of the European Association for research on adolescence* (pp. 93–9). Bologna, Italy: Medimond.

Côté, J. E. (2013a). A stranger in paradise: Fitting in, managing identities, and reaching out. In J. Brooks-Gunn, R. M. Lerner, A. C. Petersen, & R. K. Silbereisen (Eds.), *The developmental science of adolescence: History through autobiography* (pp. 97–103). New York: Psychology Press.

Côté, J. E. (2013b). The importance of resources in work transitions in late-modern contexts. In H. Helve & K. Evans (Eds.), *Youth, work transitions and wellbeing* (pp. 97–117). London: The Tufnell Press.

Côté, J. E. (2014a). The identity capital model: Functional adaptations in late-modern contexts. In S. Mizokami & K. Matsushita (Eds.), *School-to-work transitions: Basics and current studies*. Kyoto: Nakanishiya.

Côté, J. E. (2014b). Towards a new political economy of youth. *Journal of Youth Studies*. Advance online publication. DOI: 10.1080/13676261.2013.836592

Côté, J. E., & Allahar, A. (1996). *Generation on hold: Coming of age in the late twentieth century*. New York: New York University Press.

Côté, J. E., & Allahar, A. (2006). *Critical youth studies: A Canadian focus*. Toronto: Pearson Education.

Côté, J. E., & Allahar, A. (2007). *Ivory tower blues: A university system in crisis*. Toronto: University of Toronto Press.

Côté, J. E., & Allahar, A. (2011). *Lowering higher education: The rise of corporate universities and the fall of the liberal arts*. Toronto: University of Toronto Press.

Côté, J. E. & Arnett, J. (2005, February). *Emerging adulthood: A time of flourishing or floundering—For whom and why?* Public debate held at *The 2nd Conference on Emerging Adulthood*, Miami, FL.

Côté, J. E., & Bynner, J. (2008). Changes in the transition to adulthood in the UK and Canada: The role of structure and agency in emerging adulthood. *Journal of Youth Studies*, 11, 251–68.

Côté, J. E., & Levine, C. (1987). A formulation of Erikson's theory of ego identity formation. *Developmental Review*, 9, 273–325.

Côté, J. E., & Levine, C. (1988a). A critical examination of the ego identity status paradigm. *Developmental Review*, 8, 147–84.

Côté, J. E., & Levine, C. (1988b). The relationship between ego identity status and Erikson's notions of institutionalized moratoria, value orientation state, and ego dominance. *Journal of Youth and Adolescence*, 17, 81–99.

Côté, J. E., & Levine, C. (1989). An empirical test of Erikson's theory of ego identity formation. *Youth & Society*, 20, 388–415.

Côté, J. E., & Levine, C. (1992). The genesis of the humanistic academic: A second test of Erikson's theory of ego identity formation. *Youth & Society*, 23, 387–410.

Côté, J. E., & Levine, C. (1997). Student motivations, learning environments, and human capital acquisition: Toward an integrated paradigm of student development. *Journal of College Student Development*, 38, 229–43.

Côté, J. E., & Levine, C. (2000). Attitude versus aptitude: Is intelligence or motivation more important for positive higher educational outcomes? *Journal of Adolescent Research*, 15, 58–80.

Côté, J. E., & Levine, C. (2002). *Identity formation, agency, and culture: A social psychological synthesis*. Mahwah, NJ: Lawrence Erlbaum.

Côté, J. E., & Schwartz, S. (2002). Comparing psychological and sociological approaches to identity: Identity status, identity capital, and the individualization process. *Journal of Adolescence*, 25, 571–86.

Dahlgren, P. (Ed). (2007). *Young citizens and new media*. London: Routledge.

Danesi, M. (2003). *Forever young: The 'teen-aging' of modern culture*. Toronto: University of Toronto Press.

Darling, N., & Steinberg, L. (1993). Parenting style as context: An integrative model. *Psychological Bulletin*, 113, 487–96.

Davies, S. (2005). A revolution in expectations? Three key trends in the SAEP data. In R. Sweet & P. Anisef (Eds.), *Preparing for post-secondary education: New roles for governments and families* (pp. 149–65). Montreal and Kingston: McGill-Queen's University Press.

Davies, S., & Guppy, N. (2006). *The schooled society: An introduction to the sociology of education.* Toronto: Oxford University Press.

Duke, L. M., & Asher, A. D. (Eds.). (2012). *College libraries and student culture: What we now know.* Chicago: ALA Editions.

Durkheim, E. (1951). *Suicide.* New York: Free Press. (Original work published in 1897).

Durkheim, E. (1964a). *The rules of sociological method.* New York: Free Press. (Original work published in 1895).

Durkheim, E. (1964b). *The division of labor in society.* New York: Free Press. (Original work published in 1893).

Durrance, C., Maggio, J., & Smith, M. (Producers). (2010). College Inc., *Frontline* PBS Retrieved from http://www.pbs.org/wgbh/pages/frontline/collegeinc/

Dusek, J. B., & McIntrye, J. G. (2003). Self-concept and self-esteem development. In G. R. Adams & M. D. Berzonsky (Eds.), *Blackwell handbook of adolescence* (pp. 290–309). Malden, MA: Blackwell Publishing.

Dyk, P. H., & Adams, G. R. (1990). Identity and intimacy: An initial investigation of three theoretical models using cross-lag panel correlations. *Journal of Youth and Adolescence,* 19, 91–110.

Ejei, J., Lavasani, M. G., Malahmadi, E., & Khezri, H. (2011). The relationship between parenting styles and academic achievement through the mediating influences of achievement goals and academic self-efficacy. *Journal of Psychology,* 15, 284–301.

Elder, L., & Paul, R. (2010). *The foundations of analytic thinking.* The Foundation for Critical Thinking. Retrieved from http://www.criticalthinking.org

Elections Canada. (2012a). *Estimation of voter turnout by age group and gender at the 2011 Federal General Election.* Ottawa: Author.

Elections Canada. (2012b). *National youth survey report.* Ottawa: Author.

Ellul, J. (1964). *The technological society.* New York: Vintage Books.

Epstein, R. (2007). *The case against adolescence: Rediscovering the adult in every teen.* Sanger, CA: Quill Driver Books.

Erikson, E. H. (1950). *Childhood and society.* New York: Norton.

Erikson, E. H. (1958). *Young man Luther.* New York: Norton.

Erikson, E. H. (1959). Late adolescence. In D. H. Funkenstein (Ed.), *The student and mental health: An international view* (pp. 66–106). Cambridge, MA: Riverside Press.

Erikson, E. H. (1968). *Identity: Youth and crisis.* New York: Norton.

Erikson, E. H. (1969). *Gandhi's truth.* New York: Norton.

Erikson, E. H. (1974). *Dimensions of a new identity.* New York: Norton.

Erikson, E. H. (1975). *Life history and the historical moment.* New York: Norton.

Erikson, E. H., & Erikson, K. T. (1957). On the confirmation of the delinquent. *Chicago Review,* 10, 15–23.

Eschbach, K. (1993). Changing identification among American Indians and Alaska Natives. *Demography,* 30, 635–52.

Eschbach, K., & Gómez, C. (1998). Choosing Hispanic identity: Ethnic identity switching among respondents to high school and beyond. *Social Science Quarterly,* 79, 74–90.

Evans, K. (2002). Taking control of their lives? Agency in young adult transitions in England and the New Germany. *Journal of Youth Studies,* 5, 245–69.

Evans, R. I. (1969). *Dialogue with Erik Erikson.* New York: Dutton.

Farthing, R. (2010). The politics of youthful antipolitics: Representing the 'issue' of youth participation in politics. *Journal of Youth Studies,* 13, 181–95.

Ferrer, A., & Riddell, W. C. (2002). The role of credentials in the Canadian labour market. *Canadian Journal of Economics*, 35, 879–905.

Fine, G. A., Mortimer, J. T., & Roberts, D. F. (1990). Leisure, work, and the mass media. In S. S. Feldman & G. R. Elliott (Eds.), *At the threshold: The developing adolescent* (pp. 225–52). Cambridge, MA: Harvard University Press.

Finnie, R., Lascelles, E., & Sweetman, A. (2005). *Who goes? The direct and indirect effects of family background on access to post-secondary education.* Ottawa: Statistics Canada, Analytic Studies Branch Research Paper Series.

Florida, R. (2012). *The rise of the creative class revisited.* New York: Basic Books.

Fornäs, J., & Bolin, G. (Eds.) (1995). *Youth culture in late modernity.* London: Sage.

France, A. (2007). *Understanding youth in late modernity.* Maidenhead, UK: Open University Press.

France, A. (2008). Risk factor analysis and the youth question. *Journal of Youth Studies*, 11, 1–15.

Frank, T. (1997a). *The conquest of cool: Business culture, counterculture, and the rise of hip consumerism.* Chicago: The University of Chicago Press.

Frank, T. (1997b). Let them eat lifestyle: From hip to hype—the ultimate corporate takeover. *Utne Reader*, November–December, 43–7.

Freeman, D. (1983). *Margaret Mead and Samoa: The making and unmaking of an anthropological myth.* Cambridge, MA: Harvard University Press.

Frenette, M. (2000). Overqualified? Recent graduates and the needs of their employers. *Education Quarterly Review*, 7, 6–20.

Furlong, A. (2013). *Youth studies: An introduction.* London: Routledge.

Furlong, A., & Cartmel, F. (2007). *Young people and social change: New perspectives* (2nd ed.). Buckingham, UK: Open University Press.

Furlong, A., & Cartmel, F. (2009). *Higher education and social justice.* Maidenhead, UK: Society for Research into Higher Education & Open University Press.

Furlong, A., Woodman, D., & Wyn, J. (2011). Changing times, changing perspectives: 'transition' and 'cultural' young perspectives on youth and adulthood. *Journal of Sociology*, 47, 355–70.

Geertz, C. (1973). *The interpretation of cultures.* New York: Basic Books.

Gergen, K. J. (1991). *The saturated self: Dilemmas of identity in contemporary life.* New York: Basic Books.

Giddens, A. (1984). *The constitution of society.* Cambridge, UK: Polity Press.

Giddens, A. (1991). *Modernity and self-identity: Self and society in the late modern age.* Stanford, CA: Stanford University Press.

Giddens, A. (1994). *Beyond left and right: The future of radical politics.* Cambridge, UK: Polity Press.

Gidengil, E., Blais, A., Nevitte, N., & Nadeau, N. (2003). Turned off or tuned out? Youth participation in politics. *Electoral Insight*, 5, 9–14.

Gilbert, D. (2003). *The American class structure* (6th ed.). Belmont, CA: Wadsworth.

Giroux, H. A. (2012). *Disposable youth: Racialized memories and the culture of cruelty.* London: Routledge.

Gitlin, T. (1995). *The twilight of common dreams: Why America is wracked by culture wars.* New York: Metropolitan Books.

Glaser, B., & Strauss, A. (1967). *The discovery of grounded theory: Strategies for qualitative research.* New York: Aldine Publishing Company.

Gomez, J. (2007). *Print is dead: Books in our digital age.* New York: Macmillan.

Gore, A. (2013). *The future: Six drivers of global change.* New York: Random House.

Gottfredson, M., & Hirschi, T. (1990). *A general theory of crime*. Stanford: Stanford University Press.

Gramsci, A. (1971). *Selections from the prison notebooks*. London: Lawrence and Wishart.

Grant, D. M., Malloy, A. D., & Murphy, M. C. (2009). A comparison of student perceptions of their computer skills to their actual abilities. *Journal of Information Technology Education*, 8, 141–60.

Greenberg, A. (2007). *Youth subcultures: Exploring underground America*. New York: Pearson Longman.

Greenberger, E., & Steinberg, L. (1986). *When teenagers work: The psychological and social costs of adolescent employment*. New York: Basic.

Griffiths, R. (2010). The gothic folk devils strike back! Theorizing folk devil reaction in the post-Columbine era. *Journal of Youth Studies*, 13, 403–22.

Halfpenny, P. (1982). *Positivism and sociology: Explaining social life*. London: Allen and Unwin.

Hall, G. S. (1904). *Adolescence*. New York: Appleton.

Hall, S., & Jefferson, T. (Eds.). (1976). *Resistance through rituals: Youth subcultures in post-war Britain*. London: Hutchinson.

Hallett, D., Want, S. C., Chandler, M. J., Koopman, L. L., Flores, J. P., & Gehrke, E. C. (2008). Identity in flux: Ethnic self-identification, and school attrition in Canadian Aboriginal youth. *Journal of Applied Developmental Psychology*, 29, 62–75.

Hamilton, L. T. (2013). More is more or more is less? Parental financial investments during college. *American Sociological Review*, 78, 70–95.

Hammelman, C., & Messard, B. (2011). Virtual public spaces: Social media and informal youth participation. *Youth activism and public space in Egypt* (pp. 20–33). Cairo: John D. Gerhart Center for Philanthropy and Civic Engagement, the American University in Cairo and Innovations in Civic Participation. Retrieved from http://www.aucegypt.edu/research/gerhart/Documents/Youth%20Activism%20and%20Public%20Space%20in%20Egypt.pdf

Harris, J. R. (2009). *The nurture assumption: Why children turn out the way they do* (revised and updated). New York: Free Press.

Hatcher, D. (1994). Critical thinking, postmodernism, and rational evaluation. *Informal Logic*, XVI, 197–208.

Hauser-Cram, P., Wyngaarden Krauss, M., & Kersh, J. (2009). Adolescents with developmental disabilities and their families. In R. M. Lerner & L. Steinberg (Eds.), *Handbook of adolescent psychology* (3rd ed.) *Volume 1: Individual bases of adolescent development* (pp. 589–617). Hoboken, NJ: Wiley.

Hayes, D. (2002). Taking the hemlock? The new sophistry of teacher training for higher education. In D. Hayes & R. Wynyard (Eds.), *The McDonaldization of higher education* (pp. 143–58). Westport, CT: Bergin & Garvey.

Hayes, D., & Wynyard, R. (2002). *The McDonaldization of higher education*. Westport, CT: Bergin & Garvey.

Heath, J., & Potter, A. (2004). *The rebel sell: Why the culture can't be jammed*. Toronto: Harper Collins.

Heinz, W. (2002). Self-socialization and post-traditional society. *Advances in Life Course Research*, 7, 41–64.

Hellman, H. (1998). *Great feuds in science: The ten liveliest disputes ever*. New York: Wiley.

Helsper, E. J., & Eynon, R. (2010). Digital natives: Where is the evidence? *British Educational Research Journal*, 36, 503–20.

Helve, H. (Ed.). (2005). *Mixed methods in youth research*. Helsinki: Finnish Youth Research Network.

Helve, H., & Holm, G. (Eds.). 2005. *Contemporary youth research: Local expressions and global connections*. Aldershot, UK: Ashgate.

Helve, H., Leccardi C., & Kovacheva, S. (2005). Youth research in Europe. In H. Helve & G. Holm (Eds.), *Contemporary youth research: Local expressions and global connections* (pp. 15– 32). Aldershot, UK: Ashgate.

Hempel, C. G. (1966). *Philosophy of natural science*. Englewood Cliffs, NJ: Prentice Hall.

Hendry, L. B., & Kloep, M. (2010). How universal is emerging adulthood? An empirical example. *Journal of Youth Studies*, 13, 169–79.

Hendry, L. B., & Kloep, M. (2011). Lifestyles in emerging adulthood: Who needs stages anyway? In J. J. Arnett, M. Kloep, L. B. Hendry, & J. L. Tanner (Eds.), *Debating emerging adulthood: Stage or process?* (pp. 77–104). New York: Oxford University Press.

Henslin, J. M., Henslin, L. K., & Keiser, S. D. (1976). Schooling for social stability: Education in the corporate society. In J. M. Henslin & L. T. Reynolds (Eds.), *Social problems in American society* (2nd ed.). Boston: Holbrook.

Herman, E. S., & Chomsky, N. (1988). *Manufacturing consent: The political economy of the mass media*. New York: Pantheon.

Hess, R. D., & McDevitt, T. M. (1984). Some cognitive consequences of maternal intervention techniques: A longitudinal study. *Child Development*, 55, 2017–30.

Hewitt, J. P. (2003). *Self and society: A symbolic interactionist social psychology* (9th ed.). Boston: Allyn & Bacon.

Hickman, G. P., & Crossland, G. L. (2004). The predictive nature of humor, authoritative parenting style, and academic achievement on indices of initial adjustment and commitment to college among college freshmen. *Journal of College Student Retention: Research, Theory and Practice*, 6, 225–45.

Hill, R. F., & Fortenberry, J. D. (1992). Adolescence as a culture-bound syndrome. *Social Science & Medicine*, 35, 73–80.

Hirschi, T. (1969). *The causes of delinquency*. Berkeley: University of California Press.

Hollinger, R. (1994). *Postmodernism and the social sciences: A thematic approach*. Thousand Oaks, CA: Sage.

Hollingshead, A. B. (1949). *Elmtown's youth: The impact of social class on adolescents*. New York: John Wiley & Sons.

Hollingsworth, L. S. (1928). *The psychology of the adolescent*. Englewood Cliffs, NJ: Prentice Hall.

House, J. S. (1977). The three faces of social psychology. *Sociometry*, 40, 161–77.

Howe, N., & Strauss, B. (1993). *13th GEN: Abort, retry, ignore, fail?* New York: Vintage Books.

Human Resources Development Canada. (2003). *Canada's youth: Who are they and what do they want?* Hull, Québec: Author.

Hutchins R. M. (1980). In *Bartlett's familiar quotations*. Boston: Little, Brown & Co.

International Labour Office. (2004). *Global employment trends for youth*. Geneva: Author.

International Labour Office. (2012). *Global employment trends for youth 2012: Preventing a deeper job crisis*. Geneva: Author.

International Labour Office. (2013). *Global employment trends for youth 2012: A generation at risk*. Geneva: Author.

Internet World Stats. (2010). *Usage and population statistics.* Retrieved from http://www.internetworldstats.com/stats.htm

Ipsos-Reid Survey. (2008). *Canadian teenagers are leading the online revolution? Maybe not...* Retrieved from http://www.ipsos-na.com/news-polls/pressrelease.aspx?id=3829

Irwin, S., & Elley, S. (2011). Concerted cultivation? Parenting values, education and class diversity. *Sociology: The Journal of the British Sociological Association, 45,* 480–95.

Jaggars, S. S. (2013). *Choosing between online and face-to-face courses: Community college student voices.* CCRC Working Paper No. 58, Community College Research Center Teachers College, Columbia University. Retrieved from http://ccrc.tc.columbia.edu/publications/online-demand-student-voices.html

Jakubowski, T. G., & Dembo, M. H. (2004). The influence of self-efficacy, identity style, and stage of change on academic self-regulation. *Journal of College Reading and Learning, 35,* 5–22.

Jones, G. (2009). *Youth.* Cambridge, UK: Polity Press.

Jones, R. M. (1992). Identity and problem behaviors. In G. R. Adams, T. P. Gullotta, & R. Montemayor (Eds.), *Adolescent identity formation: Advances in adolescent development* (pp. 216–33). Newbury Park, CA: Sage.

Jones, R. M. (1994). Curricula focused on behavioral deviance. In S. L. Archer (Ed.), *Interventions for adolescent identity development* (pp. 174–90). Newbury Park, CA: Sage.

Jones, R. M., & Hartmann, B. R. (1988). Ego identity: developmental differences and experimental substance use among adolescents. *Journal of Adolescence, 11,* 347–60.

Jordan, W. D. (1978). Searching for adulthood in America. In E. H. Erikson (Ed.), *Adulthood.* New York: Norton.

Juris, J. S., & Pleyers, G. H. (2009). Alter-activism: Emerging cultures of participation among young global justice activists. *Journal of Youth Studies, 12,* 57–75.

Kalleberg, A. L. (2007). *The mismatched worker.* New York: Norton.

Kaplan, H. (1997). The evolution of the human life course. In K. Wachter & C. Finch (Eds.), *Between Zeus and the Salmon: The biodemography of longevity* (pp. 175–211). Washington: National Academy Press.

Keay, D. (1987, October 31). Aids, education and the year 2000! *Women's Own,* pp. 8–10. Retrieved from http://www.margaretthatcher.org/speeches/displaydocument.asp?docid=106689

Kegan, R. (1994). *In over our heads: The mental demands of modern life.* Cambridge, Mass: Harvard University Press.

Kelly, G. A. (1955). *The psychology of personal constructs.* New York: Norton.

Kelly, P. (2006). The entrepreneurial self and youth at risk: Exploring the horizons of identity in the twenty-first century. *Journal of Youth Studies, 9,* 17–32.

Kennedy, G., T., Dalgarno, J. B., & Waycott, J. (2010). Beyond natives and immigrants: Exploring types of net generation students. *Journal of Computer Assisted Learning 26,* 332–43.

Kerr, M., & Stattin, H. (2000). What parents know, how they know it, and several forms of adolescent adjustment: Further support for a reinterpretation of monitoring. *Developmental Psychology, 36,* 366–80.

Kimberlee, R. (2002). Why don't British young people vote at general elections. *Journal of Youth Studies, 3,* 85–98.

King, P. M., & Kitchener, K. S. (1994). *Developing reflective judgment: Understanding and promoting intellectual growth and critical thinking in adolescents and adults.* San Francisco: Jossey-Bass.

Kirkham, R. L. (1992). *Theories of truth.* Cambridge, MA: MIT Press.

Kirschner, P. A., & Karpinski, A. C. (2010). Facebook and academic performance. *Computers in Human Behavior, 26,* 1237–45.

Klein, N. (2000). *No logo: Taking aim at the brand bullies.* Toronto: Knopf.

Kohn, M. (1977). *Class and conformity: A study in values* (2nd ed.). Chicago: University of Chicago Press.

Kolikant, Y. B.-D. (2010). Digital natives, better learners? Students' beliefs about how the Internet influenced their ability to learn. *Computers in Human Behavior, 26,* 1384–91.

Kroger, J. (2003). Identity development during adolescence. In G. R. Adams & M. D. Berzonsky (Eds.), *Blackwell handbook of adolescence* (pp. 205–26). Malden, MA: Blackwell Publishing.

Kroger, J. (2005). Critique of a postmodernist critique. *Identity: An International Journal of Theory and Research, 5,* 195–204.

Kroger, J., Martinussen, M., & Marcia, J. E. (2010). Identity status change during adolescence and young adulthood: A meta-analysis. *Journal of Adolescence, 33,* 683–98.

Kuczynski, L., Marshall, S., & Schell, K. (1997). Value socialization in a bi-directional context. In J. E. Grusec & L. Kuczynski (Eds.), *Parenting and the internalization of values: A handbook of contemporary theory* (pp. 23–50). Toronto: John Wiley & Sons.

Kuhn, T. S. (1970). *The structure of scientific revolution* (2nd ed.). Chicago: University of Chicago Press.

Lamborn, S., Mounts, N., Steinberg, L., & Dornbusch, S. (1991). Patterns of competence and adjustment among adolescents from authoritative, authoritarian, indulgent, and neglectful homes. *Child Development, 62,* 1049–65.

Lanier, J. (2010). *You are not a gadget: A manifesto.* New York: Knopf.

Lanier, J. (2013). *Who owns the future?* New York: Simon & Schuster.

Lareau, A. (2002). Invisible inequality: Social class and childbearing in black families and white families. *American Sociological Review, 67,* 747–76.

Lareau, A. (2003). *Unequal childhoods: Class, race, and family life.* Berkeley, CA: University of California Press.

Lareau, A. (2011). *Unequal childhoods: Class, race, and family life. Second edition with an update a decade later.* Berkeley, CA: University of California Press.

Lareau, A., & Weininger, E. (2007). Class, culture and child rearing: The transition to college. Retrieved from http://www.hks.harvard.edu/inequality/Seminar/Papers/Lareau07.pdf

Larson, R. W. (2000). Toward a psychology of positive youth development. *American Psychologist, 55,* 170–83.

Lasch, C. (1995). *The revolt of the elites: The betrayal of democracy.* New York: Norton.

Lee, E. F. (2010). *Enfranchising American youth.* Washington, DC: Project Vote. Retrieved from http://www.whatkidscando.org/youth_on_the_trail_2012/pdf/2010_Policy_Paper-Enfranchising_American_Youth.pdf

Lennards, J. L. (1983). Education. In R. Hagedorn (Ed.), *Sociology* (2nd ed.). Toronto: Holt, Rinehart and Winston.

Lerner, R. M. (2002). *Concepts and theories of human development* (3rd ed.). Mahwah, NJ: Lawrence Erlbaum.

Lerner, R. M., Brown, J. D., & Kier, C. (2005). *Adolescence: Development, diversity, context, and application.* Toronto: Pearson Education Canada.

Lerner, R. M., Lerner, J. V., von Eye, A., Bowers, E. P., & Lewin-Bizan, S. (2011). Individual and contextual bases of thriving in adolescence. *Journal of Adolescence, 34,* 1107–14.

Lerner, R. M., & Steinberg, L. (Eds.) (2009). *Handbook of adolescent psychology* (3rd ed.) *Volume 2: Contextual influences on adolescent development.* Hoboken, NJ: Wiley.

Lesko, N., & Talburt, S. (Eds.). (2012). *Keywords in youth studies: Tracing affects, movements, knowledges.* New York: Routledge.

Levidow, L. (2002). Marketizing higher education: Neoliberal strategies and counter-strategies. In K. Robins & F. Webster (Eds.), *The virtual university? Knowledge, markets and management* (pp. 227–48). Oxford, UK: Oxford University Press.

Levine, C. (2005). What happened to agency? Some observations concerning the postmodern perspective on identity. *Identity: An International Journal of Theory and Research, 5,* 175–85.

Levitt, C. (1984). *Children of privilege: Student revolt in the sixties.* Toronto: University of Toronto Press.

Linn, S. (2004). *Consuming kids: The hostile takeover of childhood.* New York: The New Press.

Liu, X., Qian, M., & Huang, Y. (2004). The family environment of freshmen in one key-university and another un-key-university. *Chinese Mental Health Journal, 18,* 541–43.

Livingstone, D., & Hart, D. (2005, Fall). Hedging our bets on the future. *Academic Matters: The Journal of Higher Education,* 6–14.

Livingstone, S. (2008). Afterword: Learning the lessons of research on youth participation and the Internet. *Journal of Youth Studies, 11,* 561–64.

Loader, B. (Ed.). (2007). *Young citizens in the digital age.* London: Routledge.

Lockhart, A. (1971). Graduate unemployment and the myth of human capital. In D. T. Davies & K. Herman (Eds.), *Social space: Canadian perspectives.* Toronto: New Press.

Maccoby, E. E., & Martin, J. A. (1983). Socialization in the context of the family: Parent–child interaction. In P. H. Mussen (Series Ed.) & E. M. Hetherington (Vol. Ed.), *Handbook of child psychology: Vol. 4 Socialization, personality, and social development* (4th ed.) (pp. 1–101). New York: Wiley.

MacDonald, R. (2011). Youth transitions, unemployment and underemployment: Plus ça change, plus c'est la même chose? *Journal of Sociology, 47,* 427–44.

MacDonald, R. (2013, April). *Marginalising the mainstream? The 'missing middle', youth studies and 'the precariat.'* Paper presented at the New Agendas on Youth and Young Adulthood Conference, Glasgow, Scotland.

Marcia, J. E. (1993). The ego identity status approach to ego identity. In J. E. Marcia, A. S. Waterman, D. R. Matteson, S. L. Archer, & J. L Orlofsky (Eds.), *Ego identity: A handbook for psychosocial research* (pp. 3–41). New York: Springer-Verlag.

Marcia, J. E., Waterman, A. S., Matteson, D. R., Archer, S. L., & Orlofsky, J. L. (Eds.). (1993). *Ego identity: A handbook for psychosocial research.* New York: Springer-Verlag.

Marcuse, H. (1972). *Counter-revolution and revolt.* Boston: Beacon Press.

Marger, M. M. (2005). *Social inequality: Patterns and processes* (3rd ed.). Boston: McGraw-Hill.

Marshall, S. K., Tilton-Weaver, L. C., & Bosdet, L. (2005). Information management: Considering adolescents' regulation of parental knowledge. *Journal of Adolescence*, 28, 633–47.

Marshall, S. K., Young, R. A., & Tilton-Weaver, L. C. (2008). Balancing acts adolescents' and mothers' friendship projects. *Journal of Adolescent Research*, 23, 544–65.

McAdams, D. (1993). *The stories we live by: Personal myths and the making of the self.* New York: W. Morrow.

McAdams, D. (2011). Narrative identity. In S. J. Schwartz, V. L. Vignoles, & L. Koen (Eds.), *Handbook of identity theory and research* (pp. 99–115). New York: Springer.

McClelland, D. (1961). *The achieving society.* New York: Free Press.

McDonald, K. (1999). *Struggles for subjectivity: Identity, action and youth experience.* Cambridge, UK: Cambridge University Press.

McLoyd, V. C., Kaplan, R., Purtell, K. M., Bagley, E., Hardaway, C. R., & Smalls, C. (2009). Poverty and socioeconomic disadvantage in adolescence. In R. M. Lerner & L. Steinberg (Eds.), *Handbook of adolescent psychology* (3rd ed.) *Volume 2: Contextual influences on adolescent development* (pp. 444–91). Hoboken, NJ: Wiley.

McQuaig, L., & Brook, N. (2011). *The trouble with billionaires.* Toronto: Penguin.

McRobbie, A. (1980). Settling accounts with subcultures: A feminist critique. *Screen Education*, 34, 37–49.

Mead, M. (1928). *Coming of age in Samoa: A psychological study of primitive youth for Western Civilization.* New York: Morrow Quill Paperbacks.

Mead, M. (1930). *Growing up in New Guinea: A comparative study of primitive education.* New York: Harper Collins.

Mead, M. (1970). *Culture and commitment: A study of the generation gap.* Garden City, NJ: Doubleday.

Merchant, G. (2005). Identity involvement: Identity performance in children's digital writing. *Discourse*, 26, 301–14.

Merton. R. K. (1938). Social structure and anomie. *American Sociological Review*, 3, 672–87.

Meyer, J., & Land, R. (2003). *Threshold concepts and troublesome knowledge: Linkages to ways of thinking and practising within the disciplines.* University of Edinburgh: ETL Project.

Michaels, W. B. (2006). *The trouble with diversity: How we learned to love identity and ignore inequality.* New York: Metropolitan Books.

Miles, S. (2000). *Youth lifestyles in a changing world.* Buckingham, UK: Open University Press.

Mills, C. W. (1959). *The sociological imagination.* New York: Oxford University Press.

Milner, H. (2010). *The Internet generation: Engaged citizens or political dropouts.* Medford, MA: Tufts University Press.

Milner, M., Jr. (2004). *Freaks, geeks, and cool kids: American teenagers, schools, and the culture of consumption.* New York: Routledge.

Ministry of Education, Finland. (2008). *The Finnish government's child and youth policy programme 2007–2011.* Helsinki: Author.

Mizen, P. (2002). Putting the politics back into youth studies: Keynesianism, monetarism and the changing state of youth. *Journal of Youth Studies*, 5, 5–20.

Molesworth, R., Scullion, R., & Nixon E. (Eds.). (2011). *The marketization of higher education and the student as consumer.* London: Routledge.

Mongardini, C. (1992). The ideology of postmodernity. *Theory, Culture & Society, 9,* 55–65.

Mørch, S. (1995). Culture and the challenge of adaptation: Foreign youth in Denmark. *International Journal of Comparative Race and Ethnic Studies, 2,* 102–15.

Mørch, S. (2005). Researching youth life. In H. Helve (Ed.), *Mixed methods in youth research* (pp. 29–56). Helsinki: Finnish Youth Research Network.

Morozov, E. (2013). *To save everything, click here.* New York: Perseus Books.

Most, T., Wiesel, A., & Blitzer, T. (2007). Identity and attitudes towards cochlear implant among deaf and hard of hearing adolescents. *Deafness & Education International, 9,* 68–82.

Murray, C. (2008a). *Real education: Four simple truths about bringing America's schools back to reality.* New York: Crown Forum.

Murray, C. (2008b, September 8). Are too many people going to college? *The American: A magazine of ideas.* Retrieved from http://www.american.com/archive/ 2008/september-october-magazine/are-too-many-people-going-to-college

Muuss, R. (1996). *Theories of adolescence* (6th ed.). New York: McGraw Hill.

Myles, J., Picot, W. G., & Wannell, T. (1988). *Wages and jobs in the 1980s: Changing youth wages and the declining middle.* Ottawa: Statistics Canada.

Nader, R., & Coco, L. (1999, January). The corporate exploitation of children. *The CCPA Monitor,* 12–14.

National Geographic Education Foundation. (2002). *National Geographic— Roper 2002 Global Geographic Literacy Survey.* Retrieved from http://www. nationalgeographic.com/geosurvey2002/download/RoperSurvey.pdf

Neuman, W. L. (2006). *Social research methods: Qualitative and quantitative approaches.* Boston: Pearson.

Nickerson, R. S. (1998). Confirmation bias: A ubiquitous phenomenon in many guises. *Review of General Psychology, 2,* 175–220.

Niedzviecki, H. (2004). *Hello, I'm special: How individuality became the new conformity.* Toronto: Penguin Canada.

Nilan, P. (2011). Youth sociology must cross cultures. *Youth Studies Australia, 20*(3), 20–6.

O'Neill, B. (2003). Examining declining electoral turnout among Canada's youth. *Electoral Insight, 5,* 15–19.

OECD. (2011). Voting. In *Society at a glance 2011: OECD social indicators.* Paris: OECD Publishing. Retrieved from http://dx.doi.org/10.1787/soc_glance-2011-29-en

Offer, D., & Offer, J. (1975). *From teenage to young manhood: A psychological study.* New York: Basic Books.

Orlofsky, J. L., Marcia, J. E., & Lesser, I. M. (1973). Ego identity status and the intimacy versus isolation crisis of young adulthood. *Journal of Personality and Social Psychology, 27,* 211–19.

Ortiz, A. (2003). Adolescent brain development and legal culpability. *American Bar Association.* Retrieved from www.abanet.org/crimjust/juvjus/factsheets_brain_ development.pdf

Osterman, P. (1980). *Getting started: The youth labor market.* Cambridge: MIT Press.

Oswald, M. E., & Grosjean, S. (2004). Confirmation bias. In R. F. Pohl (Ed.), *Cognitive illusions: A handbook on fallacies and biases in thinking, judgment and memory* (pp. 79–96). Hove, UK: Psychology Press.

Pakulski, J., & Waters, M. (1996). *The death of class*. London: Sage.

Palfrey, J., & Gasser, U. (2008). *Born digital: Understanding the first generation of digital natives*. New York: Basic Books.

Parsons, T. (1959). The school class as a social system: Some of its functions in American society. *Harvard Educational Review, 29*, 297–318.

Parsons, T. (1961). Youth in the context of American society. In E. H. Erikson (Ed.), *The challenge of youth* (pp. 110–41). Garden City, NY: Doubleday Anchor.

Parsons, T., & Platt, G. M. (1973). *The American university*. Cambridge: Harvard University Press.

Pascarella, E. T., & Terenzini, P. T. (2005). *How college affects students: Volume 2. A third decade of research*. San Francisco: Jossey-Bass.

Pastore, N. (1949). *The nature–nurture controversy*. New York: King's Crown Press.

Paul, R., & Elder, L. (2006). *Critical thinking: Concepts and tools*. The Foundation for Critical Thinking. Retrieved from http://www.criticalthinking.org

Paus, T. (2009). Brain development. In R. M. Lerner & L. Steinberg (Eds.), *Handbook of adolescent psychology* (3rd ed.) *Volume 1: Individual bases of adolescent development* (pp. 95–115). Hoboken, NJ: Wiley.

Payne, M. (2001). Limitations unlimited: Interrogating some finer points of the 'scientific study' of adolescence. *Journal of Youth Studies, 4*, 175–94.

Petersen, A. C. (1993). Creating adolescents: The role of context and process in developmental trajectories. *Journal of Research on Adolescence, 3*, 1–18.

Phillips, T. M., & Pittman, J. F. (2003). Identity processes in poor adolescents: Exploring the linkages between economic disadvantage and the primary task of adolescence. *Identity: An International Journal of Theory and Research, 3*, 115–29.

Phinney, J. S. (1989). Stages of ethnic identity development in minority group adolescents. *Journal of Early Adolescence, 9*, 34–49.

Phinney, J. S. (2005a). Ethnic identity in late modern times: A response to Rattansi and Phoenix. *Identity: An International Journal of Theory and Research, 5*, 187–94.

Phinney, J. S. (2005b). Ethnic identity development in minority adolescents. In C. B. Fisher & R. M. Lerner (Eds.), *Encyclopedia of applied development science*, Vol. 1 (pp. 420–2). Thousand Oaks, CA: Sage.

Phinney, J. S. (2006). Ethnic identity exploration in emerging adulthood. In J. J. Arnett & J. Tanner (Eds.), *Emerging adults in America: Coming of age in the 21st century* (pp. 117–34). Washington: American Psychological Association.

Phinney, J. S., Jacoby, B., & Silva, C. (2007). Positive intergroup attitudes: The role of ethnic identity. *International Journal of Behavioral Development, 31*, 478–90.

Phinney, J. S., & Rosenthal, D. A. (1992). Ethnic identity in adolescence: Process, context, and outcome. In G. R. Adams, T. P. Gullotta, & R. Montemayor (Eds.), *Adolescent identity formation: Advances in adolescent development* (pp. 145–72). Newbury Park, CA: Sage.

Phoenix, A. (2010). Ethnicities. In M. Wetherell & C. T. Mohanty (Eds.), *The Sage handbook of identities* (pp. 297–320). Los Angeles: Sage.

Phoenix, A., & Rattansi, A. (2005). Proliferating theories: Self and identity in post-Eriksonian context: A rejoinder to Berzonsky, Kroger, Levine, Phinney, Schachter, and Weigert and Gecas. *Identity: An International Journal of Theory and Research, 5*, 205–25.

Picot, G. (1998). *What is happening to earnings, inequality and youth wages in the 1990s?* Ottawa: Statistics Canada.

Prensky, M. (2001). Digital natives, digital immigrants. *On the Horizon, 9.5*, 1–6.

Prensky, M. (2006). *Don't bother me, mom—I'm learning: How computer and video games are preparing your kids for twenty-first century success—and how you can help!* Saint Paul, MN: Paragon House Publishers.

Proefrock, D. W. (1981). Adolescence: Social fact and psychological concept. *Adolescence*, 26, 851–8.

Pryor, F., & Schaffer, D. (1999). *Who's not working and why: Employment, cognitive skills, wages, and the changing U.S. labor market.* New York: Cambridge University Press.

Puuronen, V. (2005). Methodological starting points and problems of youth research. In H. Helve (Ed.), *Mixed methods in youth research* (pp. 15–28). Helsinki: Finnish Youth Research Network.

Quart, A. (2002). *Branded: The buying and selling of teenagers.* New York: Perseus.

Raby, R. (2005). What is resistance? *Journal of Youth Studies*, 8, 151–71.

Raby, R. (2012). Age: Decentring adulthood. In D. Brock, R. Raby, & M. P. Thomas (Eds.), *Power and everyday practices.* Toronto: Nelson Education.

Rattansi, A., & Phoenix, A. (2005). Rethinking youth identities: Modernist and postmodernist frameworks. *Identity: An International Journal of Theory and Research*, 5, 97–123. Reprinted from Bynner, J., Chisholm, L., & Furlong, A. (Eds.) (1997). *Youth, citizenship and social change in a European context.* Aldershot, UK: Ashgate.

Rifkin, J. (1995). *The end of work.* New York: G.P. Putman's Sons.

Rivard, R. (2013, April 25). MOOCs may eye the world market, but does the world want them? *Inside Higher Ed.* Retrieved from http://www.insidehighered.com/news/2013/04/25/moocs-may-eye-world-market-does-world-want-them

Roazen, P. (1976). *Erik H. Erikson: The power and limits of a vision.* New York: Free Press.

Roberts, K. (2007). Youth transitions and generations: A response to Wyn and Woodman. *Journal of Youth Studies*, 10, 263–69.

Roberts, K. (2009). *Youth in transition: Eastern Europe and the West.* Houndmills, UK: Palgrave MacMillan.

Roberts, S. (2011). Beyond 'NEET' and 'tidy' pathways: Considering the 'missing middle' of youth transition studies. *Journal of Youth Studies*, 14, 21–39.

Rokeach, M. (1960). *The open and closed mind.* New York: Basic.

Roksa, J., & Potter, D. (2011). Parenting and academic achievement: Intergenerational transmission of educational advantage. *Sociology of Education*, 84, 299–321.

Rosenberg, M. (1965). *Society and the adolescent self-image.* Princeton, NJ: Princeton University Press.

Rosenberg, M. (1981). The self-concept: Social product and social force. In M. Rosenberg & R. H. Turner (Eds.), *Social psychology: Sociological perspectives* (pp. 593–624). New York: Basic Books.

Rotheram-Borus, M. J., & Wyche, K. F. (1994). Ethnic differences in identity formation in the United States. In S. L. Archer (Ed.), *Interventions for adolescent identity development* (pp. 62–83). Thousand Oaks, CA: Sage.

Rowntree, J., & Rowntree, M. (1968). The political economy of youth. *Our Generation*, 6, 155–90.

Rubab, G. A., Marshall, S. K., & Shapka, J. D. (2010). A domain-specific approach to adolescent reporting of parental control. *Journal of Adolescence*, 33, 355–66.

Rushkoff, D. (Producer) (2001). The merchants of cool (video cassette). *Frontline*, PBS. Available for free online viewing, Retrieved from http://www.pbs.org/wgbh/pages/frontline/shows/cool/view/

Rushkoff, D. (2013). *Present shock: When everything happens now.* New York: Penguin Group.

Rushkoff, D., & Purvis, L. (2011). *Program or be programed: Ten commandments for the digital age.* Berkeley, CA: Soft Skull Press.

Sartre, J.-P. (1969). *Being and nothingness.* London: Routledge.

Savin-Williams, R. C. (2011). Identity development among sexual-minority youth. In S. J. Schwartz, V. L. Vignoles, & L. Koen (Eds.), *Handbook of identity theory and research* (pp. 671–89). New York: Springer.

Schlegel, A., & Barry, H. (1991). *Adolescence: An anthropological inquiry.* New York: Free Press.

Schlosser, E. (2001). *Fast food nation: The dark side of the all-American meal.* New York: Perennial.

Schoeni, R. F., & Ross, K. E. (2005). Material assistance from families during the transition to adulthood. In R. A. Settersten, F. F. Furstenberg, & R. G. Rumbaut (Eds.), *On the frontier of adulthood: Theory, research, and public policy* (pp. 396–416). Chicago: University of Chicago Press.

Schor, J. (2004). *Born to buy: The commercialized child and the new consumer culture.* New York: Scribner.

Schunk, D. H., & Meece, J. L. (2006). Self-efficacy development in adolescence. In F. Pajares & T. Urdan (Eds.), *Self-efficacy beliefs of adolescents* (pp. 45–69). Greenwich, CT: Information Age Publishing.

Schwartz, S. J. (2001). The evolution of Eriksonian and neo-Eriksonian identity theory and research: A review and integration. *Identity: An International Journal of Theory and Research*, 1, 7–58.

Seeman, M. (1981). Intergroup relations. In M. Rosenberg & R. H. Turner (Eds.), *Social psychology: Sociological perspectives* (pp. 378–410). New York: Basic Books.

Seidman, S. (1994). *The postmodern turn: New perspectives on social theory.* Cambridge: Cambridge University Press.

Seidman, S. (2004). *Contested knowledge: Social theory today* (3rd ed.). Malden, MA: Blackwell.

Sennett, R., & Cobb, J. (1972). *The hidden injuries of class.* New York: Vintage Books.

Sercombe H. (2010). The 'teen brain' research: Critical perspectives. *Youth and Policy*, 105, 71–80.

Sercombe, H., & Paus, T. (2009). The 'teen brain' research: An introduction and implications for practitioners. *Youth and Policy*, 103, 25–38.

Shackel, N. (2005). The vacuity of postmodernist methodology. *Metaphilosophy*, 36, 295–320.

Shankman, P. (2009). *The trashing of Margaret Mead: Anatomy of an anthropological controversy.* Madison, WI: University of Wisconsin Press.

Sherif, M. (1958). Superordinate goals in the reduction of intergroup conflict. *American Journal of Sociology*, 63, 258–349.

Siraj-Blatchford, I. (2010). Learning in the home and at school: How working class children 'succeed against the odds'. *British Educational Research Journal*, 36, 463–82.

Small, A., & Cripps, J. (2012). On becoming: Developing an empowering cultural identity framework for deaf youth and adults. In A. Small, J. Cripps, & J. E. Côté (Eds.), *Cultural space and self/identity development among deaf youth* (pp. 29–41). Toronto: Canadian Cultural Society of the Deaf.

Small, A., Cripps, J., & Côté, J. E. (2012). *Cultural space and self/identity development among deaf youth.* Toronto: Canadian Cultural Society of the Deaf.

Small, G., & Vorgan, G. (2008). *iBrain: Surviving the technological alteration of the modern mind.* New York: Collins Living.

Smart, B. (1993). *Postmodernity.* London: Routledge.

Smetana, J. G., & Asquith, P. (1994). Adolescents' and parents' conceptions of parental authority and personal autonomy. *Child Development,* 65, 1147–62.

Smetana, J. G., Metzger, A., Gettman, D., & Campione-Barr, N. (2006). Disclosure and secrecy in adolescent–parent relationships. *Child Development,* 77, 201–17.

Snarey, J., Kohlberg, L., & Noam, G. (1983). Ego development in perspective: Structural stage, functional phase, and cultural age-period models. *Developmental Review,* 3, 303–38.

Sorell, G. T., & Montgomery, M. J. (2001). Feminist perspectives on Erikson's theory: Its relevance for contemporary identity development research. *Identity: An International Journal of Theory and Research,* 1, 97–128.

Spera, C. (2005). A review of the relationship among parenting practices, parenting styles, and adolescent school achievement educational. *Psychology Review,* 17, 125–46.

Spradley, J., & Mann, B. (1975). *The cocktail waitress.* New York: John Wiley & Sons.

Stattin, H., & Kerr, M. (2000). Parental monitoring: A reinterpretation. *Child Development,* 71, 1072–85.

Steger, M. B., & Roy, R. K. (2010). *Neoliberalism: A very short introduction.* Oxford: Oxford University Press.

Stein, L. M., & Hoopes, J. L. (1985). *Identity formation in the adopted adolescent: The Delaware family study.* New York: Child Welfare League of America.

Stein, M. R., Vidich, A. J., & White, D. M. (1960). *Identity and anxiety: Survival of the person in mass society.* New York: The Free Press.

Steinberg, L. (1990). Pubertal maturation and parent–adolescent distance: An evolutionary perspective. In G. R. Adams, R. Montemayor, & T. P. Gullotta (Eds.), *Biology of adolescent behavior and development.* Newbury Park, CA: Sage.

Steinberg, L. (1996). *Beyond the classroom: Why school reform has failed and what parents need to do about it.* New York: Simon & Schuster.

Steinberg, L. (2001). We know some things: Parent–adolescent relationships in retrospect and prospect. *Journal of Research on Adolescence,* 11, 1–19.

Strasburger, V. C., & Donnerstein, E. (1999). Children, adolescents, and the media: Issues and solutions. *Pediatrics,* 103, 129–39.

Sukarieh, M., & Tannock, S. (2011). The positivity imperative: a critical look at the 'new' youth development movement. *Journal of Youth Studies,* 14, 675–91.

Sum, A., Khatiwada, I., McLaughlin, J., & Palma, S. (2011). No country for young men: Deteriorating labor market prospects for low-skilled men in the United States. *The ANNALS of the American Academy of Political and Social Science,* 635, 24–55.

Sum, A., & McLaughlin, J. (2011). *Changes in the weekly and annual earnings of young adults from 1979–2010: Progress and setbacks amidst widening inequality.* CDF Policy Brief #3. Retrieved from http://www.childrensdefense.org/child-research-data-publications/changes-in-the-weekly-and.pdf

Sundar, P. (2008). 'Brown it up' or to 'bring down the brown': Identity and strategy in second-generation, South Asian–Canadian youth. *Journal of Ethnic & Cultural Diversity in Social Work: Innovation in Theory, Research & Practice,* 17, 251–78.

Swartz, D. L. (2003). From correspondence to contradiction and change: Schooling in capitalist America revisited. *Sociological Forum,* 18, 167–86.

Swedish Institute. (1993). *Fact sheets on Sweden: Facts and figures about youth in Sweden.* Stockholm: Author.

Swedish National Board for Youth Affairs. (1999a). *Statistics on youth people in Sweden: Tables.* Stockholm: Author.

Swedish National Board for Youth Affairs. (1999b). *Review of national youth policy.* Stockholm: Author.

Swedish National Board for Youth Affairs. (2011). *Fokus10: On youth influence.* Stockholm: Author.

Swidler, A. (1986). Culture in action: Symbols and strategies. *American Sociological Review*, 51, 273–86.

Syed, M., & Azmitia, M. (2008). A narrative approach to ethnic identity in emerging adulthood: Bringing life to the identity status model. *Developmental Psychology*, 44, 1012–27.

Syed, M., & Azmitia, M. (2010). Narrative and ethnic identity exploration: A longitudinal account of emerging adults' ethnicity-related experiences. *Developmental Psychology*, 46, 208–19.

Tanner, J. (2010). *Teenage troubles: Youth and deviance in Canada* (2nd ed.). Toronto: Nelson.

Tannock, S. (2001). *Youth at work: The unionized fast-food and grocery workplace.* Philadelphia: Temple University Press.

Tapscott, D. (2009). *Grown up digital: How the net generation is changing your world.* New York: McGraw-Hill.

Taylor, C. (1991). *The malaise of modernity.* Toronto: Anansi.

Thomas, W. I., & Thomas, D. (1929). *The child in America* (2nd ed.). New York: Alfred Knopf.

Thompson, W. E., & Bynum, J. E. (2010). *Juvenile delinquency: A sociological approach.* Boston: Allyn & Bacon.

Thorbecke, W., & Grotevant, H. D. (1982). Gender differences in interpersonal identity formation. *Journal of Youth and Adolescence*, 11, 479–92.

Thorndike, E. L. (1904). The newest psychology. *Educational Review*, 28, 217–27.

Tilleczek, K. (2011). *Approaching youth studies: Being, becoming, and belonging.* Toronto: Oxford University Press.

Torche, F. (2011). Is a college degree still the great equalizer? Intergenerational mobility across levels of schooling in the United States. *American Journal of Sociology*, 117, 763–807.

Trow, M. (2010). Academic standards and mass higher education. In M. Burrage (Ed.), *Martin Trow: Twentieth-century higher education élite to mass to universal* (pp. 241–68). Baltimore: Johns Hopkins University Press.

Turner, E. A., Chandler, M., & Heffer, R. W. (2009). The influence of parenting styles, achievement motivation, and self-efficacy on academic performance in college students. *Journal of College Student Development*, 50, 337–46.

Turner, J. H. (2006). Explaining the social world: Historicism versus positivism. *The Sociological Quarterly*, 47, 451–63.

Tyyskä, V. (2009). *Youth and society: The long and winding road* (2nd ed.). Toronto: Canadian Scholars Press.

Unger, R., Draper, R., & Pendergrass, M. (1986). Personal epistemology and personal experience. *Journal of Social Issues*, 42, 67–79.

U.S. Census Bureau. (2011). *Statistical Abstract of the United States: 2011.* Washington, DC: Author.

Vaidhyanathan, S. (2008, September 19). Generational myth: Not all young people are tech-savvy. *Chronicle of Higher Education*. Retrieved from http://chronicle.com/free/v55/i04/04b00701.htm

Van de Werfhorst, H., & Andersen, R. (2005). Social background, credential inflation and educational strategies. *Acta Sociologica*, 48, 321–40.

Van Hoof, A. (1999). The identity status field re-reviewed: An update of unresolved and neglected issues with a view on some alternative approaches. *Developmental Review*, 19, 497–556.

Vedder, R., Denhart, C., & Robe, J. (2013). Why are recent college graduates underemployed? University enrollments and labor-market realities. Washington: Center for College Affordability and Productivity. Retrieved from www.centerforcollegeaffordability.org

Veenhof, B., & Timusk, P. (2009, August). Online activities of Canadian boomers and seniors, *Canadian Social Trends*. Retrieved from http://www.statcan.gc.ca/pub/11-008-x/2009002/article/10910-eng.pdf

Vromen, A. (2003). 'People try to put us down…': Participatory citizenship of 'Generation X'. *Australian Journal of Political Science*, 38, 79–99.

Walker, L. J., & Henning, K. H. (1999). Parenting style and the development of moral reasoning. *Journal of Moral Education*, 28, 359–74.

Walsh, J. R. (1935). Capital concept applied to man. *The Quarterly Journal of Economics*, 49, 255–85.

Walters, D. (2004). The relationship between postsecondary education and skill: Comparing credentialism with human capital theory. *Canadian Journal of Higher Education*, 34, 97–124.

Waterman, A. S. (1988). Identity status theory and Erikson's theory: Communalities and differences. *Developmental Review*, 8, 185–208.

Waterman, A. S. (1992). Identity as an aspect of optimal psychological functioning. In G. R. Adams, T. P. Gullota, & R. Montemayor (Eds.), *Adolescent identity formation* (pp. 50–72). Newbury Park, CA: Sage.

Waterman, C. K., & Nevid, J. S. (1977). Sex differences in the resolution of the identity crisis. *Journal of Youth and Adolescence*, 6, 337–42.

Weigert, A. J., Teitge, J. S., & Teitge, D. W. (1986). *Society and identity: Toward a sociological psychology*. Cambridge: Cambridge University Press.

Weininger, E. B., & Lareau, A. (2009). Paradoxical pathways: An ethnographic extension of Kohn's findings on class and childrearing. *Journal of Marriage and the Family*, 71, 680–85.

Weinstock, D. (2012, November). Equality of opportunity, equality of means: An argument for low tuition and the student strike. *Academic Matters: OCUFA's Journal of Higher Education*, 16–18.

Wells Fargo. (2010). *Youth and tech savvy not always related*. Retrieved from https://www.wellsfargo.com/press/2010/20100121_Tech_Survey

Wertheimer, M. (1972). *Fundamental issues in psychology*. New York: Holt, Rinehart & Winston.

Wetherell, M. (Ed.). (2009). *Theorizing identities and social action*. Houndmills, UK: Palgrave MacMillan.

Wetherell, M., & Mohanty, C. T. (Eds.). (2010). *The Sage handbook of identities*. Los Angeles: Sage.

Wexler, P. (1983). *Critical social psychology*. London: Routledge & Kegan Paul.

Whelan, A., Walker, R., & Moore, C. (Eds.) (2013). *Zombies in the academy: Living death in higher education*. Chicago: University of Chicago Press.

White, J. M. (2000). Alcoholism and identity development: A theoretical integration of the least mature status with the typologies of alcoholism. *Alcoholism Treatment Quarterly*, 18, 43–59.

White, R. (2007). Paradoxes of youth participation: Political activism and youth disenfranchisement. In L. J. Saha, M. Print, & K. Edwards (Eds.), *Youth and political participation* (pp. 65–78). Rotterdam: Sense Publishers.

White, R., Wyn, J., & Albanese, P. (2011). *Youth & society: Exploring the social dynamics of youth experience* (Canadian edition). Toronto: Oxford University Press.

Wilkinson, R., & Pickett, K. (2010). *The spirit level: Why greater equality makes societies stronger.* New York: Bloomsbury Press.

William T. Grant Foundation. (1988). *The forgotten half: Non-college youth in America.* Washington: Author.

Williamson, H. (1997). Status Zero youth and the 'underclass': Some considerations. In R. MacDonald (Ed.), *Youth, the 'underclass' and social exclusion.* London: Routledge.

Willingham, D. T. (2009). *Why don't students like school?* San Francisco: Jossey-Bass.

Willis, P. (1977). *Learning to labour.* Farnborough Gower.

Willis, P. (1978). *Profane culture.* London: Routledge & Kegan Paul.

Wiltfang, G., & Scarbecz, M. (1990). Social class and adolescents' self-esteem. Another look. *Social Psychology Quarterly*, 53, 174–83.

Wintre, M. G., & Yaffe, M. (2000). First-year students' adjustment to university life as a function of relationships with parents. *Journal of Adolescent Research*, 15, 9–37.

Wolf, A. (2002). *Does education matter? Myths about education and economic growth.* London: Penguin.

Wolf, M., Blomquist, C., Huq, R., Kovacs, E., Williamson, H., & Lauritzen, P. (2004). *Youth policy in Norway.* Strasbourg: Council of Europe Publishing.

Wrong, D. (1961). The oversocialized conception of man in modern sociology. *American Sociological Review*, 26, 188–92.

Wyn, J. (2008). New patterns of youth transition in education in Australia. In R. Bendit & M. Hahn-Bleibtreu (Eds.), *Youth transitions: Processes of social inclusion and patterns of vulnerability in a globalised world* (pp. 73–83). Opladen, Farmington Hills: Barbara Budrich Publishers.

Wyn, J. (2012). Peer groups. In N. Lesko & S. Talburt (Eds.), *Keywords in youth studies: Tracing affects, movements, knowledges* (pp. 92–97). New York: Routledge.

Wyn, J., & Woodman, D. (2006). Generation, youth and social change in Australia. *Journal of Youth Studies*, 9, 495–514.

Wyn, J., & Woodman, D. (2007). Researching youth in a context of social change: A reply to Roberts. *Journal of Youth Studies*, 10, 373–81.

Yoder, A. E. (2000). Barriers to ego identity status formation: A contextual qualification of Marcia's identity status. *Journal of Adolescence*, 23, 95–106.

Zhikun, J., & Xiong, Y. (2005). Contemporary trends in youth and juvenile studies in China. In H. Helve & G. Holm (Eds.), *Contemporary youth research: Local expressions and global connections.* Aldeshot: Ashgate.

Index

Printed and bound in the United States of America